When the Great Abyss Opened

When the Great Abyss Opened

Classic and Contemporary
Readings of Noah's Flood

J. DAVID PLEINS

OXFORD
UNIVERSITY PRESS

2003

OXFORD
UNIVERSITY PRESS

Oxford   New York
Auckland   Bangkok   Buenos Aires   Cape Town   Chennai
Dar es Salaam   Delhi   Hong Kong   Istanbul   Karachi   Kolkata
Kuala Lumpur   Madrid   Melbourne   Mexico City   Mumbai   Nairobi
São Paulo   Shanghai   Taipei   Tokyo   Toronto

Published by Oxford University Press, Inc.
198 Madison Avenue, New York, New York 10016

www.oup.com

Oxford is a registered trademark of Oxford University Press

Library of Congress Cataloging-in-Publication Data
Pleins, J. David
When the great abyss opened : classic and contemporary readings of
Noah's flood / J. David Pleins.
p.   cm.
ISBN 0-19-515608-0
1. Noah (Biblical figure)   2. Deluge.   3. Noah's ark.   I. Title.
BS580.N6   P58   2003
222' .1106—dc21   2002015356

1 3 5 7 9 8 6 4 2

Printed in the United States of America
on acid-free paper

For Shannon

O Lord, methought what pain it was to drown!
What dreadful noise of waters in my ears!
What sights of ugly death within my eyes!
Methoughts I saw a thousand fearful wracks;
A thousand men that fishes gnaw'd upon;
Wedges of gold, great anchors, heaps of pearl,
Inestimable stones, unvalued jewels,
All scatt'red in the bottom of the sea.
                              Shakespeare, *Richard III*

Don't you understand, I replied, that we begin by
telling children stories, which, taken as a whole,
are fiction, though they contain some truth?
                    Socrates speaking in Plato, *The Republic*

The antagonism of science is not to religion, but to
the heathen survivals and the bad philosophy
under which religion herself is often well-nigh
crushed. And, for my part, I trust that this antagonism will never cease; but that, to the end of time,
true science will continue to fulfil one of her most
beneficent functions, that of relieving men from
the burden of false science which is imposed upon
them in the name of religion.
            T. H. Huxley, *Science and Hebrew Tradition*

Preface

Asking the Right Questions

This book asks: What is the truth of Noah's flood story, and how is that truth to be found? This question provides us with an intriguing opportunity to explore new links between archaeology and myth, literary methods and the Bible, and science and belief. The old story is taking on a refreshing look in many quarters. While our focus throughout will be on the variety of readings of the flood story that are emerging today, our inquiries will also open a window that looks out onto shifting currents in science, myth, and religion. In the course of this book we will challenge old assumptions about the Bible, investigate a variety of ways to interpret the text, and ultimately forge a new horizon between sparring partners who have not always seen eye to eye on matters of truth, reason, and belief. The tale of Noah's flood offers a unique and compelling case study into timeless and timely questions of fact and faith.

The immediate occasion for this book is a request I received from the National Geographic Society to comment, from a religious studies point of view, on the importance of the Black Sea discoveries for people today. Doing background work for a video entitled "The Quest for Noah's Flood," associate producer Ann Conanan raised the kinds of questions that anyone curious about the connections between history, myth, and the Bible might ask. First and foremost, she wanted to know, "Why is it important for people today that legends such as the Mesopotamian tales of Gilgamesh and stories in the Bible, such as Noah's account, are validated?" This question goes to the heart of the matter. The issue of "validation" says that the story might carry a truth, but that we moderns no longer take ancient tales at face value. We need facts. This book is an attempt to wrestle with some of those facts.

Conanan's next question summed up the issue: "Why do people care?" Why, indeed. Why spend all that money mucking about in the Black Sea or digging up the mounds of the Middle East? Why bother about the ebb and flow of such a distant past? Why dress up the program with references to "Noah's flood"? Why not just call it "Black Sea Neolithic Tidal Shifts and Topographical Analysis"?

People care because at a very basic level we want to see how faithful those tales have been about that land long ago and far away. Or, as a friend of mine more bluntly stated it while we were downing tapas at a local Mexican restaurant: "People care because they want to know if the stories they have heard about since they were kids are true." The game of faith, archaeology, and history is a high-stakes one. Even the poker-faced agnostic cares to know the human dimensions of the question. That is why so many avowed secularists find archaeological dig sites so fascinating and why tourism to the Holy Land abounds. To hold in one's hands artifacts from the Neolithic, the Bronze Age, or the Iron Age (the age of the Bible) throws our own age into sharp relief. We find ourselves asking, Are we really all that different from our ancestors? There is a truth to be found only by getting on our hands and knees, not to pray but with trowel in hand to dig deep into the sands of time to find the meaning of a past that is at once foreign and also our own.

Another question raised the specter of religious doubts and rumblings: "Does this validation of events in the Bible change the way people interpret the Bible? How does it affect one's faith or spirituality?" Believers in the Bible are continually caught in a struggle between fact and faith. It will take us many chapters to sort out this difficult question. Let us simply observe for now that in the case of the Black Sea discoveries, while faith might not absolutely need facts, a few reassuring archaeological finds can certainly give us food for theological thought.

The questions became rather pointed: "Why do people look for tangible evidence of God's presence in our world?" This question will lurk in the back alleys through most of the book, but we will tackle it directly in the last chapter, asking in light of all our archaeological and literary work, Can we really dig up God? We need first to get ourselves in a better position to think about this question, but having it in mind throughout might help us to consider the respective roles of dig data and divine dogma when we approach the God equation. Archaeology holds out hope of a faith rooted in fact. We ought at least to examine the claims the archaeologists are making.

The last of the questions put the frosting on the cake when Conanan asked me to "describe the relation between science and religion. . . . How does one affect the other?" This is a battleground today. In Kansas, we have seen state educational institutions forced to reconsider the evolution-creationist controversy, first throwing out and later reinstating the testing of students on this fundamental scientific view. In Ohio, controversy has raged over "intelligent design." Those who thought these issues were settled long ago by the Scopes "Monkey Trial" are in for a bit of a shock. The battles continue. For some, all talk about archaeological and scientific results flies in the face of the plain claims of sacred scripture. For others, it seems best to let the test tube and the telescope, or, in our current case, the archaeologist's trowel, do the talking and not outmoded Holy Writ. How much religious truth should be brought into the classroom? Is this even truth that has scientific relevance? While this book focuses on one small slice in this larger controversy, the question of the relative weight of science and religion hangs over our entire discussion. Perhaps either-or is not the answer. But a simple addition of the two—science plus religion—will not do either. It is definitely not the case that science and religion are saying the same thing only in different words. We will nonetheless find that they have interesting things to say to each other. If we can at least keep this unhappy couple talking, we will perhaps have done the best we can for what, over the last several centuries, has been a rocky relationship. The best therapist will learn to ask the right questions. This book seeks to do just that.

I am grateful to Marijo Dowd (executive producer) and Ann Conanan (associate producer) at Wiley-Dowd Productions for prompting me to ask some of these questions. They have led me to discover some surprising and refreshing answers. I am deeply indebted to Cynthia Read, executive editor at Oxford University Press, for seeing beyond the crude initial drafts of this work to envision the final product. I am especially grateful for the deft ways she brought clarity to my overly purple prose. Since she will not let me use such words elsewhere, I must reserve adjectives like "amazing," "stunning," and "wondrous" for this gifted editor who truly deserves such praise. Warmest thanks go out to Scott Rains and Patty Narciso for many years of thoughtful theological conversations over good food and Shoreline walks. Ditto to Jeff Wild. I also wish to acknowledge the gracious generosity of Ron Numbers, whose careful reading of the material in chapters 4 and 5 saved me from a number of distortions. Those that remain are, of course, my own, the product of not being able to plumb the depths or scale the heights that this explorer in our field so readily commands. I am likewise grateful to Kim Warren, doctoral candidate at Stanford University, for her insightful comments on an early draft of chapter 7. Her research into slavery and education in nineteenth-century America is destined to open up new vistas in the field. As always, thanks to my wife, Teresa, who sustains me along the way and through those last-minute corrections. I dedicate this book to our wonderful daughter Shannon, whose lively mind, quick wit, and commitment to social progress give me hope for the future. Finally, I am especially grateful to my research assistant, Claire Elam, for seeing the humor in the right places and for pointing out lines that needed mending. My wish is that the reader will find this book as enjoyable and as thought-provoking as she did.

Contents

When the Great Abyss Opened

I

Of Angels, Mangers, and Arks

Black Sea Flooding and Mountain Mania

Just survey the shelves of the New Age boutiques, and you will learn the whole story. Or so they would have you believe.

In the popular spiritual imagination, the biblical images that stand out are angels, manger scenes, and Noah's arks. The pictures and figurines that line the walls of New Age shops attest to a fascination with the Bible's more dramatic episodes. What on earth causes eager credit card–carrying religious consumers to snap up such paraphernalia?

Sequestered as I often am in my academic ivory tower, poring over ancient languages and archaeological facts of a duller sort, I was ill prepared for the New Age craze for Bible kitsch. There I was in a New Age establishment in Ashland, Oregon, staring at the idols of postmodern spirituality and wondering what it was all about. The gray-haired clerk, who did not really fit in with the store's clientele, summed up the disparities between pop images and Bible realities as she leaned across the checkout counter and, indicating the angels, whispered, "They're not really like the ones you find in the Old Testament, now are they?"

By which, I suppose, she may have meant the Angel of Death who spread the plagues of God in Egypt!

No, the New Age cherubs speak of more fanciful sensibilities.

Which brings us to the continuing fascination with Noah's flood and its possible archaeological dimensions. Some think a flood at the Black Sea 7,500 years ago accounts for the biblical tale. Others think that remains of Noah's ark have been found on Mount Ararat. Do these finds, if such they are, bring us closer to the Bible's truth? Is the popular image of Noah and his boat a valid historical vision of the past? Or are there other ways to understand this very ancient tale? How are we to make sense of the latest discoveries?

Rather than settle for Bible baubles or ark-eology, we must dare to go to the heart of the question: prompted by the aging clerk who secretly chooses to remain out of step with the New Age, we must ask what realities lie behind one of the best-known stories in human history, the flood story of Noah in the Book of Genesis.

The Hydrological Hubbub at the Black Sea

Two prominent geoscientists have posed a daring theory to account for Noah's flood story and other ancient flood legends. They offer a compelling scientific tale of rising Mediterranean floodwaters that burst through the Bosporus to create the vast Black Sea. This theory views the great Neolithic Black Sea flood as the Rosetta stone of ancient myth, unlocking secrets long hidden in cryptic flood legends known to us from the ancient Middle East and the Bible. Since their theory has captured a lot of attention, leaving a best-selling book and a National Geographic special in its wake, let us begin our journey by considering what the Black Sea discoveries are telling us about the Bible. What is the hydrological hubbub all about?

In their recent book, *Noah's Flood: The New Scientific Discoveries about the Event That Changed History*, William Ryan and Walter Pitman suggest a surprising reconstruction of the story behind the flood story. They argue from marine archaeological finds along the north shore of the Black Sea that in roughly 5600 B.C.E., some 7,600 years ago, climatic and geological conditions created a catastrophic situation that caused massive amounts of water from the Mediterranean to surge across the Bosporus and inundate the Black Sea coastline. The ancient freshwater lake was transformed into a massive salt sea. Everything on the Black Sea coast was devastated in the tidal rising that spread for nearly a year. The prosperous village life that had its eco-niche along this Neolithic lake was wiped out in a relatively short period of time.

The story behind this discovery is fascinating.

In 1970, Ryan had studied cores dug deep in the Mediterranean Sea. These cores revealed a desertlike past and a sudden resurgence of the sea several million years ago. Walter Pitman had done pioneering work related to plate tectonics and continental drift. A fellow researcher asked Ryan somewhat sarcastically, "Bill, do you suppose the catastrophe that filled the Mediterranean [millions of years ago] might have been the one Noah escaped in the ark?"[1]

Of course, a Mediterranean flood millions of years back could not explain the biblical tale, but Ryan and Pitman could not help but take this curious query as a "challenge." Might there not have been such a flood in the more memorable and not so distant human past? If so, what would have been the telltale signs of such a disaster?

They identified the hypothetical markers of such an event: an initially "arid setting"; "entrenched river valleys"; shifting flora and fauna; and the "caves and campsites abandoned as hunters and gatherers were induced to migrate elsewhere for survival."[2]

Was there such a time and place that might be identified with Noah's flood?

Some of the answers were already coming from a different quarter, although Ryan and Pitman nearly overlooked the key article in *Science* magazine in 1970 that put them on the Black Sea trail.[3]

The article in *Science*, based on the work of the research vessel *Atlantis II*, hypothesized that the Black Sea was "a former sea that had turned into the world's largest freshwater lake and then back to a sea" and that "the reentry of salt water had occurred some time between twelve and seven thousand years ago."[4] The dim outline of a set of cataclysmic events was already emerging. It would be another twenty years, however, before studies aboard the Russian vessel *Aquanaut* put the rest of the puzzle in place, confirming many of Ryan and Pitman's initial suspicions, clarifying a number of oddities in the ancient geological record of the last 20,000 years, and providing a new window into the origins of the biblical flood story.

Sophisticated sonar readings and deep-sea core drilling by the *Aquanaut* team drew back the veil of time to reveal a clear picture of the Neolithic flooding that engulfed the once freshwater lake, creating what we now call the Black Sea. The investigators were able to detect vast ancient beaches, numerous river channels, and intact sand dunes that for millennia have lain submerged well beneath the surface of the Black Sea.[5] They also found evidence of an abrupt transition from freshwater fauna to saltwater marine life.

Most telling of all, the sea researchers were able to pinpoint the century of the flood. Accelerator mass spectrometry, the process that uses a particle accelerator to count long-lived radiocarbon atoms in a sample to determine its age, unlocked the date of the very shells of the newly arrived marine creatures from the Mediterranean Sea: some 7,500 years before the present.[6]

All that remained was to discover how rapidly this shift from the freshwater Ice Age lake to salt sea occurred. The soil cores brought up from across a wide area told one consistent and compelling story: the inrush of water from the Mediterranean was a catastrophic event.

"Someone escaping the onslaught of the rising tide on this [western] shelf would have had to travel, on the average, a quarter mile per day to keep up with the inundation. If fleeing up the very flat river valleys, they would have had to move half a mile to a mile per day."[7] One can only imagine the havoc wreaked on a region where "one's village could have disappeared beneath the abyss in a matter of weeks."[8] It was an event of epic proportions, a disaster that indelibly altered the landscape and the lives of those who inhabited the shores of the ancient lake.

Was there anyone who witnessed the flood? Can we say who fled the scene of this aquatic crime? There was no shortage of people in the overall region during the Neolithic era. Those interested in "biblical archaeology," for example, point with fondness to the city of Jericho, the site that is so famous from the account of Joshua's conquest of Canaan. Jericho is one of the oldest cities in the world, and its inhabitants resided there throughout the Neolithic. It is true that climate changes did force population movement and created occupation gaps at various junctures. By and large, however, the entire Near East, Anatolia, and areas around the Black Sea yield evidence of sophisticated farmers and fishing peoples pursuing sedentary life in their villages.

One key factor affecting population shifts between 6200 and 5800 B.C.E. was a major "cold snap" or "second mini Ice Age," during which many of these peoples were forced into more restricted areas.[9] The Black Sea would have been an "ideal refuge" around which diverse peoples would have clustered and flourished.

Until the flood, that is.

So where did the refugees go? With the flood, civilized folk living around the lake would have moved on to new homelands, bringing their culture along with them.[10] Their loss was in one sense the world's gain, for the dispersal of these highly civilized peoples would have served as a cultural stimulus wherever they settled.

For Ryan and Pitman, the geological data, archaeological artifacts, genetic tests, blood samples from later population groups, and vestiges of vocabulary words in a variety of far-flung languages lead to one stark conclusion: the Black Sea flood was a watershed historical and cultural event that forced the fleeing survivors to set up shop in lands near and far from the epicenter of the disaster.[11] They believe that

> the Semites and Ubaids fled southward to the Levant and Mesopotamia; the Kartvelians retreated to the Caucasus; the LBK [Linearbandkeramik = linear pottery farmers] dashed across Europe, leapfrogging from one site to the next, pushing ahead their frontier for reasons never adequately explained; the Vinča retreated upsteam to the enclosed valley of the Hungarian plain. Others went to the Adriatic and the islands of the Aegean. Some refugees migrated into the heartland of Eurasia via the Don. Still others used the Volga as access to the distant steppes of the southern Ural Mountains. In due course the Indo-Europeans soon occupied an arc extending from the Adriatic, western Europe, and the Balkans across Ukraine to the Caspian Sea. From somewhere in this strip the Tocharians struck out east to settle one day in the Tarim basin at the edge of what was to become the Old Silk Route.[12]

The role given to the Ubaids is critical to the handing on of the flood story in the Middle East. As the ancestors to the Sumerians in ancient Mesopotamia, the Ubaid poets and wandering bards could have kept alive a memory of the flood event for the peoples of that region, thereby preserving for all time news of ancient days locked inside their memorable myths.[13]

Until recently, the connection of this diaspora with a Black Sea flood was only a hypothesis.[14] More hard evidence has been needed, particularly of the people who fled before the flood. Most recently, however, the theory has received a boost from the Black Sea expeditions of Robert Ballard. If anyone is destined to find "Noah's flood," Ballard would seem to be the man for the job. Should we expect anything less from the famed discoverer of the *Titanic*, the *Bismarck*, the *Yorktown*, sunken Phoenician trading vessels, and PT-109? Ballard's work in the Black Sea was the focus of the 2001 National Geographic special entitled "The Quest for Noah's Flood" (see Preface).[15]

Ballard's first expedition in 1999 revealed the outlines of the ancient southern shore of the Black Sea as it appeared prior to this inundation. "It looked like any beach, anywhere on Earth—except it was under 550 feet of water!"[16] The mixture of freshwater and saltwater mollusks serves as a telling sign that the once freshwater Black Sea had been overcome by salt waters pouring in from the Mediterranean Sea.

In his subsequent expedition in the fall of 2000 aboard the research ship *Northern Horizon*, Ballard was out in search of evidence that the habitations of those who once lived along the shore had been destroyed. His finds were again suggestive but unfortunately still ambiguous. Underwater searches by the robotic submersibles *Argus* and *Little Hercules* revealed more of the now submerged ancient coastline and some sort of structure, possibly a house. At first, it was hoped that the wood from the site might date back to the Neolithic. Through the undersea cameras of the submersible, the rectangular structure looked like the remains of a wattle-and-daub hut. Unfortunately, conjecture was leaping ahead of the facts. Upon further investigation, it turns out that the wood was no more than 200 years old and simply represents the sort of sea debris that one might expect in a heavily trafficked maritime zone. The nature of the associated structure, if such it is, is still a mystery.

The big find of the season, earning *Scientific American*'s Greatest Archaeological Discovery of 2000 award, was a well-preserved 1,500-year-old Byzantine period trading vessel, from an era far removed from the flood. Ironically, Ballard was not even aboard the ship when his crew made this discovery. He had departed, disappointed at the apparent failure of the project. For the Neolithic side of the question, the fall 2000 hunt saw the quarry slip through the hunter's hands. It must be left to another season to search out signs of Neolithic habitation around the ancient shores of the Black Sea. It is hard to imagine that people would not live along such a huge freshwater lake prior to the flood. Without the hard evidence, though, this part of the puzzle must remain unsolved.

It is safe to presume, however, that further probing of the Black Sea will bring us face-to-face with those who perished in the flood and with those who survived to tell their harrowing tale. The evidence of submerged ancient beaches and demolished homes will suggest a disaster that spelled tremendous trouble for numerous peoples of the region. The massive scale of the event is such that Fredrik Hiebert, a University of Pennsylvania archaeologist attached to the expedition, described it as "a major discovery that will rewrite the history of civilization in this key area between Europe, Asia, and the Middle East."[17]

The possible link between this Neolithic flood and later flood tales stirs the imagination. Fleeing a coast that was disrupted beyond recognition, the displaced peoples carried away with them a few belongings and their unforgettable tale of destruction, a tale that may have been passed down to us through the ancient Middle Eastern myths of the flood. Bill Newcott, a writer for *National Geographic*, goes so far as to boast, "Robert Ballard has found conclusive proof that a flood of Biblical proportions inundated an area north of Turkey about 7,500 years ago—a timetable and location that virtually match the Old Testament account of Noah."[18]

The theory is very clever. Certainly something happened in the Neolithic. Of that there can be little doubt. Still, roughly 3,500 years separate that event from the first known recorded flood stories (see chapter 6). The sheer length of time raises at least a few red flags. Despite this obstacle, the latest reconstruction captures the imagination as the flood story has so often done. Perhaps that is all that we can hope for. Focusing on truth and proof may actually divert us from the most interesting aspect of this story, namely, the attraction it holds for scholars, students of myth, religionists, book publishers, the "Discovery Channel," and, as we shall see next, dreamy mountain explorers. Let us take a trip up Mount Ararat in search of Noah's ark.

Mountain Mania: Finding the Ark

Persistent rumors of a large vessel washed up on the mountain of Ararat in Turkey have led many pilgrims and explorers over the centuries to visit that fabled peak. However, this is not the only mountain with a claim to being the site of the landing of the ark. According to Josephus (37–101 C.E.), the ancient Greek historian Nicolaus of Damascus (first century B.C.E.), author of a 144-volume universal history, places the boat on Mount Baris, a site that has been identified with Mount Elburz in Armenia.[19] Muslims locate the landing at Jebel Judi deep in the Arabian Peninsula. While there are literally dozens of candidates for the site, it is the Ararat region that has captured the imagination of Christian pilgrims over the centuries.[20] The devout wayfarer at Ararat encounters two volcanic mountains that dominate the landscape, the conelike Lesser Ararat, which reaches 14,000 feet, and the saddle-shaped Greater Ararat, which rises to 17,000 feet. The ark-seeking wayfarer also runs into mountains of lore connected with the ark.

The oldest tales tell of a monk who repeatedly tried to reach the top of Mount Ararat to find the ark. One version of this story, from Faustus of Byzantium (fourth century c.e.), tells of a certain Bishop Jacob of Nisibis, who, on one of his ascents, was miraculously given wood from the ark and ordered by God to cease his incessant climbing.[21] A later version of the monk's tale comes from Vincent of Beauvais (1184–1264), who tells of an unnamed monk who fell asleep during each ascent and wound up back at the bottom of the mountain. Once, however, God permitted a successful ascent during which this monk found a beam from the ark. After descending the mountain, he established a monastery to house the relic.[22] Later writers tend to conflate and confuse these two stories, but two features stand out. One is that the mountain mysteriously prevents the curious from entering its sacred sphere. The other is that one lucky soul in the past found all the evidence anyone might need, putting to rest speculation about the ark on Mount Ararat.

The vague reminiscences of medieval pilgrims and travelers such as Marco Polo and others have given way in more recent times to scientific climbs by skilled mountaineers.[23] While there are some doubts that any of these figures actually made the climbs that they claim, most agree that Friedrich Parrot (1791–1841) in 1829 became the first modern to ascend Ararat.[24] He has been followed by a series of climbers, not all of whom found on Ararat the "solitude, silence, and snow" that Major Robert Stuart experienced in 1856.[25] On the contrary, most report facing terrible storms, sleet, and severe cold as they braved the summit. Claims of ark sightings, as one might imagine, are rare given the treacherous climbing conditions and the general honesty of the climbers. Some might wax eloquent about "standing on the spot where the ark of gopher rested, where first the patriarch alighted on the face of an earth renewed," as does Henry F. B. Lynch in 1893.[26] But very few assert, as did James Bryce in 1876, that they found actual wood from the ark.[27] On that score, Bishop Jacob's ancient legacy remains intact.

Early attempts to climb Ararat paved the way for more recent endeavors such as the 1952 ascent of Abbé Pierre and a series of climbs by Fernand Navarra, who, together with polar explorer M. J. de Riquer, ventured yet again to seek the ark. Abbé Pierre made his trek and left a Turkish flag but found no boat. Navarra hardly fared any better, but he did leave some stirring accounts of the challenges faced in attempting to conquer what he calls "the forbidden mountain."

Fernand Navarra was the quintessential romantic adventurer. A chance glance at an illustrated Bible in a bookshop and a picture of Noah's ark were all the inducement he needed to set off on the hunt for history's elusive prize. Moreover, the fact that Navarra's name had exactly the same number of syllables as "Ararat" seemed more than mere coincidence to this mountain dreamer. Coincidence became reality shortly thereafter when Navarra was called on by his friend Raymond Zubiri to join in an attempt on Ararat.[28]

There was hardly a more willing convert to search for mountaineering's holy grail.

The aim? To "confirm" the "evidence" from reports over the centuries that the ark was truly resting somewhere on that great mountain.[29] With grim determination (and appropriate bribes and gifts), Navarra and his team from France, joined by Turkish soldiers and attendants, made the first in a series of treks up the mountain in 1952.

Describing his initial view of "the old mountain, access to which is forbidden by angels," Navarra writes: "No other mountain is more perfectly formed or more beautiful, and we know none which gives greater illusion of rising so close to the sky."[30]

For Navarra, love *before* first sight was renewed by first sight itself. Earnest hopes of finding the ark drip from Navarra's pen:

> We should be the first Frenchmen to storm its ice cap, to come to grips with its seracs, to sound its lakes and its névés. And perhaps the ark would be within range of our cameras. . . . Or perhaps, lying beneath a covering of ice, it would be the dumb and invisible witness of our victory.[31]

If Navarra's heartfelt convictions alone could produce an ark on Ararat, he certainly would have found it there. Short of that, the 1952 ascent at least allowed him to express his French pride by unfurling his homeland's flag on the summit.

Navarra's claims of having seen the outlines of the ark beneath the ice have never been substantiated.[32] Nonetheless, his ark fever propelled him on to subsequent expeditions in 1953, 1955, and 1969 to seek evidence for his claims. The result? A few pieces of wood, purported to be 5,000 years old, hand cut and squared in Noah's maritime workshop, or so Navarra would have us believe. Independent carbon dating of the various fragments put them between 300 and 800 C.E., far later than anyone's date for Noah.[33] Navarra has also constructed a detailed model of the ark. His heightened literalism sees what it wishes in the bits and pieces of mountain wood, but the gap between those fragments of late date and the vast vessel he harbors in his imagination is large indeed.[34] While others in more recent times have made valiant attempts on the mountain in search of the ark, none have done so with the grit and the gusto of Navarra (although Montgomery's 1970 outing seemed better stocked with Kronenbourgs and Moëts!).[35]

Thus the ark continues to remain elusive despite rumors in fundamentalist circles of "top secret" government photos. The only fact that is certain in all of this ark-eology is that no concrete proof of an ancient vessel perched somewhere on Mount Ararat (or anywhere else, for that matter) has ever emerged from the murky depths of history. One cannot help but sympathize with the skepticism of missionary traveler Rev. Frederick G. Coan, who encountered Archdeacon Nouri, a Nestorian Christian who not only claimed to be a "lineal descendant of Nebuchadnezzar" but also purported to have found and measured the ark. Coan said, "I could not but ask a rather mean question at this point, whether he saw Mrs. Noah's corset hanging up in her bedroom."[36] The arch-deacon was apparently unmoved by the jibe, as are so many who wish to believe the ark is on Ararat despite the lack of evidence. Coan recounts Nouri's sadness at his failure to enlist the services of a Belgian firm to transport the ark to the Chicago World's Fair: "He was much disappointed, for he knew it would be a great attraction, and that people from all over the world would go to see it."[37]

Here are two curious sidebars in this mountain mania. Not all searches for the ark are what they seem. A British major who was stationed in Palestine during World War II tells me in a private communication that in at least one instance after the war British troops were sent to learn advanced mountain-climbing tech-niques in the region of Ararat, feigning to the Americans that they were on an archaeological expedition to find Noah's ark. The training expedition was quite successful, and the Americans were none the wiser for it.

In 1946, just after the war, Benjamin Franklin Allen (1885–1960) of the defunct Deluge Geology Society and fellow Seventh-day Adventist Clifford L. Burdick worked on a "top-secret project" known as the Sacred History Research Expedition to find the ark. As R. L. Numbers explains, "The conspiratorial Allen planned to keep news of the anticipated discovery secret until 'M-Day' (Mes-sage Day), when the find would be announced to the world in repeated interna-tional broadcasts followed by sound newsreels."[38] The project came to naught as the climb was delayed and the ark was never found.

The Dividing Wall of Hostility: Science versus the Bible?

One irony of seventeenth-century Christian scientific speculation about the flood would seem also to be true of Navarra's adventures. As one scholar of that early modern era so keenly observes, "The more the Bible was defended by science, the more it had to be defended."[39] The science of Copernicus and Galileo offered exciting new vistas but posed grave challenges to those who wished to put his-tory and the Bible together in some sensible fashion. Every insight produced a challenge, which in turn led to more sophisticated schemes for saving the Bible. As the proposals to defend the Bible became more and more elaborate, the in-terpretation of the text moved far afield from the simple moral tale of Noah's flood in terms of both the science and the tale's literary dimensions. Creating a science of the flood has not necessarily helped to shore up biblical belief. In fact, the preposterous character of so many of the proposals made belief in the Bible seem ludicrous. Navarra's continual climbing has not helped out the literal side of the story very much, and neither has he done scientific and historical studies any favors by insisting that the ark is on Ararat.

As a result of the intellectual stalemate, many have preferred to erect a wall between science and the Bible. On the one side of the wall are the scientists who feel that science has moved well beyond the Bible, and that the Bible can safely be discarded as a source of scientific or historical information of any substance. On the other side are the biblicists who rail against the sciences, defending a literal reading of the Bible at all costs.

Despite the advances in the archaeology of the Middle East and the Holy Land throughout the nineteenth and twentieth centuries, the perception became entrenched that keeping the wall in place is probably in the best interests of both parties. As a result, the secularists stole away the sciences, while the believers bagged a rather tattered Book. The evolutionary theories of the nineteenth century and the quantum physics of the twentieth century seem finally to have interred religion beneath the scrap heap of history's worn-out ideas.

Yet just when the divorce between religion and science seemed to have been finalized and the unhappy couple taken up residence in separate intellectual houses, with science settled deep in the valley of learning and religion pitched far away on Holy Hill, the jury brings in new findings that have forced the two back to the negotiating table. If one is willing to have more modest expectations about the biblical record than the obsessive Navarra seems to have had, then the new theories will be heartening. They are not trying to force-fit the scientific findings into the straitjacket of biblical "truth." There is room for dialogue between science and belief in a place where Navarra only ran into dead ends. On that score, the work of Ryan and Pitman on the Black Sea flood can help hammer an opening through the wall that so often separates secular scientists from people of faith.

The delicate balance they strike is central to their project. The key for the scientist and the historian is to focus on what archaeology can offer us from the Middle East and its contiguous regions. This is the domain of science. This is the playground of history. Yet in the process, their work encourages us to pore anew over the ancient texts to see what insights emerge when we read these tales as fragments of still more ancient cultural memories. If the Bible is going to be rescued from the clutches of myth, it would seem that an escape can be effected only in connection with good hydrological investigation. At least that is the direction that their work encourages.

Ryan and Pitman's more circumspect methods and cautious observations keep them from the flights of fancy that have driven Navarra and others up and down the mountain. Yet their approach does not separate them entirely from all who are religiously minded. The focus on actual floodwaters and reliance on careful scientific analysis has precursors in a number of nineteenth-century theological interpreters who attempted to harmonize the Bible with geology by arguing that the flood was a local event rather than the universal catastrophe that the Bible describes (see chapter 5). While today's marine archaeology is far more sophisticated than the sciences relied on by these nineteenth-century religious interpreters, in another sense their modern counterparts are following the lead of previous synthesizers in seeking to ground the stories in sensible geological and material processes. This approach has the distinct advantage of allowing the background event to emerge as a historically significant but geographically limited occurrence that may have sparked the flood legends found in the Bible and in other traditions. Just as many theologians in the nineteenth century were open to geological developments in that era, allowing them to find renewed religious insights in those discoveries, perhaps the Black Sea flood theory will jar renewed reflection on the Bible and ancient myth today.

Their account does not harmonize in the literalistic fashion desired by our medieval religious forebears or by fundamentalist mountaineers today. This will be disconcerting to some. Yet their studies stand on surer ground than previous efforts precisely because the theory is not seeking to protect the Bible from a critical reading. This may make the theologically timid feel uneasy but will come as a breath of fresh air to others. For those who are more open, the proposal that the story of the flood has a plausible ground is worth considering, both out of historical curiosity and for religious belief.

If nothing else, Ryan and Pitman's work will spur further discussion. Since neither Navarra nor anyone else has found an ark, students of the Bible and ancient myth might rather benefit from a seagoing quest that puts geological history first, offering a reasoned explanation for the origins of the later biblical and Middle Eastern flood legends. Good archaeological thinking about the Bible can restore the book's historical respectability and rescue myth from psychologized readings. While Ryan and Pitman take us into a geological world that stands in the background to the Bible and other ancient flood stories, we find insight into how science can constructively connect with the Bible and ancient myth. We will certainly never read the Genesis flood story or ancient flood myths in the same way after encountering their book. This is all to the good for persons of faith and students of myth.

Enthusiasm for this theory, however, ought not to obscure another kind of danger here. For all the insight archaeological investigation might bring to a reading of the Bible and ancient myth, even the casual reader will recognize that Ryan and Pitman's discussion shifts our attention away from the ancient flood story to focus on the cities that were destroyed, the populations that moved about, and the process by which the flood traditions were passed on to their descendants from that rather tumultuous time. The reader who fears for the Bible, or values the Book as a work of great literature in its own right, or is simply sympathetic to the power of myth will be left wondering if the hydrological story is the only side that matters. Surely there must be more to the story than a vague reminiscence of a Black Sea catastrophe?

Does the Bible Need a Bodyguard?

One fundamentalist Web site, appropriately entitled www.answersingenesis.org, accuses Ryan and Pitman of trying to destroy the Bible. Tas Walker argues that the Bible plainly speaks of a flood of global proportions.[40] For Walker, the Bible's facts speak for themselves. Taking to task the Black Sea flood theory, Walker writes, "Their link with Noah's Flood is totally arbitrary. They need a flood, so presto, pluck Noah's Flood out of the air." The notion of a global flood is definitely not lacking defenders in fundamentalist circles, despite the Black Sea finds. Dennis Gordon Lindsay goes so far as to say that those who do not acknowledge a global flood but rely on evolutionary models "know neither Scripture nor God's power."[41] He credits Satan with clouding the minds of those who might seek to reconcile science and scripture on a basis other than his own.[42] A strong charge indeed!

Another Web site, this one nonfundamentalist and decidedly anticreationist in orientation, entitled www.talkorigins.org, unwittingly supplies those who want to believe in a global flood with all the ammunition they need through its extensive collection, "Flood Stories from around the World."[43] Here they are in endless detail, synopses of tales spanning the globe from Europe, Africa, and the Near East, to the Far East, Australasia and the Pacific Islands, and the Americas. All but the !Kung peoples in Africa seem to know of a great watery catastrophe in the distant past. As for the !Kung, the Web pages explain that they possess no such story, "The very idea is ludicrous." In the face of such overwhelming evidence, any talk of a rather limited Black Sea flood necessarily pales by comparison for the fundamentalist.

Going for the jugular, Walker of www.answersingenesis.org argues that the Black Sea archaeologists and scientists miss the *moral* point of the Bible's story. Walker declares, "By saying that Noah's Flood was a local flood, do they think they can dismiss the implications of the real global Flood described in the Bible, viz. that God judges human sin?" As far as this fundamentalist is concerned, the secular archaeologist's spade heaps up piles of dissembling dirt on the Bible's plain message. Walker is saying, in effect, that there is a real flood behind the story, but the archaeologists have yet to find it. His message is clear: keep digging and ye shall find!

For fundamentalists such as Walker, the Bible is to be read as if it were a scientific textbook regarding events that are supposed to have taken place "at 2348 BC, [when] the Ice Age peak would have been around 1850 BC and the melt back complete by 1650 BC at which time the Black Sea area flooded."

Walker's fundamentalist science and flood archaeology stand everything Ryan, Pitman, and Ballard are saying right on its head!

So which is it? A local flood? A universal flood? Or perhaps no flood at all? How are we to read the Bible's flood story? The many answers that truth seekers offer to these questions will no doubt entertain and confound the reader. In the next chapter I will begin by sizing up the basic options.

2

For the Bible Tells Me So!

Competing Ways to Read Genesis

I have on my office bookshelf a pamphlet that I like to pull out on occasion regarding the coming end of the world. On the cover is a scene that depicts in rather stark fashion the return of Jesus to the earth as he is joined by people who fly up into the air to meet him in the clouds. Below, a series of car accidents are seen taking place because the drivers have flown out of their seats into the sky. I keep the pamphlet not for the artwork but for the date. It boldly announces the end of the world: "RAPTURE, OCT. 28 '92." Since the projected date has long since passed, either I missed one of the biggest events of all time or the pamphleteers got their Bible wrong.

These end-times enthusiasts went astray in a fundamental way. When reading the Bible, we need to know when a passage is to be understood literally and when it is to be taken more figuratively. By insisting on reading the poetic and mystical Book of Revelation in the Christian Testament as if it were tomorrow's newspaper, our doomsayers were destined to misunderstand the very book they hold so dear. Because it is so important how we read the various texts of the Bible, we need to consider the possibilities with respect to the flood story. Based on the end-times example, one can say that there are essentially two ways to read the flood story: it either is to be treated at face value and read literally, or it must be considered a myth. Since the wrong sort of reading can lead to laughable results, we should spell out what each sort of reading might net us.

The Bible Tells Me So: Exact Literalism

Among the literalists there are both the "exact literalists" and what I would call the "loose literalists." The exact literalists believe that the Bible's events happened just the way the Bible says and at just the moment in history to which the Bible dates them. For D. G. Lindsay, for example, this means taking the Bible "at face value."[1] The exact literalist's rallying cry is "The Bible tells me so!" Such a person might cautiously make room for an "ark science," but only to the extent that hints of a global geological catastrophe in the past specifically corroborate what is known from the Bible. Exact literalists will doubtless endorse the seemingly precise mathematical calculations of J. Woodmorappe's *Noah's Ark: A Feasibility Study*, whose ark carries 15,754 animals that require a total of 2,500 tons of dried food (less if hibernating) and produce 12 tons of "excreta" daily, not to mention giving off 241 tons of biomass heat at a ventilation clearing rate of 210,000 cubic meters per hour (thus coping with "explosive manure gases"). Despite the accumulation of details, the guiding vision is provided by a literal reading of the biblical text.

Certainly, not all literal readings lead to the misguided prophecies with which I began this chapter or to the excesses of Woodmorappe's calculations. In fact, there can be real advantages to insisting that biblical texts be taken as they stand. For years, for example, people have been arguing over whether or not the ancient Israelites crossed the Red Sea when they escaped from Egypt under the guidance of Moses. In a liberal effort to save the credibility of the text, many scholars suggested that the Hebrew words *yam suph* were best translated "Reed Sea" rather than "Red Sea." Thus, instead of thinking that the huge Red Sea one day was split asunder, as happens in Cecil B. DeMille's film *The Ten Commandments*, the modern scientific reader could rest content knowing that a stiff breeze simply dried a path across the Sea of Reeds, allowing the Israelites to flee without muddying their sandals.

Even on the face of it, this rereading of the Hebrew text seems patently ridiculous, as if the Egyptian army drowned under a few inches of water when it followed after the Israelites. This is a case where a failure to take the text at face value fails to do justice to the story. The *yam suph* is the Red Sea elsewhere in the biblical text. No amount of special pleading will make it otherwise in the Book of Exodus.[2] The story was designed not to allay the doubts of moderns but to elevate the authority of the Bible's God over that of Pharaoh, and for that the Red Sea crossing and the utter devastation of Pharaoh's forces were essential. In the Bible, God commands the forces of nature and the floodwaters of the world. We may choose to doubt that the Red Sea ever parted, but let us not rob the Bible of this dramatic and triumphant tale. Here, a literal reading is the only one that truly respects the text, regardless of what we might make of the story scientifically.

However, too much literalism can distort and flatten the text. The fundamentalist apologist Harold Lindsell got into a real muddle when he overanalyzed Peter's denials of Jesus in the Christian Gospels. Finding that the different Gospels presented some seemingly irreconcilable details regarding the events surrounding the trial of Jesus, Lindsell felt constrained to argue that the traditional story of Peter's threefold denial of Jesus should be thrown out in favor of the "true" count, which he fixed at six denials.[3]

When it comes to exact literalism, we need to consider when exactness is appropriate and when another sort of reading might be our best bet.

Vetus Testamentum Supplement: Loose Literalism

There is, however, another type of literalist, the "loose literalist." This is the one who accepts something of the surface story of the Bible but suggests that science and archaeology provide the cues as to how best to read it. A loose literalist may suggest, for example, that the six days of creation talked about in the first chapter of Genesis are to be read as six epochs of history, which might have been much vaster in their time scale than the Bible lets on. For the loose literalist the Bible can be read in a way that harmonizes the text with modern science's picture of the past. The story of Noah's flood will thus be thought to correlate with some ancient catastrophe that changed civilization in some decisive way. The loose literalist's rallying cry is "The Bible tells me so, but science tells me so much more!"

Ryan and Pitman may be more sophisticated, but they really are loose literalists as well. They are telling us that the story that has come down to us may not be correct in all its details but can be unpacked in ways that marine archaeology now helps us to see: "The strategy is to search the mythology to check for any credible Black Sea fingerprints. Are there clues within the myths that might point to a Black Sea origin?"[4] Such a loose literalism has great advantages when one is reading much of the Bible. The endless conundrums that have been created, for example, as people have tried to connect the tales of Joshua's conquests of Canaan with the archaeological record are a case in point. Far too much ink has been spilled trying to fit together the tall tale of the fall of Jericho's walls with the meager archaeological finds from that historical moment. Perhaps if we see the story as a legend reflecting the disruptions at the end of the Bronze Age (c. 1200 B.C.E.) rather than as a videotape of the past, we will be less troubled when the archaeological record does not precisely correspond to the Bible. The loose literalist will still find behind the story a fascinating archaeological picture that reveals the turmoil that preceded the establishment of the ancient kingdom of King David. But the loose literalist will not confuse the details of the biblical story with historical facts, except perhaps in the broadest of brush strokes.

The trouble with loose literalism is that what tends to capture our attention is the clever explanation rather than the story itself. We quickly move on from the flood story or the tales of Joshua's conquests to the seemingly more interesting archaeological problems that stand back of the Bible.

We catch Ryan and Pitman falling into this trap in a section of the book that extols the virtue and power of ancient myth:

> For a myth to survive unscathed from repeated recitation, it needs a powerful story. . . . Oral tradition tells such stories. But so does the decipherment by the natural scientist who works from a text recorded in layers of mud, sand, and gravel from the bottom of lakes and seas using all the tools and principles of physics, chemistry, and biology. The scientific plot can then be given richer detail and new themes from the supporting contributions of the archaeologist, the linguist, and the geneticist.[5]

Figures such as Noah and the Mesopotamian survivor of the flood, Utnapishtim, are thus relegated to the supporting cast in a grander scientific drama that has as its dramatis personae scores of dislocated village dwellers put on the move by a Neolithic conflagration.

Ryan and Pitman's Hollywood epic of ancient humans on the run makes for an impressive script. Yet loose literalism leaves more than a few literary stones left unturned. Should the mythic story as such fade from the stage so quickly? Is there nothing lost when we fail to grasp the power of the tale in and of itself for the peoples who passed on those legends over the millennia?

These stories are powerful tales in their own right. They are, at their core, myths. We ought not to let the loose literalist's scientific reading upstage the mythic characters entirely.

Myths as Nonsense: The Secularist's Safety Valve

What does the mythic reading offer that literalism does not? The mythic reading of the flood tales represents a clear alternative to literalism, of both the exact and the loose varieties. In the mythic camp there are also two subtypes. In the first place, there are those for whom myths are simply nonsense. They prefer the scientific view over the mistaken explanations of past civilization. For the "myth as nonsense" school, our scientific knowledge of the earth's past reveals a picture that is so totally at odds with anything in the Bible that we must abandon the Bible altogether as a source of knowledge about the earth's origins, human evolution, and the later rise of civilization. The rallying cry of this crowd is "Science tells me: no way!"

The "myth as nonsense" school has been with us for a long time. When the ancient Greek natural philosophers started giving materialistic explanations for the workings of the universe in terms of the properties of earth, air, fire, and water, the challenge to belief in humanlike gods such as Zeus, Hera, Ares, and the others soon arose. Stories of the gods and their love affairs and temper tantrums quickly became an embarrassment.

It even became possible to offer rational explanations for the phenomenon of religion. Euhemerus (fourth century B.C.E.), for example, argued that cultures simply create gods out of their all-too-human heroes. The later Greek and Roman philosophers came to prefer more complex understandings of the gods, if they continued to believe in them at all. The Epicureans, who thought all things to be composed of atoms, maintained that gods were just made of finer atoms than humans. The gods sat in distant repose and never interacted with mere mortals, who were made of cruder atoms. The Stoics, opponents of the Epicureans, dispensed with humanlike gods entirely, arguing that the spherical planets were divinities and that the entire universe was governed by one vast Mind, the great Logos.

The Epicurean and Stoic conceptions represent an intellectual turn that Western culture has never been able to reverse. Despite the ascendancy of Christianity, the West's scientists would eventually come to prefer scientific theories over ancient myths to explain the workings of nature. As a result, especially with the European Enlightenment, many learned to disregard the Bible in whole or in part as just another outdated myth. Thomas Paine, in his 1794 treatise *The Age of Reason*, dismissed the flood story in one line by saying: "The story of Eve and the serpent, and of Noah and his ark, drops to a level with the Arabian nights, without the merit of being entertaining."[6]

The modern approach to the "myths as nonsense" view is summed up well by one of the famed discoverers of the genetic double helix, Francis Crick, who writes that "the myths of yesterday, which our forebears regarded as the living truth, have collapsed. . . . Yet most of the general public seems blissfully unaware of all this, as can be seen by the enthusiastic welcome to the Pope whenever he travels."[7]

Theoreticians like Crick may not have the last word on the interpretation of Genesis, but the secularist view that myths are nonsense stands as a barrier between today's readers and the ancient mythmakers.

The Literature of the Spirit

There is another side to the mythic approach, one with strong scientific claims of its own. There are those who see myths as powerful tales, tales that provide insight into the living of our lives, tales that create and sustain whole civilizations, tales that reach into our deepest selves to draw out a recognition of the divine element at work in this world. On this reading, Noah's flood story is not fundamentally about science, archaeology, or hydrology but about the human heart and the living of a life in this tumultuous world. The rallying cry of this camp is "The myth tells me: know thyself!"

For this camp, myths are not simply the mistaken ideas of a bygone age but, in Joseph Campbell's phrase, the "literature of the spirit" with which we desperately need to connect if our world is not to lose its psychic roots in the past and the present.[8] On this reading, myths supply us the wisdom of the ancients, albeit in an encoded form. Thus, where Crick sought to debunk the ancient myths, other scientists today would offer a different reading. Roger Jones, theoretical physicist and author of *Physics for the Rest of Us: Ten Basic Ideas of Twentieth-Century Physics That Everyone Should Know and How They Have Shaped Our Culture and Consciousness*, draws a different line between myth and science:

> The philosophies, myths, and cosmologies of earlier times may seem
> completely inadequate and naive nowadays because they fail to
> provide an accurate and verifiable description of the natural world.
> But based on their ability to add meaning and significance to human
> life, they may indeed score higher than does modern science.[9]

Jones's confession is an eye-opener. There need be no hard-and-fast line in the sand between science and mythology when it comes to the living of a human life. The fluid character of this line provides an occasion for thinking about the continued relevance of ancient myth to an age that speaks more in terms of genes, quanta, and the big bang than of the old stories of gods battling to create new worlds or heroes surviving terrible floods.

Perhaps if we learn how to decode the myths, we can journey with the ancient heroes and benefit from the insights they have to offer about death, sexuality, love, honor, survival, and joy. The Epic of Gilgamesh, as we shall see, does not pass on just the tale of an ancient flood but also the wisdom that the great warrior and king Gilgamesh brought back from his visit with the survivor of the flood, the hale Utnapishtim. The message of the myth endures. Those who treat mythology as the literature of the spirit understand the humanistic worth of such stories.

This is not to say that mythography does not have its blinders and excesses. The most bizarre explanation of the flood comes from Freudian interpreters. Insisting that myths have psychological and biological rather than archaeological roots, Otto Rank, for example, suggested that the waters of flood myths can be traced back to dreams that result from bladder troubles! The myth, according to the Freudians, merely speaks to another sort of dangerous overflow.[10] P. Vandermeersch explains that psychoanalysis has seen encoded in flood stories all manner of human urges and animalistic needs, including urination, nighttime weeping and bed-wetting, and even male womb envy.[11] While Vandermeersch might be justified in saying that psychology restores to us the "dirty mind" that we need to really understand myths and dreams, it is also clear that the psychoanalytic approach to the flood story has been rife with uncontrolled speculation.

We stand warned that without good theories of myth, the reading of the flood story can be distorted under the guise of analytic respectability.

Charting a Course

Let us consider each of these four views in greater detail. Perhaps no one camp has the whole truth. What contribution can each make to the unfolding of the meaning of the story? Surprises await. In the kaleidoscope of readings that we will explore in this book, fresh possibilities will emerge to challenge each camp and bring greater insight to those who are ready to navigate waters that science and religion are learning to cross together.

3

Not as Seamless as It Seems

The Literalist's Lens

The Bible's flood story seems so seamless.

God becomes angry at all the evil on the earth and charges the one righteous man, Noah, to construct a boat, built to very detailed specifications, and to head inside with his family and countless animals to await the rainwaters. The storm gates of the heavens are opened, the boat floats away, and the wicked of the earth are blotted out forever.

Eventually the waters begin to subside and the boat comes to rest on the mountains of Ararat, from which place Noah sends out first a raven, then a dove. When the dove brings back a fresh olive leaf, Noah knows that it is about time to disembark. When the dove is sent out again and fails to return, the family and animals emerge from the boat with God's blessing. Noah completes the story by offering up a fine sacrifice to the glory of God.

The more dedicated reader who proceeds a bit further will find the strange episode of Noah's naked drunkenness, leaving the distinct impression that paradise has not exactly been restored even after God's scouring of the sinful planet. In any event, the tale seems rather straightforward and complete. The events unfold in a logical sequence and lead to their expected conclusion. The way is paved for humans to rebuild and for the animal kingdom to be restored.

But is it so seamless?

Wenham's Seamless Garment

At least one interpreter thinks that the seamlessness extends to the very fibers of the story's literary structure. Labeling each segment carefully, Wenham discerns a clear and deliberate pattern to the story, one that betrays the deft hand of a skilled author with a distinct message.[1]

Wenham finds that the story is arranged in a mirror pattern around a centrally located pivot point. In other words, it works toward the central point in a very ordered and deliberate fashion and then works backward from that point step-by-step, the second half mirroring the first. Wenham charts the story as follows:

A. Noah (vi 10a)
  B. Shem, Ham and Japheth (10b)
    C. Ark to be built (14–16)
      D. Flood announced (17)
        E. Covenant with Noah (18–20)
          F. Food in the ark (21)
            G. Command to enter ark (vii 1–3)
              H. 7 days waiting for flood (4–5)
                I. 7 days waiting for flood (7–10)
                  J. Entry to ark (11–15)
                    K. Yahweh shuts Noah in (16)
                      L. 40 days flood (17a)
                        M. Waters increase (17b-18)
                          N. Mountains covered (19–20)
                            O. 150 days waters prevail (21-24)

                          P. GOD REMEMBERS NOAH (viii 1)

                            O' 150 days waters abate (3)
                          N' Mountain tops visible (4–5)
                        M' Waters abate (5)
                      L' 40 days (end of) (6a)
                    K' Noah opens window of ark (6b)
                  J' Raven and dove leave ark (7–9)
                I' 7 days waiting for waters to subside (10–11)
              H' 7 days waiting for waters to subside (12–13)
            G' Command to leave ark (15–17(22))
          F' Food outside ark (ix 1–4)
        E' Covenant with all flesh (8–10)
      D' No flood in future (11–17)
    C' Ark (18a)
  B' Shem, Ham and Japheth (18b)
A' Noah (19)

Notice the pivot of the story for Wenham. The key verse, the one with Wenham's all-important theological message, is the central statement: "God remembered Noah." No doubt Wenham regards the story as historical, but he also sees in its seamless retelling a vital theological message for Noah's descendants: God remembers God's people even when they might think that God has abandoned them.

The literary structure that Wenham discerns, with its pyramidal mirror shape, is certainly impressive at first sight. The sheer number of balancing elements makes it appear that the story was very carefully constructed. Names balance names, one covenant parallels another covenant, comings match goings, entries find echoes in exits. The balancing pairs seem to give evidence of one overall design by one key author or editor.

Yet is everything so neat and tidy? Note that the analysis is achieved at the expense of certain passages that are omitted. Where, for example, are the verses in 6:11–13 that speak of the corruption of the world? Why not include the actual departure from the ark (Genesis 8:19–21), unless it is that this factor disrupts the neat balancing of J and J'? Note, too, that Noah's sacrifice in 8:20–22 has disappeared from sight along with God's promise not to destroy the world again, which would inconvenience Wenham's "balancing" of similar sentiments in D and D'. What happened to 8:2, which mentions the closing of the floodgates? If Wenham had left it in, one might have noticed that its corresponding passage, namely, 7:11, was way out of kilter in terms of the mirror pattern. Furthermore, as J. A. Emerton has observed, certain elements, such as references to "forty days," actually occur elsewhere in the story.[2] Emerton rightly asks why one should pick out the particular instances that Wenham does, as if they are of greater importance than other occurrences of the same words or phrases. Has Wenham, in other words, created a "contrivance"—to use Emerton's word—that masks the counterevidence, polishing the mirror more than it deserves?

Wenham's theory is riddled with holes. It is nothing more than analytic Swiss cheese, tasty perhaps in the first bite, but ultimately critically unsatisfying on its own. We are justified, therefore, in suspecting that Wenham is up to some literary sleight of hand, trying to outflank those who argue that, to the contrary, the Bible's story is hardly seamless and that its real message is only to be found when the story is broken down into its background sources. The literary pyramid that Wenham has built is more like a house of cards ready to fall. Contemporary scholars have, in fact, found in the Bible's flood story a reshuffled deck of fragments that, when studied carefully, can be sorted into tales that were at one time quite distinct. More on this detective work in just a bit.

Before I turn to this dissection of the text, there is another ingenious way of imagining an ancient and rather unified story behind the Genesis flood tale that shows us how far some will go to protect the historicity of the text. This one comes from a Dutch Webmeister, Cees van Arnhem, who goes even further than Wenham to argue that the unity (assumed rather than proven) of the Genesis tale is the result of the "fact" that it represents the "captain's log" kept during the voyage of Noah's ark.³ On the basis of Genesis 10:1, which mentions the *toledot* of Noah's sons Shem, Ham, and Japheth, a Hebrew word that means "lines of descendants" but which Arnhem takes to mean "histories" as in "history book," he argues that each of the sons of Noah took turns writing the ship's log. The fact that the Bible does not ascribe writing to the sons of Noah (nor to Adam, another of Arnhem's antediluvian "authors") hardly ruffles this fanciful fundamentalist reconstruction, a reconstruction that Arnhem finds totally "logical." One cannot help but feel that there must be another way to look at the flood story and its composition.

The God of the Gaps

There are those who consider the flood story a seriously fractured fairy tale strung together not so neatly from sources that were originally separate. This effort to break the Bible down into its original parts gets its impetus from a more careful reading of the text than even the fundamentalist might perform. Whereas the fundamentalist might be impressed by the way that Wenham or Arnhem seems to show that the whole story fits together well and is terribly ancient, the modern biblical scholar reads even more closely to find that the story hardly fits together at all and is in fact two stories that have been merged. These inklings have been discussed by scholars for the last two and a half centuries but can still come as something of a shock to pew sitters, who often find the hypothesis initially rather disturbing. Most, however, are glad to move on from a kindergarten view of the Bible to something that exhibits a more subtle historical awareness.

The rabbis of the Middle Ages suspected that something was not quite right with the traditional view that Moses wrote the first five books of the Hebrew Bible, Genesis, Exodus, Leviticus, Numbers, and Deuteronomy. Any thinking reader of the last chapter of Deuteronomy has to pause at least for a second in reading of Moses' death: "Moses, the servant of YHWH, died there in the land of Moab at the command of YHWH" (Deuteronomy 34:5). Is it reasonable, I ask my students, to think that Moses penned the story of his own death, speaking of his bodily disappearance? The rabbis, too, knew this deserved explanation. One medieval talmudic tradition stemming from Rabbi Judah (others say from Rabbi Nehemiah to remind us how rabbinic tradition delights in diversity) suggests that Moses' successor, Joshua, added the bit about Moses' death after Moses died.⁴ Disagreement breaks out when another rabbi (Rabbi Simeon), uncomfortable with the idea that Moses did not write the last chapter, demands to know, "Can we imagine the scroll of the law being short of one letter?"⁵ Apparently unable to imagine such a thing, Rabbi Simeon goes on to picture what must have happened as God dictated the last chapter of Deuteronomy to Moses: God dictated while Moses wrote. Moses wrote chapter 33 as coolly as ever. Then he heard the bad news of chapter 34. Doggedly, he continued to write but did so with tears in his eyes. Such an explanation creatively saves the tradition but stretches our credulity as we are forced to imagine the ink on the last page of the Torah scroll smudged by bitter teardrops. However clever Rabbi Simeon might be, something is clearly not right with the traditional view of Deuteronomy.

The oddities multiply. Just a few verses later in the same chapter of Deuteronomy, we read this resounding judgment concerning Moses' life and work: "Never again did there arise in Israel a prophet like Moses—one who knew YHWH face to face" (Deuteronomy 34:10). Those words "never again" beg the question of how long it takes to make such a judgment. How much time has to elapse before one can extol Moses' eternal greatness? Does Joshua, Moses' immediate successor, really have enough years under his belt to make such a claim? Or, as my students more often observe, does it take *centuries* before such a judgment can be rendered? Perhaps these words were penned at the end of Judah's history, during the time of the exile, when the related books of Joshua, Judges, 1 and 2 Samuel, and 1 and 2 Kings appear to have been pulled together hundreds of years after Moses' day. The ancient rabbis, who were at least perplexed by Moses' death story, do not attempt to explain this time-lapse problem. Presumably Moses did not write about his own future greatness. We are left wondering who did and when. The traditional view of the so-called Books of Moses clearly needs to be revised.

The modern realization that Genesis might represent a compilation of texts rather than one continuous story goes back to the brilliant French physician Jean Astruc (1684–1766). Astruc had puzzled over the question of how the Genesis stories came into the hands of Moses. Like many in his day, Astruc thought that Moses was in some way responsible for the first five books of the Hebrew Bible. He wondered whether the stories in Genesis had been passed down orally or if the ancient patriarchs had kept written records that eventually made their way into Moses' hands.

Suspecting a reliance on written records, Astruc also wondered if the careful eye might discern the outlines of those memoirs in the Book of Genesis. The good doctor decided to conduct a little textual vivisection to see what literary realities might lie deep inside the biblical body.[6]

Astruc's alert medical mind carefully probed the patient. He concluded that various anomalies signaled the presence of at least four sources within the Book of Genesis. Three bits of data tipped him off. First, there were unnecessary repetitions of stories, such as two creation stories in Genesis 1 and 2. Second, alternating segments, which Astruc termed "A" and "B", made use of different names for God, namely, Elohim ("Dieu," or God) and Jehovah ("l'Éternal," Lord, or in Hebrew YHWH). Third, the alternating A and B present many chronological reversals. It seems as if the text is moving forward and backward in time for no apparent reason.

How did Astruc explain these anomalies? He saw in his A and B two different "memoirs" passed down by the ancestors. These memoirs were split apart
by Moses and shuffled together to make one more or less continuous book.
Astruc saw in the repetitive stories, the name disparities, and the chronological
reversals strong indications that Moses had quilted together distinctive retellings
of Israel's most ancient stories.

In addition to A and B, Astruc thought that he could disentangle two other
sources in Genesis. His source "C" consists of segments that repeat details
found in the other sources, but in the case of C neither of the names for God
is used. Finally, source "D" gave facts about non-Israelite peoples. Astruc even
suspected that D might represent a number of fragmentary sources, perhaps
yielding a total of as many as twelve memoirs that Moses drew on to write
Genesis.

Astruc published his findings anonymously. Today, one can sense in his
work something of a Sherlock Holmes flavor. Why, though, publish it anonymously? Astruc presented the results of his detective work cautiously because
he knew the ideas could appear antireligious. After all, he treats Genesis as a
human compendium rather than a work that has dropped out of the sky. Given
that even today fundamentalists greet the current incarnations of Astruc's source
theory with outrage and derision, one can understand his caution.[7] Yet one cannot help but be impressed by the simple logic of his far-reaching investigations.
If Genesis consists of diverse materials at Moses' disposal or, as scholars now
think, draws on sources from various points in Israel's history, centuries after
the time of Moses, we have before us a rich tapestry that deserves closer inspection. If we could decipher the dates and authors behind the sources, we could
rewrite the history of Israel.[8]

What do the sources tell us about the flood story?

The divisions that Astruc held to exist in Genesis overall are seen in the
biblical flood story itself, with one curious twist. The flood story is one place
where A and B do not simply alternate. The seemingly singular flood story of
Genesis looks to be a fusion of two different stories (see the appendix). Astruc
noted many oddities inside the Genesis flood account. As with Genesis as a
whole, so also in the flood tale there are large sections of the story that use different names for the Deity exclusively. Some use Elohim (God), whereas others
use the divine name YHWH (Lord or Jehovah).[9] But the differences go beyond
the use of the divine names. The segments call for different numbers of animals to go into the ark. Is it two pairs of animals as the Elohim section prescribes
(Genesis 6:19–20; 7:9), or two pairs of clean animals *plus* seven pairs of unclean as the YHWH segment commands (Genesis 7:2–3)? Furthermore, the
segments offer different amounts of time to account for the events. The YHWH
segment is more stylized, with its forty days and forty nights (Genesis 7:4, 17),
while the God segment offers more "realistic" lengths of time spelled out in terms
of a calendar of events (Genesis 7:24; 8:3–5, 13–14).

My favorite example is how the segments portray the differently named deity. In Astruc's B segment, we find a YHWH who is rather temperamental and reactive. Caught seemingly off guard by the continuing misdeeds of humans, this YHWH angrily seeks to destroy the earth (Genesis 6:5–7). However, after the flood this same YHWH is readily appeased by Noah's fragrant sacrifice, much as a human king might be pacified by his petitioners, forswearing further destructive deeds (Genesis 8:20–22). The writer of this portion of the Bible is referred to as the "Yahwist" writer, reflecting the use of the name YHWH. This narrative commences in Genesis 2 with the creation of Adam in the garden and includes the expulsion from the garden, the Cain and Abel struggle, and the Tower of Babel judgment. Often this author is more simply designated by the letter "J" after the Germanic version of YHWH, namely, Jahwe. On the positive side, J's YHWH is a god of angry justice. On the negative side, this figure suffers from a dangerous divine distemper.

By contrast, the God (Elohim) of Astruc's A segment is ever detached but continually in control. This divine figure, who dictates the tediously verbose and excruciatingly detailed plan of the ark to Noah (Genesis 6:11–16), is depicted much like Aristotle's Prime Mover, a rather detached lawgiver who governs Nature by means of higher plans and dispassionate knowledge (Genesis 6:11–22). Scholars typically label the author of this portion of the Bible the "Priestly" writer (abbreviated "P"), since many of the "details" that are of concern to this writer (or group of writers) elsewhere in the first five books of the Hebrew Bible have to do with sacrifices, rituals, and matters of cultic purity. This writer's vision of Elohim is revealed at the start of the P record in the first chapter of Genesis, wherein the story of the six days of creation presents us with a highly ordered series of events that culminates step-by-step in the seventh day of Elohim's rest. The day of rest is a rather transparent reference to the Priestly writer's Sabbath day of worship. The orderliness of creation, in other words, is mirrored in P's ritual system. P's deity is a god of order.

If we can invoke an analogy from the Greek world, we can say that whereas the Elohim segments of the flood story offer us the dispassionate and logical Prime Mover of the Priestly writer, the YHWH sections of the Yahwist writer present us with a hotheaded Zeus who is also responsible for booting Adam and Eve out of the Garden of Eden. My students readily recognize the distinctions between these two portraits of God in the flood story, especially when I ask them which of the two deities they would rather have design their house and which one would be a good choice as the bouncer at a local bar. They can easily see that Elohim is the Grand Planner and that YHWH is the temperamental Deity of Doom. Elohim gets to build the house, or at least draws up the plans and tells his devoted servant how to build it. YHWH sees that no loser gets into the bar. (Consider the alternative: YHWH would just as soon knock over your house, while Elohim would compose endless writs against minor barroom infractions as business steadily declined.)

These distinctions represent more than simply two ways of portraying the Deity. There are two different theological conceptions of the divine at work. The ancient Israelites were as broad in their views as the Greeks, some of whom loved the lusty gods of the *Iliad* and the *Odyssey*, while others revered the grand God of the philosophers. The same distinction seems to hold true for the Bible. Only the most conservative of readers resists what appears obvious to the sensitive theological observer, at least since the time of Jean Astruc in the mid–eighteenth century.

By making this distinction between the Planner and the Bouncer, my students have discovered some fundamentals about the flood story that the most careful fundamentalist seems to miss: the Genesis flood story weaves two different tales and two different theologies into one, producing a final story that allows competing conceptions of the divine to sit rather awkwardly side by side. Should we favor one view over the other? While some might prefer the Priestly image of Elohim as an Aristotelian Planner to the Yahwist's Lord of Doom and Gloom, I ask my students not to choose between these images of God. The tradition may be wise in giving us two pictures. Each is, after all, only a likeness or a metaphor. Neither exhausts all that God might be. Indeed, each picture has served as a vehicle of insight for countless generations. Competing portraits can serve complementary aims. Perhaps neither a detached God nor a totally attached Deity should have the final place in our thinking. In any event, the tradition insists that God is not easily stuffed into one theological box.

Travels to Kardu: A Kaleidoscope of Rabbinic Readings

Interestingly, later Jewish tradition brings us yet another approach to reading the Genesis flood tale. Whereas Christian fundamentalists retreat into the one true meaning of the text, and Christian liberals endlessly dissect the origins of the text, Jewish tradition's strength is its willingness to constantly reinvent itself rather than be limited by the biblical text or confined to particular readings of it. Fundamentalist efforts to oversimplify the story or liberal attempts to break it down into a few component parts fall far short of the kaleidoscope rabbinic Judaism offers when reading and rereading the flood tale: the rabbis ask us to live inside the story, inhabit its inner recesses, and observe what may be found. What they discover is tantalizing and imaginative, offering a real alternative to both fundamentalist and modernist readings.

The medieval rabbinic rereading of the text was not without precedent in Jewish tradition. Long before the Talmud arose, the community at Qumran developed intriguing expansions of the Genesis flood story, which have been recovered through the discovery of the Dead Sea Scrolls. For the inhabitants of Qumran, Noah was more than a watery witness; he was a "founder, leader, and lawgiver of a new humanity," a prototype of the supreme lawgiver, Moses.[10] Key documents such as the Genesis Apocryphon, 1 Enoch, and Jubilees—the latter two known also from fuller Ethiopic versions—provide insight into the Jewish willingness to reinvent the tradition for the needs and issues that beset the community long after the completion of the Torah.

In the Qumran imagination, the pre-flood world was a place of violence and forbidden knowledge, terrorized by the so-called Watchers, offspring of wicked angels who had mated with mortal women (1 Enoch 15:1–8; 86:4–5; 106: 13–14; Jub. 7:21–25; cf. Genesis 6:1–8). The resultant half-breeds, divine and mortal, wreaked havoc on the earth. Only the miraculous birth of Noah, himself initially suspected of being a Watcher, brought relief to humankind (1 Enoch 106:16–18). Noah, either endowed with angelic powers or through actual angelic assistance, built the boat that saved the world from this trial of agony, much as the Qumran community saw itself saving the Jewish world from its theological trials at the end of the time (1 Enoch 67:2; 89:1; 93:4–10). The ties that members of the Qumran community saw between their day and Noah's time were made to seem even closer as they recalibrated the chronology of the flood to conform to Qumran's solar-based liturgical calendar, rather than the lunar calendar that dominates the Hebrew Bible (Jubilees 7). While Noah's deeds spared the world divine annihilation, evil persisted after the flood. As a result, true believers must continue to rely on the sacrifices and medicines that Noah bequeathed to the world (Jub. 21:10).[11]

Building on this legacy of hermeneutical openness, the rabbis of late antiquity and the early Middle Ages take the traditions of the Torah into unexplored literary and theological territory. The rabbinic translations of the Hebrew Bible into Aramaic, the Targums (second–fourth centuries C.E.), provide a first glimpse of the creative direction the flood story would take in rabbinic exegesis. The Targums, in other words, were more than translations. They were acts of theological imagination.[12]

It is curious, for example, that the Targums give us a completely different landing spot for the ark, namely, the Kardu Mountains of Kurdistan and Armenia south of the favorite Mount Ararat. Reflecting the location also known to the Jewish writer Josephus (37–101 C.E.), this alternative identification has caused consternation for those Christian fundamentalists who insist the ark is on the more traditional mountain.[13] Other fundamentalists relish these alternatives, thinking that Josephus and the Targums preserve clues to explain why the Ararat searches have failed. They are looking for the boat in the "wrong" place! This may explain why still others have been spurred farther afield to Iran in search of the lost ark.[14] Rabbinic interpretation is literally taking the Bible to new places. We may treat travels to Kardu as a metaphor for the entire rabbinic enterprise.

The Targums offer changes great and small to the story. Unlike the Qumran documents, the Targums downplay any talk of fallen angels cohabiting with human women. Instead, they speak of "great sons" or "sons of judges," that is, humans, who committed evil and thereby caused the flood. By contrast, many later rabbinic interpreters will restore talk of the angels (see later discussion).

One item found in the Targums that figures into later rabbinic interpretation is the issue of God's compassion. Any sensitive reader of the biblical text would have to admit that the flood story complicates the assessment of God as merciful, especially when the entire world has been wiped out through God's wrath. Is this not overkill? In response, the Targums tinker with the text by modifying the reference to the human life span of 120 years (Genesis 6:3), transforming the period into the number of years that God allotted for repentance before sending the flood. Granting people well over a century to mend their ways was considered a sign of God's mercy. The flood almost seems like a grievous afterthought. It is as if corrupt humanity had left God no choice.

Closely related to this notion of compassion, the Targums also anticipate the later negative rabbinic estimates of Noah's character. The rabbis resisted the idea that Noah had done something special to deserve his rescue (Tg. Genesis 6:3). Instead, they follow the Targums, which attribute the deliverance of Noah solely to God's mercy and grace. The reader will not be surprised to find Noah drunk after the flood. His survival is a sign of God's care, not Noah's goodness. The tone reflects the view that humans are corrupt, but also that God's saving intent is assured despite our waywardness. Whatever the original biblical text intended to convey in the drunkenness tale (see chapter 8), the rabbis felt free to refashion the text to speak to the theological dilemmas of a later age.

Already in the Targums, then, the rabbis were beginning to show us how to live inside the story, kneading the biblical dough into all manner of theological delights. But the Targums offer only hints of things to come. The great body of rabbinic lore known as the Talmud takes the story much further to create a living storytelling tradition. As Howard Schwartz explains,

> These stories retained their immediacy because subsequent generations gave themselves to projecting themselves into the biblical archetypes and reliving the myths in themselves. In this way it was possible for the *Aggadah* [i.e., medieval Jewish legends and allegories built closely on biblical stories] to become a vehicle for the personal and mythic expressions of the people that could then be absorbed into the tradition, as well as the means of permitting the religion to evolve, which it did.[15]

This approach, which Schwartz dubs "reading between the lines of the Torah," allowed the rabbis "to discover the answer to all of their unanswered questions" and "to fill in the gaps in the biblical narrative."[16] The flood story serves as fodder for the rabbinic reworking of the tradition to meet the needs of later generations.

There is, for example, in talmudic tradition a fascination with the generation that lived before the flood, especially the intermingling of divine beings with human women. This no doubt stems from tales of the Watchers like those found at Qumran. The medieval period, however, saw further developments. In one rabbinic text, the angels Shamhazai and Azzael (figures found in the Qumran texts) demand that God allow them to live among humans to show what good can be made of the earth.[17] Presumably humans were doing an unsatisfactory job. Reluctantly, God permits the angels to try their hand at earthly matters. God's apprehension proves to be well-founded, for soon the angels become sexually involved with human women, and Shamhazai has two children, named Hiva and Hayya. Then the announcement of the flood goes forth. Shamhazai is grieved to learn that his children are to be destroyed by the coming flood. However, he and his half-human descendants are comforted when they learn that their names will be shouted out by laborers and sailors as they go about their tasks, exclaiming, "Hiva" and "Hayya," much as we might shout out "Heave ho!"[18] This tale of boundary crossings by divine beings expresses the morality of the rabbis, who in other texts seek to strictly regulate matters of sexual purity and gender interaction. Here the legend serves a similar purpose but roots such values in the twists and turns of the more ancient flood tradition. In other words, the recasting of the story serves to update the biblical traditions in light of more contemporary concerns.

Some of the rabbinic commentary seeks to tie the flood story more closely to the story of creation earlier in Genesis. The rabbis offer observations about both creation's "light" and creation's "waters" to this end. They taught that the proclamation in Genesis 1 that the light of creation was good really meant that the light was "for the good," which is to say that the light was for "good people." This light was withdrawn from the wicked when God saw the evil generation of the flood. This good light for good people has since been set aside for the just in the Garden of Eden.[19] Some taught that the waters of the second day of creation were not called "good" because God knew ahead of time that those waters would one day be used to punish humankind.[20]

We see in these interpretations a rabbinic effort to ground the flood more consciously into a theology of creation. The flood does not stand as an anomalous event in the flow of history but is a clear embodiment of principles at work since the foundation of the world. The flood as an instrument of judgment may seem to be out of step with the ordering of creation as laid down in Genesis 1, but in actuality, according to the rabbis, it is the logical counterpart to the world's ordered structures. Although disruption seems at times to gain the upper hand, there is an ordered dimension to the world that is breaking through even in times of chaos. God's ultimate intention is to bring order out of the chaos.

The rabbis use the figure of Noah to represent the order that displaces disorder. Before the time of Noah, the planting of wheat and barley yielded only thorns and thistles. But after Noah, so say the rabbis, when wheat was planted, wheat is what grew. The era before Noah was a time of heavy labor: the ground had to be worked with bare hands. But the bringer of order, Noah, is said to have invented the tools needed to make the ground more workable, namely, plows, hoes, and the like. Agriculture was once impeded because the heifers would disobey the plowmen, but after Noah's appearance the heifers did as they were supposed to do.[21] In each case, the rabbinic picture goes into far greater detail than the biblical story, which simply said the world before Noah was corrupt. In practical terms, the rabbis expand on the notion that the world before the flood was in severe disrepair and that Noah was somehow especially endowed by God to bring cosmos out of chaos.

This is not to say that all rabbis were in agreement regarding the character of Noah. Some thought that although the Bible says that Noah was righteous for his own generation (Genesis 6:9), he would not have stood out in other ages. To Rabbi Hanina, Noah was like a jar of wine amid jars of vinegar, a common wine jar that in other places would go unnoticed. Rabbi Oshaia taught otherwise, deeming Noah a fragrant flask of oil lying in the midst of excrement, an oil that would have been noticed even among other spices.[22] When Genesis says that Noah "walked with God" (Genesis 6:9), some took this as a sign of his weakness, for when the Bible chooses to characterize the patriarch Abraham, it says instead that Abraham walked "before" God, an apparent mark of his strength, according to the rabbis.[23] All this is probably designed to anticipate the troubling episode of Noah's drunkenness that closes the Genesis flood story. Somehow Noah's justice and his depravity have to be made to gel, and thus the rabbis suggest that hints of Noah's less redeeming qualities must also be embedded in the earliest parts of the text.

The rabbis make heavy weather of the fact that God was quite patient in waiting to send the flood against that evil generation. A reading of the Bible's own story might lead one to think otherwise. As we have seen, the Yahwist's version puts great emphasis on YHWH's regret and temperamental anger, while the Priestly version proceeds matter-of-factly from God's decision to the rather swift sending of the flood. Over time, however, it seems that this made God look less than compassionate. By filling in gaps in the story, the rabbis subtly but significantly offer to their generation a God who is at heart compassionate while remaining the Bible's God of justice.

Thus, the rabbis tell us that God warned the people for 120 years before telling Noah to make the ark of a particular type of wood. Noah, in turn, bought that generation additional time for repentance by planting the trees and warning them all the while the trees were growing. Even while he was sawing the beams for the ark and assembling the vast boat, Noah offered more warnings.[24] During that time, the rabbis recount that the people responded to Noah with sharp ridicule and a plan of action, claiming they had iron plates that would cover the rising waters. They also boasted of possessing a fungus that could be worn on their heads as a covering to ward off the rain.[25] Elsewhere, God is said to have grieved a further seven days at the very last before actually sending the flood.[26] Likewise, the fact that God allowed ten generations to pass between Adam and Noah is taken as a sign of divine patience, since each generation had sinned grievously against God.[27] Essentially, the rabbis teach that divine compassion makes ample room for sinners to recant their unbelief, but also that there is a limit to divine tolerance. Thus, in the final moments, so the rabbis tell us, when the people tried to tip over the ark, God surrounded it with lions to seal their doom.[28]

Through such elaborations on the flood tale, the Bible's picture of the God of judgment gives way to the rabbinic vision that God is essentially compassionate. The rabbinic additions to the tale are not simply tasteful flourishes to an otherwise complete tale; they represent a dramatic transformation of the theology of the more ancient and primitive tales of Genesis. We see in the rabbinic retellings of the flood tale a brilliant set of theological moves to keep the tradition alive for a medieval generation of dispersed Jews, offering them a vision of a God who is deeply involved in the world. This God wills that people work to mend the world and gives them every opportunity to prove themselves in this endeavor.

Some rabbis were bothered by the fact that animals perished in the flood because of human sin. Why did God choose to destroy innocent animals along with sinful humanity? Some argued that God's action was analogous to that of the man who destroyed his son's bridal canopy when his son tragically died soon after the wedding. Just as the canopy, which had been made for the son, was no longer needed, so also the animals, which had been made for humankind, were no longer needed by God.[29] The amorality of this analogy is countered by another tradition, which contends that the animals were not so innocent after all. How bad were those days? Some rabbis taught that when the Bible says all flesh was corrupt, it means just that. Even the animals bred in perverse ways, so that "the dog mated with the wolf, the rooster with the peacock."[30] The earth itself produced weeds from wheat. All was confused, and all came under divine condemnation. According to some rabbis at least, nothing on earth deserved to escape God's judgment. In this and in other places, we find the rabbis bringing theological consistency and reasonableness to a story that has some rather gaping moral holes.

Beyond such moral musing, the rabbis also had a taste for literary embellishment. What, they asked, were conditions like on the ark?

Behind the solid walls of the boat, Noah had no need for lamps because he had installed a special pearl that gave off the appropriate light for day and night.[31]

Maintaining the animals aboard the ark would have been an enormous task. The rabbis expand on the possibilities. In one tradition, Abraham's servant Eliezer, who was puzzled about daily life on the ark, learned from Noah's son Shem that feeding the animals was a terrific chore because some animals ate only during the daytime and others ate at night.[32] Feeding them around the clock was a grueling task. One tradition suggests that Noah's hectic schedule left him no time for rest, but miraculously he did not need to sleep during his time on the ark.

Shem reports that Noah had no idea what to feed the chameleon until it ate a worm that had injudiciously emerged from a pomegranate. Problem solved!

The phoenix was rewarded with eternal life for not bothering Noah about its feeding times—an understandable reward from a man who was doubtless terribly wearied by his labors. The basic diet for the animals appears to have been vegetarian, according to the rabbis, except for the ostrich, which was given glass to munch (an obvious folkloric element).

Certainly the labors were taxing on poor Noah. In addition, he was said to have been attacked by a lion whose feeding time he had missed. Needless to say, one rabbinic tradition suggests that Noah fell seriously ill because of the animals' heavy feeding demands.[33]

On one score, at least, Noah was spared. A large whalelike creature, the re'em, was apparently not brought onto the ark but was simply tethered to its hull.[34] Whether the ark was up to the task of actually carrying such an animal on board seems to have troubled the rabbis. Some thought that the creature was too large; its excrement was said to have been big enough to stop up the Jordan River.[35] There was no way such a creature could have been inside the ark. Perhaps, others thought, only a young re'em was brought on board, or else the behemoth was tied to the outside of the ark, allowing only its head or even the tip of its nose to poke inside. Presumably it fed on the fish that were left to roam the flood's currents, although here there were other difficulties because some taught that the people of the world were boiled to death as an appropriate divine response to their hot and passionate sexual misdeeds.[36] The ark was spared by a ring of cool water that surrounded it, but one wonders about all those fish. If they were boiled to death, then this means that Noah would also have needed to transport the world's fish aboard the ark in some sort of aquarium. The rabbis do not take these questions much further. Theirs was an age of moral musing and not scientific speculation. Literary embellishment in the service of religious truth was one thing; historical certitude was not their primary intent.

In all this, the early medieval rabbis create a sense of moral depth and narrative realism out of a story that otherwise is rather brief and fanciful. By elaborating on Noah's arduous labors, they made it possible for hearers to relate to a figure who is otherwise seemingly beyond their own time and place. Rather than turn Noah into a distant superman, the rabbis make him a mensch among men to inspire us. The long-term message is clear: we should not shirk the labors of the moment, for in them we are doing Noah-like service, bringing life to a world that totters on the brink of destruction. Only those in the boat know the way forward. The survival of Jewish life and culture, in other words, rested squarely on the shoulders of observant Jews and their revered teachers. How right they were. The reinventing of the story was integral to the survival of the tradition.

As the floodwaters dissipate, the well-known story of the sending forth of the birds receives new twists. The rabbis saw in the raven's flitting to-and-fro signs of the fowl's contentiousness. The raven is said to have complained that Noah was risking the extinction of all ravens, since he was sending out one of only a pair of unclean birds. What should happen if the male raven perished? The raven's line would cease. Some suggested that the raven even feared that Noah was lusting after the raven's mate and was just trying to get him off the boat so that Noah could have his way with her![37] Later, Noah sends forth the dove. The dove brings back the olive branch, a fact that caused even our prescientific rabbis to wonder where the branch came from if all things on earth had perished. The ready-made explanation was that the very gates of Eden were opened for the dove.[38]

After the flood, the rabbis berate Noah for planting a vineyard rather than the decidedly more useful figs or olives. In this way, Noah is credited with profaning the landscape (Genesis 9:20). Another tradition adds that Satan assisted Noah in planting the vineyard. In the process Satan slaughtered a ewe lamb, a lion, a monkey, and a pig, using their blood to irrigate the vineyard. The net effect is seen when people drink:

> The charade was Satan's way of saying that when a man drinks one
> cup of wine, he acts like a ewe lamb, humble and meek. When he
> drinks two, he immediately believes himself to be as strong as a lion
> and proceeds to brag mightily, saying, "Who is like me?" When he
> drinks three or four cups, he immediately becomes like a monkey,
> hopping about giggling, and uttering obscenities in public, without
> realizing what he is doing. Finally, when he becomes blind drunk, he
> is like a pig, wallowing in mire and coming to rest among refuse.[39]

Poor Noah. Though he secures the survival of the human race, after the flood he is thought of as no more than a beggar and a thief. He has saved the world, but the divine curses against creation are not undone. Thus, the rabbis leave him in a rather dejected state, reminding us that without God's sense of balance and order, we humans are bound to make drunkards of ourselves and pigsties of the world. Through the creative imagination of the rabbis, the story is transformed from a quaint and dated legend about the ancient Noah into a moralistic anecdote about public life and social decorum.

In this sense, then, Noah's age prepared the way for the necessity of Torah, the written code of instruction given to Moses by God on Sinai. The rabbis taught that the six commandments given to Noah (some say seven) had to yield to the comprehensive 248 positive commandments and the 365 negative commandments given to Moses.[40] For the rabbinic tradition, in other words, the flood story and its aftermath underscored the relevance of the legal system of the Jewish Bible. Without those commandments we would relapse into the time of Noah—decidedly not a pleasant prospect, according to the rabbis.

In this way, later tradition acknowledged that Noah, in part, nurtured the order that was needed for life outside God's garden. Yet only the house of Torah, remodeled time and again through sound rabbinic reinterpretation, could provide the safe house needed for the survival of God's people in the post-flood world. For the rabbis, a tradition that continually reinvents itself is the best option for preserving Jewish faith and practice. In Schwartz's words, "Each time this takes place, the tradition is transformed and must be reimagined. And it is this very process that keeps the tradition vital and perpetuates it."[41] Thus, Noah's era becomes ours; Noah's struggles attest to the enduring Jewish struggle; Noah's survival signals medieval Jewish hope; Noah's God represents the divine designer of every rabbinic age.

Patterns, Pieces, or Pundits? Decrypting the Bible Code

So which is it? A seamless story? A fractured fairy tale? A tradition always in transition?

The perspective that we choose determines to a great extent how we understand the flood story's religious significance and ultimate theological role. For the fundamentalist, if the story does not hang together, then God cannot be behind it. The fundamentalist's view of the Bible is that God breathes out every detail of the Book and oversees the preservation of the tradition. Since God is a God of truth, the Book cannot lie in whole or in part. The Bible's flood story is the truth, the whole truth, and nothing but the truth—truth, that is, in a historical and factual sense. The patterns that Wenham discerns in the text are signs to the fundamentalist that God is the ultimate author of the Book.

Doubtless it is this fascination with divine patterns that has made books like Michael Drosnin's *The Bible Code* and Jeffrey Satinover's *Cracking the Bible Code* so popular. Appearing at virtually the same time, these two books draw on statistical theories about the Hebrew Bible to claim that hidden messages and divine prophecies are embedded in biblical books such as Genesis. This kind of literalism makes Wenham's mirror pattern look tame. *The Bible Code* and *Cracking the Bible Code* popularize the theories of Doron Witztum, Eliayahu Rips, and Yaov Rosenberg, who in 1994 offered up the puzzles of "Equidistant Letter Sequences in the Book of Genesis."[42] By skipping through the Hebrew Books of Moses and reading every third letter, or tenth letter, or fiftieth letter (or whichever spacing pattern the decoder desires), the modern reader can suddenly discern hidden words and phrases. The idea goes back in recent times to Rabbi Weissmandel, who "noticed that if he skipped fifty letters, and then another fifty, and then another fifty, the word 'Torah' was spelled out at the beginning of the Book of Genesis."[43] It is as if Moses, or whoever wrote Genesis and the other so-called Books of Moses, were a spy working for the Central Intelligence Agency of the ancient Judaean Security Services.

Both Drosnin and Satinover discern hints of newsworthy events of our own time locked away in the Hebrew words of the Books of Moses, secrets only modern cryptographers armed with sophisticated computer programs can ever hope to uncover. Drosnin argues, for example, that news of Prime Minister Yitzhak Rabin's assassination was tucked away in the Book of Deuteronomy, awaiting the observant eyes of later decoders. While much of his book is taken up with dire predictions for the fate of Israel and the world today, Drosnin also sees many twentieth-century events encoded in the Hebrew Bible: the 1995 Oklahoma City bombing; the 1991 Gulf War; *Apollo 11*'s landing on the moon; President Kennedy's assassination; Hitler's slaughter of the Jews; the Great Depression; the Wright brothers' first air flight; and even Edison's invention of the lightbulb! Yet Drosnin's primary focus is on the "end of days," the end of the world, an event that is somehow linked with 1995–96 (Hebrew 5756) but also delayed. He finds even greater terrors for the years 2000 and 2006 and offers up comet collisions in 2006, 2012, and 2126. The hidden messages Satinover finds tend to be mild by comparison, but he does occasionally add such items as the AIDS crisis and the assassination of Anwar Sadat.[44]

Are we to thank God for giving us the software to finally be able to read the literal meaning of the letterspacing of the Hebrew Bible? Of course, relying as they are on the consonantal Hebrew text (shorn of its traditional vowel points), Drosnin and Satinover are working with such flexible parameters that any clever computer programmer can make many such "encrypted messages" appear. If the consonants of the name or the word we are looking for can be 2, 3, 78, or any other number of spaces apart, whether forward, backward, or diagonally, in any size sentence array that we care to produce, there is no doubt that most lengthy books can be made to offer up a variety of supposed prophecies. The mathematical ruse, thus, becomes clearer when we turn to these other books for hidden messages. As a way to debunk this sort of misguided literalism, Shlomo Sternberg asked Australian mathematician Brendan McKay to search *Moby Dick* for hidden messages. We now know that *Moby Dick* "predicted" such infamous events as the assassinations of John F. Kennedy, Indira Gandhi, and Martin Luther King Jr. Even the attack on New York's World Trade Center can be "found" in Melville's veiled work.[45]

That debunkers can find similar "predictions" in other works of literature doubtless will not diminish the enthusiasm of those who claim to find God in the patterns of scripture or in the spaces between its letters, but such literalism can hardly be said to do justice to the flood story or any other story in the Hebrew Bible. The sort of intense literalism that Drosnin and Satinover offer no doubt takes the text very seriously. In the process, however, it dispenses with the surface story of the text in favor of the deep underlying codes that only we moderns with sophisticated computer programs can recover. One wonders what these authors make of the Bible's stories as such or the meanings they have had for observant Jews and believing Christians over the centuries. On Drosnin's and Satinover's reading, the Bible was a pointless agglomeration until now, when its sense has become apparent. One feels sorry for all those readers over the centuries who thought that the surface story had some bearing on religious insight and spiritual practice.

The second group, namely, those who fracture the fairy tale into many sources such as the Yahwist and Priestly writers, find God not in the larger edifice (as does Wenham) or in the arrangement of the individual bricks (as do Drosnin and Santinover) so much as in the mortar that separates the courses in the walls. They believe that the diversity of scripture is its strength. They revel in the old Jewish adage that where there are two rabbis there are three opinions. They see in the fragmentation of scripture, with its many flood stories, not a sign of divine neglect but proof that God is to be found in the rough-and-tumble of our collective dialogue and disputes over who God is. They are very much aware that God is not to be trapped inside one story or metaphor. For those who find more than one flood story in the Genesis tale, these diverging stories set cheek by jowl are not simply "apparent contradictions" to be harmonized at all costs, as they are to the fundamentalist, but a sword of knowledge and the whetstone of truth that, when struck together, yield even sharper insights into the mystery of Israel's God.

Of course, to the fundamentalist this liberal project is like wandering through a forest without a compass or a map. The fundamentalist thinks of modern biblical scholars as hopelessly lost without the North Star of God's undivided truth to guide them, namely, the seamless Bible in all its patterns. However, to the modern biblical investigator, our ability to listen to the different writers who have contributed to the formation of scripture, in this case the Yahwist writer and the Priestly writer, makes the quest for the divine also a very human quest.

This does not mean that liberals deny a divine dimension to scripture but rather that we should not look for God apart from ancient Israel's diverse theological responses to war, exile, and history. Whereas the fundamentalist seeks truth from a Bible that is historically accurate in all its details, the liberal finds truth in a Bible that emerges from the fractured historical experiences of ancient Israel and the ancient debates about God's justice that ensued from these experiences.

There is, however, a third way to read scripture, supplied by the rabbis. Those who see the flood story as a tradition always in transition, as did the medieval rabbis, realize that living off the past, whether through fundamentalist patterns or liberal dissection, is not enough. The rabbis of the Middle Ages tapped the elasticity of the tradition to use the stories to speak to the changed conditions of the Jewish community of medieval Europe and the Middle East. Where the fundamentalist wants us to go back to the perfect Bible and re-create its patterns in the here and now, and where the liberal wants us to enter the fragmented dialogue of the Bible to discern the deeper truth, the rabbis teach us that we are always living inside the infinite variations of the biblical stories. Each retelling opens up new possibilities and new vistas. There is not one pattern to re-create and live by, as the fundamentalist thinks. There are not just two, three, or four voices from the past who have left us to puzzle out for ourselves where God is in the world today, as the liberal maintains. Rather, for the rabbis, the infinitely multifaceted character of this biblical diamond is precisely what keeps the stories shimmering generation after generation.

To grasp the vitality of the biblical tradition as the rabbis do, we must seek to live inside the nooks and crannies of the tradition, not simply replicate the fundamentalist's primal pattern or the liberal's splintered kerygmas. This is the practical legacy that the medieval rabbis offer those in church, synagogue, and mosque who continue to rely on the biblical text for guidance and inspiration. The tradition lives on in a vital way, so the rabbis tell us, only if it finds ways to reinvent itself. While today there is a tendency for religious communities to rely on bite-sized morsels of scripture as if the tradition were frozen in time, the rabbinic rescripting of the old tales can work to kindle our theological imaginations and whet our spiritual appetites.

The question I raised earlier comes back to hound us: Is the Genesis story seamless, fractured, or a tradition continually under reconstruction? While each view is possible depending on our angle of vision, the fact is that no single approach exhausts the meaning of the text. Certainly, fundamentalist "literalism" misses much that can be said about the text. So if God does not weave an entirely seamless web, then perhaps neither should we, at least not out of the flood story. In probing the tale with an intensity that is not altogether unlike that of the fundamentalist—though without insisting on finding a singular meaning for the text—both the modern biblical critic and the ancient rabbis help us to uncover some of the many hidden treasures of scripture to challenge our thinking today. We are reminded by these acts of literary investigation and theological imagination that not all answers are found by means of the dirt archaeologist's spade. Sometimes deep and persistent textual archaeology is required to probe the meaning of the religious tradition and its ancient tales, though, as we shall see, our literary excavators, regardless of ideological stripe, do not have the last word either.

4

Just after Breakfast on Sunday, October 23, 4004 B.C.

Fundamentalist Literalism and Creation "Science"

The problem for those who wish to take the Genesis story literally is that the facts tend to get in the way. We have seen this in the case of the literary facts of the Genesis flood narrative, where our detection of divergent editorial strands undermined the attempt to read the story in a seamless way. But it is not just the texts that have created problems for the Bible reader. Terra firma has her own peculiar story to tell. With the unearthing of prehistoric geological layers and ancient fossils the world over, the facts of nature and evolution began to rear their heads, insisting on a hearing of their own. As explorers, naturalists, fossil hunters, and geologists have learned to read the book of nature more attentively, perplexing insights have emerged along with new readings of the Bible. Reacting negatively to the trends, fundamentalists have outdone themselves in offering up their own peculiar spin on scientific advances. In this chapter I take up their more recent interest in a young earth and a global flood, and in the next chapter I will look back to their early scientific predecessors. Conservative Christianity turns out to be a more complex phenomenon than recent trends in those circles might lead one to imagine.

Pioneers of Biblical Flood Geology

For readers who might have thought the issues were settled by geologists and biologists long ago, let us begin with an eye-opening view of the current version of the debate between science and religion. What is all the fuss about "fundamentalist flood geology"?

Despite the advances in our understanding of millions of years of human evolution, there are those in fundamentalist circles who remain devoutly committed to Whitcomb and Morris's view that the catastrophe of the flood is sufficient to explain the odd shape of the world we know today. In their book, *The Genesis Flood: The Biblical Record and Its Scientific Implications*, a text that has achieved near-legendary status among fundamentalists, J. C. Whitcomb and H. Morris conjure up a detailed defense of the basic views of Christian "flood geology." To their fans, Whitcomb and Morris are the "Davids who slew the Goliath of evolution."[1] However, these fundamentalist heroes did not suddenly appear from nowhere in 1961. Such ideas began to percolate early in the twentieth century, although not always with the narrow-minded bent of Morris and Whitcomb. What were the steps along the way?

The fundamentalist movement sought to define itself fairly early on in the century through a major publication effort that brought its ideas to millions of ministers, missionaries, and general readers around the globe. Published between 1910 and 1915, the influential though diminutive twelve-volume collection of essays known as *The Fundamentals: A Testimony to the Truth* quite literally defined the movement in America. These writings ranged across a broad slice of issues dear to the hearts of conservative Christians at the time, especially as they faced the challenges of the modern world and the rise of more liberal forms of biblical interpretation. The scope of the essays was threefold: defense of Christian doctrine, resistance against modernizing trends, and personal testimonies on behalf of the conservative Christian life.

The Fundamentals defended traditional Christian teachings about Christ's virgin birth and divinity, the reality of miracles, the truth of fulfilled biblical prophecy, the genuineness of the Bible's divine inspiration, and the like. With regard to modernizing trends, the collection identifies such diverse dangers as Mormonism, Eddyism (Christian Science), socialism, spiritualism, destructive biblical criticism ("higher criticism"), and Darwinism. In fact, several essays challenge the atheistic tendencies of the evolutionary model, defending the historical truth of the early chapters of Genesis.

One anonymous article entitled "Evolutionism in the Pulpit: By an Occupant of the Pew" denounces ministers who seek to link Darwinism and Christian faith.[2] The writer attacks Darwinism as a system of thought that was "conceived in agnosticism, and born and nurtured in infidelity."[3]

Another essay entitled "Decadence of Darwinism" sounds a note that recurs throughout the collected essays, specifically that modern liberal biblical interpretation is destructive of the Bible's authority.[4] If the Bible cannot be trusted in matters of science, so the argument goes, then it cannot serve as a moral authority either. As H. H. Beach explains, "We cannot depend on the Bible to show us 'how to go to heaven' if it misleads us as to 'how the heavens go.'"[5] This essay also heralds a theme that will echo in the later Scopes trial and down to the present day in fundamentalist circles, namely, whether to permit the teaching of evolution in the public schools. For the writer of "Decadence of Darwinism," the answer was obvious: a view that is so speculative and morally corrupt ought not to be thrust on unsuspecting schoolchildren.

Theologian and geologist G. F. Wright takes a different line of attack in his contribution to *The Fundamentals*. His is an all-out assault against atheistic construals of Darwinian theory, specifically when "variation" and "advantage" are relied on as the key ingredients in the evolutionary process.[6] He argues that no one really knows why variations occur. He points to theistic evolutionists like Asa Gray and Alfred Russell Wallace as examples of Darwinians who have been forced by the facts to acknowledge that reference to God is needed to explain how evolution occurs. Wright also contends that there is just not enough geological time for all this random evolutionary development to take place. Furthermore, he points out that some supposed variations give the recipient no apparent added advantage; human nakedness increases our vulnerability; it does not lessen it. Finally, he thinks it is ridiculous to imagine that life arose spontaneously out of inorganic matter. Better to believe that humans came about by "special creation" than to be taken in by the materialist credo. While Wright was well aware that the secularized reading of evolutionary ideas had a strong following, he felt confident enough of the weakness of this school of thought to entitle his essay "The Passing of Evolution." Wright is a complex figure, one who long championed a kind of Christian Darwinism but resisted its naturalistic tendencies. While by the time of the 1925 Scopes trial the nation's press will identify fundamentalism with the wholesale rejection of evolution, Wright's example shows us that rejectionism was not always the stance taken by conservative Christians in the late nineteenth and early twentieth centuries.[7]

Elsewhere in *The Fundamentals*, J. Orr senses that believers err when they turn the Bible into "a text-book of the newest scientific discoveries." He insists that with respect to the composition of the solar system Copernicus was right, whereas the Bible uses an imprecise "language of appearances" regarding sunrise and sunset. Nevertheless, when it comes to the question of human origins, Orr defends the biblical idea of a sudden creation of humans by God.[8] This, he thinks, is the true scientific significance of Genesis 1–11. Furthermore, he argues that this segment of the Bible is entirely different than the corrupt myths of the ancient Babylonians.[9]

From the point of view of later fundamentalists, Orr is far more progressive than one might at first recognize. Like Wright, he does not cling to the Bible's chronology, which seems to put the earth at no more than 6,000 years old. He treats the six days of creation of Genesis 1 as symbolic days, roughly paralleling the "age and gradual formation of the earth" known to science.[10] He is an evolutionist of sorts, though one who relies on God's purposive providence rather than random variation. However, concerning the flood story, Orr adheres to a strictly historical interpretation of Genesis. He treats the flood as an event that accords quite well with what science tells us about the great catastrophes that attended the glacial and early postglacial periods.[11] In Orr's estimation, this geological era is doubtless reflected in the Bible's narrative. While becoming more literalistic with regard to the flood story, we still see Orr trying to blend the discoveries of science with a nuanced reading of scripture.

Among the writers of *The Fundamentals*, Orr makes the strongest case for science and the Bible to be considered partners. He thinks of science as providing confirmation of the Bible in three important regards: humans as the crown of creation, the unity of the human race, and our common origins in Babylonia. He reminds us that many great pioneers in science were Christian and that the view that religion must battle science is an invention of writers such as J. W. Draper and A. D. White. Fundamentalist circles will not always retain such openness.

Thus, long before Morris and Whitcomb, we find many fundamentalists meshing science and religion, though unlike Morris and Whitcomb these conservative apologists saw affinities between Darwinian evolution and Christian belief. Which raises a key question: How did the antievolutionary mind-set come to dominate fundamentalist discussions of science? We must credit three major voices in the earlier part of the twentieth century for reframing the questions for fundamentalists. These three were the strident John the Baptists of their day, paving the way in the geological wilderness for the messianic arrival of Whitcomb and Morris on the fundamentalist scientific scene.

One key voice was Arthur I. Brown (1875–1947), author of *Evolution and the Bible* (1922) and *Men, Monkeys and Missing Links* (1923), who gave up "his lucrative surgical practice in order to devote his full time to lecture on science and the Bible."[12] Touring the East Coast and the midwestern United States for several years, Brown sought to save the Bible from being turned into a batch of "nursery yarns."[13] His attack was two-pronged. Against evolution, he argued that Darwin's basic ideas had become outmoded among scientists: no transformation of species had ever been attested.[14] On behalf of the Bible, he argued that the creation language of Genesis is simple but accurate, and "fits in amazingly with every modern discovery."[15] If Darwin was dated and the Bible was the best resource for knowledge of the past, why would anyone try to build on the quicksand of "a man-made hypothesis unproven by science" when one might rely on "a simple, God-given record, supported by every known scientific discovery"?[16] Shunning the "mass of moonshine" called evolution, Brown preferred to rely on Moses as "one of the outstanding figures of all time."[17]

Brown's particular brand of antievolutionism made room for an ancient earth but not for men descended from apes. This accommodation to an archaic earth may seem peculiar when compared with current fundamentalist predilections for a young earth, but it appears that most fundamentalists of the time had few problems with an ancient geological record. What Brown battled was not the antiquity of the fossil record but the view that humans shared roots with the apes. On Brown's reading of the record, when humans appear among the fossils, they arrive "complete."[18] Brown summarily dismisses as illusory the evidence for apelike ancestors among the fossils: "That this so-called 'science' has appropriated so much self-certified dignity, and has fooled so many 'educated' men, will ever remain one of the mysteries of this ouija-board age."[19] A line from Brown's poem "'Bunk' and the 'Monk'" tersely sums up his views: "And this 'brain-stormy' theory can't answer my query;— / Not one ape roosts in my family tree!"[20] Not exactly great science or elegant poetry, but it was the sort of lingo that made Brown popular with the crowds and secured the sales of his twenty-five-cent pamphlets.

The next key pioneer was Harry Rimmer (1890–1952). Schooled on the Scofield Reference Bible, with its literal twenty-four-hour days of creation, Rimmer could be found in the 1920s and 1930s in "agitation against evolution."[21] Rimmer produced pamphlets like *Monkeyshines: Fakes, Fable, Facts concerning Evolution*, texts that were "designed to illustrate to high school students the dissimilarity between gorilla and human skulls."[22]

While Rimmer pushed an antievolutionary message, as did many fundamentalists of the time, he did allow for the possibility of an old earth before the seven days of creation (we would say "re-creation") at the time of Adam. Rimmer also thought that the flood of Noah was only a local affair, not a global catastrophe. An aging earth and a local flood is all the ground that Rimmer would give the evolutionists and secular historians. In terms of origins, human fossils may be old, but they are not conjoined to apelike ancestors. To defend his view, Rimmer threaded together three interrelated cords of thought. One was that all animal and human species are established from the start. The second was that the bones of apes and humans (whether ancient or modern) are not related genetically but only by pattern. The third was that there are no links between apes and humans in the fossil record, "missing links" or otherwise.

Of the separate descent of apes and humans Rimmer states rather bluntly: "We would rather a thousand times trace our descent up to God through Adam than down to a sea jelly through wormy ancestors whose children were apes."[23] Ape and human species are fixed, and the twain have never and shall never meet: "No monkey ever gave birth to any creature that in time became man!"[24]

Of the disparities between the bones, Rimmer offers picture after picture to demonstrate to his own satisfaction that humans and apes are quite different: "Even a child can tell the difference."[25] But what, then, are we to make of the seemingly obvious anatomical similarities between apes and humans (such as the sharing of the same number of teeth) despite the gross differences? In Rimmer's view, "resemblance does *not* mean relationship."[26] The similarities reflect the fact that the same Designer made use of similar designs, not that the two creatures are connected genetically to one another: "Into one container He put a human, in the other He put a brute."[27]

Of the so-called missing links, Rimmer makes room for the antiquity of human beings. However, he argues that humans were always humans. Indeed,

Cro-Magnons were "our mental superior"![28] Rimmer understood Neanderthals
to be true humans, not apes as the museums liked to depict them.[29] Rimmer
was annoyed that evolutionists would create whole animal types out of fragmentary evidence such as a single jawbone: "And then they laugh, and say that God
could not make a wife out of a man's rib!"[30]

Reading Rimmer's own whimsical words, we can easily see why so many
found his views persuasive in sound if not in substance:

> Without bones enough to fill a soup dish, but with plenty of plaster
> of Paris, thoroughly mixed with imagination and prejudice, evidence
> can be manufactured. *The fatuous and infantile credulity of the
> evolutionary public are certainly astounding.* Barnum was right. Partly
> at least. He said: "There is a sucker born every minute." He was
> wrong to this extent: There are two born every minute. Barnum got
> one–then evolution gets the other![31]

From plaster of Paris to P. T. Barnum, Rimmer's rousing message carried
the day with the crowds, although as Rimmer's son confessed, "Dad never won
the argument; he always won the audience."[32] He wrote his *Monkeyshines* book-
let "in non-technical language for the average lay reader who can use his eyes
and brain." It was the language of the layperson rather than his cloak of scientific jargon that won Rimmer a popular following.

In many ways, however, the failure of creationists to move beyond pyro-
technics that pleased spectators, but fell short of convincing well-trained scientists, long remained the Achilles' heel of the movement. Rimmer's approach to
the sciences of his day was hardly flattering. He castigated the evolutionists for
fudging the evidence and for choosing to "bludgeon" themselves into conform-
ing to "the bigoted, opinionated, arbitrary demands of a self-elected educational
hierarchy."[33] Despite the invective, Rimmer liked to create an air of scientific
respectability for his own work. He argues rather fiercely that he has gathered
his own set of ape and human skulls–through collection and by his own excavations—allowing him to make an independent analysis of evolutionary claims.[34]
Despite the rhetoric, the lack of properly credentialed scientists among the fundamentalist proselytizers of early twentieth-century creationism would dog the
movement for decades.

The third pioneer of fundamentalist creationism was Seventh-day Adventist
George McCready Price (1870–1963). The cantankerous Price went much further than other fundamentalists of his day, putting a literal seven-day creation
together with a global flood model. Under the influence of Seventh-day Adventist
founder, Ellen G. White (1827–1915), Price stood against both the "gap view"
(which said that the creation of the universe in Genesis 1 occurred long before
the rest of the days in Genesis 1) and the "day-age view" (which said that the
"days" in Genesis 1 were really long epochs of time) to rescue a literal reading
of the Bible from the onslaughts of loose-minded fundamentalists who in Price's

estimation had given too much over to the evolutionists. While someone like Price, when pressed, might accept an ancient earth, he could not agree with the view that life on earth is more than 6,000 years old. Hence, the evolution of humans from common animal ancestors is both a scientific and a theological impossibility. A variety of books put Price on the theological map, including *Illogical Geology: The Weakest Point in the Evolution Theory* (1906); *Q.E.D. or New Light on the Doctrine of Creation* (1917); and his monumental geological textbook, *The New Geology* (1923).

In Price's *Q.E.D.*, the key biblical watchwords were "In the beginning God" and "after its kind." These phrases encapsulate in a nutshell Price's view that only the Divine Magician could pull the protoplasmic rabbit out of the hat of inorganic matter. After living beings were created by God out of inanimate matter, they did not evolve in the Darwinian sense but varied only according to traits dominant or latent in the parent (as Mendel discerned). Life, in other words, comes from God's hand and not randomly out of inorganic matter. Life also perpetuates itself in a species-specific way, not through the gradual accumulation of variations as evolutionists have mistakenly taught.

When it came to matters of geology, Price took issue with two major features of the evolutionary argument. Making the observation that geologically more "ancient" rocks can be found on top of supposedly more "recent" rocks (a feature that geologists explain by the overthrusting of the more ancient layers), Price felt that geologists were not being honest about the mixed-up character of the geological record. He castigates "this theory of Successive Ages which drives otherwise competent observers to throw away their common sense and cling desperately to a fantastic theory in the very teeth of such facts."[35] Furthermore, while geologists posited that such formations can be entirely flipped over because of the movement of the earth's crust (with fossil sequences found in reverse order), Price argued that the supposed direct line of fossils from ancient to modern was shown by the mishmash not to be the neat linear sequence that evolutionists purported.

Like many fundamentalists of the time, Price put money behind his words with the offer that he was "willing to give a thousand dollars to any one who will . . . show me *how to prove* that one kind of fossil is older than any other."[36] Price preferred to explain the entire fossil record by the flood. Would it not be better, he argued, to believe that the flood churned the earth, laid out the strata in a mixed-up fashion, and put fossils willy-nilly in the landscape, sometimes in roughly one sequence and sometimes upside down?

Price stands alone among early twentieth-century fundamentalists. He saw himself on the cusp of a new era in which a true science would emerge to confirm the ancient claims of the Bible regarding human origins and the geological catastrophe of the flood. Drawing his metaphor from the world of banking, Price contended he was living at a time when "the stock of the central holding company [of evolution] itself is still quoted at fictitiously high figures."[37] He imagined that the fortunes of evolutionary science were soon to wane, especially as his writings moved out to a wider public who would see that "the doctrine of Creation is established by scientific discoveries almost like the conclusion of a mathematical problem."[38] Science, in other words, would soon have to confront the literal truth of the biblical flood story.

Ironically, as R. L. Numbers notes, the popularity of Price's geological gospel among fundamentalists was not entirely deserved. Many who hailed the book as a blow against evolution failed to recognize that Price's views about a young earth and a global flood ran counter to common fundamentalist beliefs regarding an old earth (the day-age and gap views) and a nonuniversal flood.[39] Others were skeptical of Price's scientific credentials. Among Latter-day Saints, for example, squabbles among leaders took the form of harangues against Price. Harvard-trained geologist Sterling B. Talmage (1889–1956) told his high-ranking father, James E. Talmage (1862–1933), that Price had "nothing 'new' or any real 'geology'" to offer in *The New Geology*, yet "*With these two corrections, the title remains the best part of the book.*"[40] Hardly a flattering endorsement of Price's work.

Regardless of their checkered career, Price's writings created the most note-worthy ripple regarding flood geology prior to the advent of Whitcomb and Morris. The Deluge Geology Society that he helped establish in 1938 carried on that message through its *Bulletin of Deluge Geology and Related Sciences* until the organization broke up in 1945, a victim of infighting regarding the age of the earth.[41] Certainly, without Price's pioneering efforts, the sea change brought about by Morris and Whitcomb would likely not have occurred. Only through Morris and Whitcomb's successes have the ideas of Price lived on, even if he has not always been acknowledged as a source for such views about the relation between science and the Bible.[42] However, before we turn to consider Whitcomb and Morris, we would be remiss if we did not discuss the watershed event of the century for fundamentalists, the Scopes "Monkey Trial."

Clashes in the Courts: The Flood Story on Trial

Ever since the Scopes trial in 1925, factions among the Christian fundamental-ist crowd have placed their bets on setting up a legislative roadblock against what they perceive as an antibiblical science. The people of Tennessee imagined they had dispelled the evolutionary demon with the Butler Act, which barred the teaching of any evolutionary view of human origins that stood in conflict with a literal reading of the Bible. Great matters of religion and education were at stake when John Scopes proved willing at the instigation of the American Civil Liberties Union (ACLU) to confess that he had broken the law. Scopes had discussed evolutionary concepts with a group of high school students as he helped them prepare for an upcoming science exam. In the mind of Scopes's ACLU defense team, the incident became an occasion to test the Tennessee law.[43]

For its part, the prosecution sought to restrict the case to the bare fact of Scopes's having broken the law (which he readily admitted), deftly avoiding any debate concerning the actual merits of evolution as a scientific theory. As Attorney General A. Thomas Stewart explained at one point in the proceedings,

> We are excepting [i.e., objecting], your honor, to everything here that pertains to evolution or to anything that tends to show that there might or might not be a conflict between the story of the divine creation and evolution, and on the same theory we will except to this scientific testimony on the ground it is incompetent, because it is, so far as this case is concerned, it invades the province of the court and jury, and ask your honor to exclude the jury while we argue this matter.[44]

The judge was quite willing to indulge the prosecution's case at every opportunity. As a result, the prolonged seesaw battle in the courtroom devolved largely around which sort of evidence would be admissible during the proceedings. The poor jurors, who presumably thought they would have a front-row seat for the entire proceeding, missed most of the action, since they were barred from actually hearing the points of dispute.

On the other hand, the defense aimed (1) to challenge the constitutionality of a law that restricted teachers from properly teaching their science and (2) to argue that a kind of Christian evolution was possible even though the Genesis creation story itself ruled out evolution. As defense attorney Dudley Malone explains,

> While the defense thinks there is a conflict between evolution and the Old Testament, we believe there is no conflict between evolution and Christianity. There may be a conflict between evolution and the peculiar ideas of Christianity, which are held by Mr. Bryan as the evangelical leader of the prosecution, but we deny that the evangelical leader of the prosecution is an authorized spokesman for the Christians of the United States. The defense maintains that there is a clear distinction between God, the church, the Bible, Christianity and Mr. Bryan.[45]

Such "distinctions" were lost on the court. The courtroom drama turned on competing understandings of religion, science, and education that failed to overturn the admitted predispositions of the court and jurors or woo jurors away from a literal reading of the Bible.

The contest reached a head with a clash of the juridical titans. A defining moment in legal and educational history was reached late on the seventh day of the trial, pitting defense attorney Clarence Darrow against that great populist politician William Jennings Bryan (who had joined the plaintiffs). The cunning Darrow, donning the mantle of academic freedom, defended the right of a science teacher to teach the best science of the day, regardless of the religious sensitivities of the school's clientele. Darrow sought to beat back Bryan, who had ridden into the sleepy town of Dayton as a crusader for biblical literalism, though not entirely the narrow literalism that Darrow envisioned as true of all conservative Christians. Bryan stood firmly by the good taxpaying Christian citizens of Tennessee who simply wanted their schoolteachers to teach only what they were contracted to teach, not contradict the community's religious beliefs. At that crucial moment in the trial, when Darrow brilliantly elected to call that great crusader himself, William Jennings Bryan, to the witness stand as his final "expert" on matters of the Bible and science, the world was assured of a courtroom clash that would reverberate to the present time.

Darrow grilled Bryan on a series of biblical absurdities. If Adam and Eve were the first people, where on earth did Cain get his wife?[46] Did the sun actually stand still as it says in the Book of Joshua? Or, more scientifically stated, wouldn't the world have suffered a meltdown if the earth had stopped spinning on its axis to make it appear as if the sun had come to a halt?[47] Was Jonah really swallowed by a whale and then spit up alive three days later?[48] How can the Bible's date for the creation of humankind be accurate if there are civilizations that are older than 4004 B.C.E., such as China and Egypt?[49] Can all the world's languages really have come about since the time of the Tower of Babel, roughly 2218 B.C.E.?[50] This cavalcade of absurdities, for Darrow, included the Bible's story of the flood.[51] How could such a story be taken literally? Could Bryan point to any reputable scientist who actually believed in a literal worldwide flood that took place in 2348 B.C.E.? After some hesitation, Bryan spoke of George McCready Price, whose work was discussed earlier in this chapter. Uncomfortably, Price was the only authority on the Bible and geology Bryan could invoke to lend an air of scientific veracity to the literalist reading of the biblical flood story.[52] Despite the jokes that Bryan made in the face of Darrow's relentless interrogation, Bryan's defense of antiscientific dogma was dismal. Darrow had, in the process, effectively demonstrated the fact that the literalist is as much an interpreter of the Bible as anyone else, if only a poorer one.

Perhaps to compensate for the sloppiness of his responses, Bryan actually took pride in expressing ignorance of books, data, and theories that might challenge or broaden his views. Consider this exchange:

DARROW   "You have never in all your life made any attempt to find out about the other peoples of the earth—how old their civilizations are—how long they had existed on the earth, have you?"

BRYAN   "No, sir, I have been so well satisfied with the Christian religion that I have spent no time trying to find arguments against it."

In the course of this combat, defense attorney Malone interjected that Bryan's Christianity was not the only sort of Christian reading of the Bible and science.[53] A more positive relation with modern views was possible in the minds of many Christians. Yet even the possibility that Christians might disagree with him and be open to evolution seemed alien to Bryan.

To his undoing, Bryan defended the view that the "days" of Genesis 1 were not literal twenty-four-hour days.[54] This view was hardly unusual in conservative Christian circles, as we have seen, but it was the kind of recasting of the text that Darrow capitalized on to demonstrate that a modern view of Genesis could not be consistently literal in the narrow sense. At some level, even Bryan knew this. Thus, for Bryan, creation "might have continued for millions of years."[55] The earth might be quite old, even if humans were created only 6,000 years ago. In Darrow's mind this led to yet another absurdity because the sun's creation on day four, which Bryan accepted as true based on the Bible's story, would have left the world without a sun for millions of years.[56] While fundamentalist interpretation left open the meaning of "day," it is clear that Bryan had not worked out the full implications of his views. Literalism alone was bad enough, but literalism linked to unreflective interpretation led to the heights of absurdity, as Bryan's testimony showed under Darrow's withering questioning.

The final acrimonious exchange of that day of the trial sums up what the debate looks like when strident secularism tangles with a narrow-minded religion:

BRYAN   "Your honor, I think I can shorten this testimony. The only purpose Mr. Darrow has is to slur at the Bible, but I will answer his question. I will answer it all at once, and I have no objection in the world, I want the world to know that this man, who does not believe in a God, is trying to use a court in Tennessee—

DARROW   "I object to that."

BRYAN   –(Continuing) to slur at it, and while it will require time, I am willing to take it."

DARROW   "I object to your statement. I am exempting you on your fool ideas that no intelligent Christian on earth believes."[57]

For Darrow's team, the Bible cannot continue to be read literally and survive in an age of science. For Bryan, the Bible has all the answers one needs; further investigation is not required.

The faltering character of Bryan's testimony in defense of biblical literalism has long convinced liberals of the nonsensical nature of fundamentalist "science." Yet this apparent stumbling results in part from the fact that not all Christian literalists were alike, nor were they as simpleminded about the Bible as Darrow may have wished. The trouble was that the nuances could hardly be reduced to courtroom sound bites. Still, it seems clear that Bryan had not thoroughly worked out his own brand of literalism, and so looseness about Genesis 1 sat awkwardly beside strictness about the flood tale. Regardless of his performance, Bryan's death shortly after the trial left conservative Christians with a martyr to hail, one who had resolutely stood against the scourge of atheism at the cost of his own life. On the other hand, Darrow's final judgment on Bryan's "fool ideas" underscores once and for all the view that Christians, no matter what their stripe, inevitably interpret the Bible. The choice for moderns is clear: literal interpretation creates absurdities; thinking people today need a nuanced nonliteral interpretation of the creation and flood stories if the stories are to retain their moral authority.

This clash of the titans has lived on in judicial lore, but the Scopes trial can actually be seen as something of a draw. Scopes was initially convicted of the misdemeanor and fined the stipulated $100. The case was later dismissed by the state's supreme court on a technicality, even as the high court continued to uphold the validity of the state statute against evolution. In the larger scheme, however, the questions raised by the trial were of great moment: Is there one science for the rest of the country and another for restrictive religious groups? Should a teacher present what science says is true or limit the curriculum to what parents insist should be taught, even if the parents are ignorant in the ways of the sciences? Is religion to have a controlling hand in the public school's science curriculum or not? Less delicately, the trial's combatants set forth the issue for public education:

> BRYAN   "The purpose [of Darrow's questions] is to cast ridicule on everybody who believes in the Bible, and I am perfectly willing that the world shall know that these gentlemen [i.e., the defense team] have no other purpose than ridiculing every Christian who believes in the Bible."

> DARROW   "We have the purpose of preventing bigots and ignoramuses from controlling the education of the United States and you know it, and that is all."[58]

States like Louisiana, Arkansas, Texas, Kansas, and Georgia have all attempted at one time or another to limit or even expunge the teaching of evolution in the name of specific religious values and preferences.[59] Numerous school boards in many other states have battled these same issues. Various fundamentalist groups continue to call for "equal time" for creationism as the appropriate course of instruction for public schools. More recently, the call has gone forth for the teaching of "intelligent-design" theory as a respectable theistic alternative to randomized "natural selection."[60] Doubtless more school board squabbles and courtroom wrangles are on the horizon.

These conflicts, however, tell us that such questions are not essentially legal questions, at least not at their deepest level. Nor can fundamentalist legal maneuvers prevent us from seeing that science does indeed have something to say about the deep age of the earth and about the descent of humans and apes from common ancestors. These are scientific matters that should not be stifled by biblical literalists or by court gag orders against biology teachers.[61] This is not to say that attempts to integrate religion and science are fruitless, but those efforts are probably best left to church, synagogue, mosque, and forums for dialogue between religion and science rather than the courtroom or the biology lab. Integration is, however, very different from transforming the Bible into a scientific textbook. Yet this, as we shall now see, is precisely what a newer breed of fundamentalism is trying to do.

Flood Geology's Dynamic Duo: Whitcomb and Morris

The hydrologist Whitcomb and the theologian Morris's "creationist science" proudly inverts everything that modern science says about the great antiquity of the big bang, the remote depths of earth's geological past, and the ancient vistas of animal and human evolution. It neatly tucks all the earth's development into the Divine Magician's bag of tricks, a bag that bears the label "rapid catastrophism." In this scheme, the Bible's brief chronology is upheld while "scientific" explanations are supplied to make the world's geological picture fit into the Bible. These views have been followed up through a spate of writings by Whitcomb, Morris, and others who are connected with the so-called Creation Research Society and the Institute for Creation Research.

Purporting to represent hydrological "science," Whitcomb and Morris actually rely a great deal on the unique and miraculous to bolster their claims. In *The Genesis Flood*, they explain that God created a "vapor canopy" during the seven days of creation (an idea found previously in the writings of the Quaker schoolteacher Isaac Newton Vail), one that does not owe its origins to the normal processes of rainfall and evaporation.[62] This canopy, "which existed only during the antediluvian period," is thought to explain where the floodwaters came from.[63] When this canopy collapsed, the massive floodwaters rained down. For Whitcomb and Morris, the Bible makes it possible for us to describe the material processes behind the flood even though, because of their miraculous character, these processes lie outside the demonstrable reach of secularized science, which they contend repeatedly misconstrues the evidence. Without the Bible, in other words, modern geologists are lost.[64]

For our purposes, perhaps the most important among the sequels to their earlier writings is Whitcomb's *The World That Perished*. I focus on this book, since it effectively blends both the science and the theology that Whitcomb and Morris have championed as their exclusive way to read and defend the Bible. The miraculous elements found at key junctures in the flood event are summarized by Whitcomb as follows:

> A careful analysis of the relevant exegetical data reveals at least six areas in which supernaturalism is clearly demanded in the doctrine

of the Flood: (1) the divinely-revealed design of the Ark; (2) the
gathering and care of the animals; (3) the uplift of oceanic waters
from beneath; (4) the release of waters from above; (5) the formation
of our present ocean basins; and (6) the formation of our present
continents and mountain ranges. Each of these supernatural aspects
of the Flood constitutes a radical break with the naturalistic presup-
positions of modern scientism, and for this reason deserves our
careful consideration.[65]

For Whitcomb, the ark's very design is miraculous; without the aid of modern technology, Noah built a boat that could remain afloat in the most dire of
circumstances and had just the right storage capacity.[66] Although Noah had a
century in which to gather the animals, God spared him this arduous task by
causing just the right number of animals to gather for the ship's maiden voyage. Thereafter, God put them into "supernatural hibernation" to simplify the
feeding chores.[67] (Never mind that the Genesis story itself does not mention
such hiberation.) Next, a miraculous uplifting of the ocean basin and a concomi-
tant collapse of the vapor canopy brought the needed downpour on an earth that
was a bit flatter then, so that less water would actually be required to destroy all
"air breathing" creatures (again, making the assumption that Noah did not take
aboard any fish despite the fact that the text says that all flesh was destroyed).[68]
To bring the flood to a close, God had to jockey the ocean floor a bit so that masses
of land heaved up to put new limits to the oceans and permit humans to re-
claim their place on the land.[69] While this is not explicitly stated in Genesis, one
of the Psalms (poetry that Whitcomb also reduces to creation science) provides
a clue that the mountains continued to rise so that the world took the shape we
now know.[70] Presto! What secular geologists vainly seek to explain, Whitcomb
solves with a seemingly logical linking of science and the Bible.

The most dangerous of all the scientific bogeymen for Whitcomb is "uniformitarianism," the view that geological processes that are at work today can
account for the world's development in the past. This is essentially the view of
the Scottish geologist Charles Lyell (1797–1875) in his *Principles of Geology*. Lyell's
system speaks of a uniformity of geological laws and processes, which, working with vast expanses of time, produces the earth as we know it today. In other
words, the incremental processes we see at work today, such as steady rivers
carving deep valleys over long periods of time, are the same slow processes
that have step-by-step shaped the world as we now know it. Lyell's system
directly challenges any view that relies on the young-earth picture presented
in the Bible. Consequently, Lyell is the geological bad guy in Whitcomb's
intellectual showdown.

The trouble is that modern geologists are not purely Lyellian. Even most
geologists of the nineteenth century were not strict uniformitarians. While Lyell
was fiercely nonprogressionist in his outlook, imagining that world geology ran

in cycles that exhibit no forward movement or direction, Whitcomb overlooks the fact that most successors to Lyell were actually progressionists, viewing the world in terms of gradualist processes that produce progressive stages of development, not the repeating nonprogressive cycles of Lyell. Thus, modern geology, like its nineteenth-century counterpart, combines both uniform processes and catastrophic events; the latter include plate tectonics and meteors colliding with the earth. Nevertheless Whitcomb insists on shadowboxing with Lyell throughout his book.[71] To grant to modern geologists elements of catastrophism and progression would mean having to acknowledge that modern geological science incorporates a variety of mechanisms to explain how the major geological marvels such as deep oceans, high mountains, vast canyons, and the like have developed over the millennia. Whitcomb is not quite ready to do that. All such phenomena have to be explained by Noah's flood, a singular catastrophe to explain a host of geological forms and the entire fossil record the world over. This view is difficult for geologists and paleontologists to accept. By contrast, modern geology, infused with both uniform processes and elements of catastrophe, seems better able than ever to posit logical explanations for earth's natural history, directly challenging the creationist view. As Whitcomb loses his corner on the market of "catastrophism," modern geology of necessity looks more attractive as an explanation of how the world has developed.

Railing against the uniformitarian specter, Whitcomb and Morris treat the Bible as if it had been intended as some sort of high school science textbook. They deny this, of course, yet at every turn Whitcomb insists that Genesis 1–11 is filled with hydrological, geological, and historical facts that reflect the Bible's essential scientific character. Here is how Whitcomb puts it:

> Evangelical Christians have long recognized that the Bible is not a "scientific textbook" in the pedantic sense of a compendium of detailed descriptions of all kinds of things and events. But it is most definitely a scientific textbook from another standpoint. It is an absolutely authoritative and infallible textbook on *the philosophy of science.* It provides for man the necessary frame of reference apart from which true science in the ultimate sense would be an impossible enterprise. But even beyond this, the Bible provides for us an accurate and objective record of events which have enormous scientific implications from the standpoint of our total world-and-life view.[72]

As he splits hairs over "uniformitarianism," which apparently has not only an atheistic but also an even more dangerous Christian variety (religionists who have succumbed to the wiles of secular geology), Whitcomb oddly attempts to save Genesis 1–11 as a historical record by placing these texts *outside* the normal realm of human history. They are set in an age of miracles quite unknown to us who live long after the flood. We shall not experience such divine intervention again, Whitcomb claims, until the fire that destroys the world at the end of time. In our era, which falls between the flood and the fire, the normal processes of physics and hydrology operate largely unchecked by a divine hand, giving us a weaker kind of uniformity of natural processes that passes Whitcomb's doctrinal muster.[73] By reading Genesis 1–11 as miraculous hydrology, Whitcomb offers us a hopelessly contradictory view that makes these stories both the *same* sort of literature as the rest of the Bible and *not* the same sort of literature as the rest of the Bible. On the one hand, the text is defended as amenable to science, but on the other hand, it is miraculous. How can one even begin to think that this is the stuff of science?

While most readers sense that Genesis 1–11 is different in scope and tone from other parts of the Bible, it is difficult to know why we should prefer a miraculous hydrological and historical reading of Genesis 1–11 to a mythic reading. The mythic reading would also make Genesis 1–11 a different sort of literary beast from other parts of the Bible, but in the mythic view such stories would more clearly conform to the symbolic character of other ancient religions and flood stories. Whitcomb defends his reading at all costs as if revelation can be effected only through "scientifically accurate" and "historical" texts.[74] He insists that "Genesis 1–11 is *detailed, accurate, prose, authoritative history!*"[75] In fact, Whitcomb goes so far as to label as enemies of God those who do not agree with his reading.[76] And then he is nonplussed when others condemn his own writing as harsh and dangerous, as if only the others are doing the name-calling.

Whitcomb's shrill insistence on flood geology as dogmatic doctrine regarding the divine shaping of the earth is also rather odd when one considers that vast canyons, steep mountains, and deep riverbeds, sometimes on a grander scale than on earth, are found on Mars, a place to which Noah's flood does not reach. It would be rather dubious for Whitcomb to suggest that modern geology cannot possibly explain such phenomena and that only a singular flood of biblical proportions must account for Martian geology. Unless one is open to the idea of a series of recent interplanetary divine judgments, then perhaps so-called Christian flood geology should be seen for what it is, an elaborate but failed attempt to salvage stories that demand a different sort of reading. A mythic reading would give insight into the texts as they stand. Even Ryan and Pitman's geological reading might point to the origin of the flood story. But in neither case, whether a mythic reading or a looser geological reading, must science be forced into the straitjacket of fundamentalist flood geology. The science of geology should be allowed to discern what it can of the earth's past while believers in the Bible learn to revise their understanding of biblical truth in light of those findings.

To the observant reader, then, Whitcomb and Morris's imaginative theorizing must be unpersuasive. In the name of literalism, the text is read in a fairly unliteral fashion. The insistence that only the convolutions of a hydrological reading of Genesis 1–11 can rescue the truth of the flood story from the storms of modern scientism is as strained as the efforts of those who tried to save the Ptolemaic view of the fixed earth from Copernicus and his sun-centered system.

But Is It Science? Creationism Cross-Examined

So, can there be a theologically credible and scientifically sensible "flood geology" or "creation science"? Three well-positioned observers think not, for both scientific and theological reasons.

The late Harvard evolutionary biologist and historian Stephen J. Gould counters fundamentalist "creation science" by arguing that "flood geology" is neither good science nor good theology. A scientific view is one that can be tested and found wrong. Likewise, good theology knows when to yield to good science. As an example of a wiser theological light on the scientific path, Gould points to the nineteenth-century studies of the Reverend Adam Sedgwick, who initially believed the fossil strata to be the product of the flood but later came to acknowledge the better geological work of his day. Like so many other believing scientists of the time, Sedgwick was compelled by the evidence to accept the view that the earth's complex strata arose over the course of vast stretches of time.[77] Gould thus reminds us that the fundamentalist does not have an exclusive claim on the way that religion and science can be put together.

From the religious side, J. R. van de Fliert, a Dutch geologist and member of the Christian Reformed Church, argues that Whitcomb and Morris misunderstand both geology and Genesis.[78] In the first place, they misunderstand the care with which geology reads and sorts out the stratigraphic remains and fossil sequences.[79] The process is not the hocus-pocus that Whitcomb and Morris imagine, says van de Fliert. They likewise misunderstand Genesis by turning faith in God into something that now must require "*scientific* proof."[80] To be fair, both Whitcomb and Morris might object that they are not using science to prove the Bible but instead see the Bible to be eminently compatible with a biblically informed reassessment of the scientific facts. In any event, van de Fliert would prefer to assign science the more modest role of putting to the "test the reliability of our ideas and conceptions about the Bible, the inspiration, and the historicity of the first chapters of Genesis."[81] This means that, unlike Morris and Whitcomb, we might revise our views of Genesis in light of science, but we would not try to use science to prove the Bible or, worse, to force science to conform to a literalist reading of the text. Van de Fliert, like Gould, finds deficient Whitcomb and Morris's fundamentalist flood geology, especially as a science of the biblical text.

Langdon Gilkey, one of the key theological consultants in the 1981 court case that struck down a creationist attempt to lay hold of Arkansas's public school system, has argued that creation science is a "changeling" that is both "half-misinterpreted religion and half-misinterpreted science."[82] In his remarkable book, *Creationism on Trial: Evolution and God at Little Rock,* he takes readers into the courtroom for a blow-by-blow account of his preparation for the trial and his intelligent performance in the witness box. Gilkey insightfully observes that creation science confuses religion's language of "*ultimate* origins" with scientific theories about "*proximate* origins."[83] Creation science has fallen into the trap of reducing all truth to "scientific" truth. As a result, its proponents have had to embark on a needless offensive against the findings of modern science, especially with regard to the processes of the earth's geohistory and the history of human evolution.[84] Many scientists fall into a comparable error with respect to religion, reducing all truth to mechanistic and materialist truth. In response to both the religious literalists and these hypersecular scientists, Gilkey rightly argues that a complementarity of truths and modes of investigation into the nature of reality is needed if we are not to be victims of biblical literalism, on the one hand, or of a narrow scientific naturalism, on the other.[85] There is a movement afoot within the mainline or traditional denominations that maintains that science and religion can have a coherent relationship. Likewise, there are scientists who hold out hope of a dialogue.[86] While fundamentalism is at war against both a theology of accommodation and a science of synthesis, Gilkey embodies the spirit of a third way.[87] If nothing else, Gilkey's presence at the Arkansas trial reminded religionists and scientists alike that their paths need not inevitably diverge. Despite his liberalism, Gilkey wrung an "Amen!" or two from spectators with his deep theological commitment, even as he gained the grudging respect of secular scientists who at first saw no reason for religionists on their side of the court case.

Imagining a Biblical Science: The Creationism Debate Today

Despite losses in the courts and the fact that the Bible no longer plays a role great or small in relation to the findings of secular geologists or evolutionary biologists, many fundamentalist Christians continue to hold out hope for a "creation science." They would maintain that the earth is not as old as most geologists claim. They would argue that the flood story of the Bible tells us of a catastrophic event in the not-so-distant past that reshaped the world into the form that we now see. They would argue that all the major fossil finds and strata go back to this singular event, bearing witness to the divine judgment of God. They would join Whitcomb and Morris in standing the world of modern science on its head. What are we to make of this development, which can be observed on popular Web sites such as www.youngearth.org and www.creation inthecrossfire.com? How is it that the battle between flood geology and secular science continues to rage in these circles?

Debating the question of whether or not Noah's flood was global, as if it were still a hot-button issue among geologists, creationist researcher Steven Austin argues that scientists fail to grasp the truth of the "evidence of the flood" in direct proportion to the "view they take on the validity of Scripture and according to the interpretive framework they adopt for conducting geologic science."[88] For Austin, the Krakatoa volcanic explosion and the resulting tidal waves of 1883 provide a miniature scientific model for the unleashing of the great deep of Genesis (Genesis 7:11). Scripture and science dovetail nicely in the fundamentalist's scheme, but only if the vast majority of modern geology's findings are thrown out of court as cases of mistaken identity.

Similarly, although fellow creationist Michael Oard confesses that "the Bible is not a textbook of science," he claims, much like Austin, that "one's reconstruction of the past will be based on the foundation of his view of origins."[89] Oard then proceeds to crush all historical climatological data into an exact literal reading of the Bible, producing an ice age that occurs after Noah's flood. Oard does this in the belief that the Bible's story is the "most reasonable" representation of a "true event," when compared to all the flood legends found worldwide.[90]

Yet is it really just their view of scripture or their "framework" that leads scientists who work without reference to scripture to come to such a divergent understanding of our human, animal, and geological past? Or is it that the evidence itself demands it? When the Bible says that Jericho's walls fell to Joshua's trumpet-blasting army, Austin and Oard might think that people's view of scripture and their scientific framework are the sole determinants of whether they accept or reject such a tale as historical. But the evidence from the ground suggests otherwise, and no amount of special pleading can produce what the archaeologist's spade cannot find.

For the fundamentalist, the case of the dinosaurs poses a particular challenge. Oddly, while Austin tells us confidently that the flood covered over the dinosaurs, he fails to tell us why Noah did not take them aboard the ark or, if Noah did have them aboard, why they apparently disappeared soon afterward, vanishing without any trace in the written records of Egypt and Mesopotamia, records that must have been contemporaneous with the last of the dinosaurs on his chronological scheme.[91] Even more strangely, Oard talks a lot about woolly mammoths but is altogether silent about the dinosaurs.[92] Intellectual honesty demands that he at least mention the issue amid his piles of charts and graphs that claim to demonstrate the reality of the so-called post-flood ice age. One fundamentalist writer, Dennis Gordon Lindsay, has Noah taking dinosaurs aboard the ark, only to have them perish soon after the flood "because of hostile environmental conditions."[93] One wonders why God put Noah through all the bother if the dinosaurs were to going die off so soon anyway.[94]

What fundamentalist flood apologists like Austin, Oard, and Lindsay refuse to see is that the evidence cries out for a different reading of the past and consequently for a different understanding of scripture. Sadly, the possibility of a revision of our view of the Bible eludes the exact literalist, even as the text is pored over for minute details and creation science "frameworks" are forced around the data. In the meantime, the big fish (or should we say crossopterygians?) get away.

The trouble with the creationist's "flood geology," then, is that, in essence, it assumes that there really is nothing new to be learned, that there can be no progress in our understanding of nature, history, or the Bible. For the creationist, so-called creation science is merely there to confirm what we already know from the Bible. There are no vistas to explore beyond what the Bible claims. In fact, the Bible must be read first to determine what the strata are saying. This is a strange state of affairs. One might have hoped that scripture and nature would speak with one voice, but when they do not, we have to wonder why the fundamentalist's reading of scripture should dictate how we read the geological record. The fundamentalist resists what the record appears to demand: a revision of our understanding of the Bible.

Those who work in the sciences will rightly ask if creation science is really science at all. Scientific naturalism will rule out creation science by definition. Yet even theists who are open to modern science will look with suspicion on a creation science that insists on having the Bible dictate what the sciences should find. The theologically minded evolutionary biologist Kenneth Miller, for example, in his influential *Finding Darwin's God*, readily endorses geologist G. Brent Dalrymple's conclusion that "the creationists' 'scientific' arguments for a young earth are absurd." For Miller, the creationist young-earth view turns God into a "charlatan" who deceives us about the age of the earth by creating a world that science can only discern to be very old.[95]

In this light, Gould was generous to consider creation science as bad science. To call it bad science is to leave open the possibility that even if we disagree with the creationists, their ideas deserve equal time in our science classrooms, if only to use the occasion to disprove the model. Rather, creation science is not science at all.

Let us consider a not altogether unrelated example. What about the view that says the earth stands still and that the sun goes around the earth, namely, the "geocentric" view that still has a following among some fundamentalists?[96] Adherents at www.biblicalastronomer.org and www.fixedearth.com promote the geocentric view as a legitimate scientific "model" that is rooted in the Bible. Should we entertain these ideas as science for us today? A thousand years ago this view may have constituted "science." Today, however, it is not "bad" science but an absurdity that any educated person ought to recognize as such. Such ideas do not deserve "equal time" in our science classrooms, as if the evidence is so ambiguous that it can be read either way. They deserve to be relegated to the dustbin of outmoded conceptions that are historical curiosities but not of serious scientific interest.

Just as the sun does not revolve around the earth, so also Noah's flood was not the sole universal cause of fossils being stuffed en masse into layer upon layer of the earth's strata. Today this view is not bad science but simply ignorance. To mandate equal time for such views in our classrooms, as some have attempted to press upon local and state boards of education, not only is a grave disservice to the natural sciences but also denigrates the progress we have made in the theological sciences.[97] The call for equal time belittles the findings of gifted scientists like Charles Darwin, Albert Einstein, and a host of others. What is more, Whitcomb and Morris's work is bad theology, as they are unable to celebrate the unlocking of the mysteries of the universe, the earth, and Nature's God.

If the Bible teaches anything, it teaches the progressive and halting character of our grasp of God's creation and our understanding of ourselves. Each step forward is a cause for rejoicing. By contrast, the house of cards that Price, Morris, and Whitcomb have built teeters precariously on the laboratory table. We can only hope that courageous evangelicals will continue to push fundamentalism beyond this impasse.[98]

Woolley's Mammoth Discovery and Mallowan's Mystery

There is yet another possible explanation for the origin of the biblical flood story. Since this explanation has gained some currency in fundamentalist circles not strictly wedded to the global flood view propagated by Whitcomb and Morris, a serious look is in order here.

During the 1920s and 1930s, while excavating in southern Iraq at Ur, the hometown of the biblical Abraham, Sir Leonard Woolley discovered flood deposits nearly four meters thick beneath Sumerian burials. In this layer, dating to the mid–fourth millennium B.C.E., roughly 3500 B.C.E., Woolley saw unmistakable evidence for the source of the flood legends of the ancient Middle East and the Bible. Likewise, from the same period, a "pluvial interval" was identified by the excavators of Nineveh, in the north of ancient Iraq. For Woolley, some sort of Mesopotamian archaeological connection to the flood stories could not be denied.[99] Many have been intrigued by his explanation.

Did a flood at Ur give rise to the biblical and Mesopotamian flood stories? Apparently Woolley thought so, although the picture was more complicated than he was willing to admit. Other interpretations of Woolley's finds were certainly possible. In fact, Woolley's protégé at Ur from 1925 to 1930, excavator Max Mallowan, husband of the dame of detective fiction Agatha Christie, took the Mesopotamian evidence and constructed a compelling alternative hypothesis.[100] While his wife was writing such detective novels as *Murder on the Orient Express* and *Death on the Nile*, Mallowan was doing some Middle Eastern detective work of his own, developing a perspective on the archaeological remains that improved on Woolley's theories.

Mallowan was convinced, like Woolley, that both the biblical and the Mesopotamian flood storytelling traditions rested on "one definite event."[101] If not a global flood, was it possible, he wondered, that some local Mesopotamian event had given rise to the stories? The dangerous reality of river floods in modern Iraq certainly made this scenario seem plausible.[102] But did Woolley get it right?

Mallowan relied in part on clues provided by ancient myth. He postulated that King Gilgamesh, who in Mesopotamian myth is said to have visited with the immortal hero who survived the flood, must therefore have lived sometime around 2650 B.C.E., not long after the flood.[103] This bit of surmising and other considerations led Mallowan to put the flood in the Early Dynastic I period of ancient Sumer (2900–2700 B.C.E.). Since this is much later than Woolley's date for the flood, Mallowan was forced to cast about for evidence of later floods in lower Mesopotamia. He did not have far to look. At Ur there was evidence, downplayed by Woolley, of later flood levels. Elsewhere, from differing time periods at various sites, such as Kish, Eridu, and Fara (Shuruppak), flood layers have come to light. What was one to make of the evidence?

Mallowan remembers Woolley's and Watelin's disagreement over the proper identification of the various flood finds: "There was some amusement watching, as I did at the time, this dispute between the masters, each claiming the authentic Flood as his own."[104] Mallowan's own sense was that Woolley's flood layer (3500 B.C.E.) was much too early to have a realistic connection to Gilgamesh. He also thought that the later layers at Ur (2700 B.C.E.) were "too near perhaps to the time at which Gilgamesh himself is now presumed to have lived" and so could not be a candidate for the layer of the flood legends.[105] In other words, Mallowan came to believe that neither the early nor the later flood layers at Ur were to be connected with the flood story traditions.

Mallowan hunted elsewhere for evidence, reconsidering the flood layers at Kish. While one of the Kish layers was later dismissed by Watelin as a candidate for the flood because clay seals of Gilgamesh were found beneath the layer, an earlier layer was taken by Mallowan to be the flood layer of the flood legends.[106] The date that fit for Mallowan was 2900 B.C.E. Putting the nail in the coffin, Mallowan also discerned a contemporaneous flood layer at Shuruppak.[107] Interestingly, Shuruppak is the reputed home of the Mesopotamian survivor of the flood, Utnapishtim. Perhaps the very layers at Kish and Shuruppak identified by Mallowan are indicative of the flood that the Sumerian king list has in mind when it says, "After the Flood had swept over (the earth) (and) when kingship was lowered (again) from heaven, kingship was (first) in Kish."[108] The dates would be right. The connections with Shuruppak would make sense. If Mallowan's detective work is on target, the flood would have been a memorable, datable, but local event.

While Mallowan's reconstruction has its merits, we may never know for sure what to make of this evidence. In any event, whether the flood is to be linked to one specific layer or more generally to a wider range of layers dating from roughly 3000 to 2800 B.C.E., the distinctive evidence of flooding marks a decisive turning point in the region's history and lore. If river floods stand in the background, then the flood myth represents a highly stylized and exaggerated account of a definable period in Mesopotamian history.[109] Taking the Mesopotamian flood layers as clues, Woolley's work and Mallowan's hypotheses leave us with provocative, albeit speculative, candidates for the origin of the biblical and Mesopotamian flood story tradition.

Even if the flood stories have some roots in Mesopotamian flood conditions, the *stories* go well beyond the scope of a local flood limited to southern Mesopotamia. It is hardly necessary to build a boat to save the entire world when everyone could just walk a few miles to escape the peril. Is the story's meaning exhausted when we link it to some flood layers in ancient Iraq? At the very least, the myth does more than simply report ancient weather conditions, even if it is traceable to some such historical event.

Ryan and Pitman, likewise, tempted us to find the real substance of the story in archaeology's still more distant watery past. The Black Sea tells a much more exciting story than the southern Mesopotamian rivers. Many would agree with Ryan and Pitman against Woolley and Mallowan that "several key elements of the basic theme of the Mesopotamian flood stories do not make sense in the context of a river flood."[110] Those elements suggest events that had world-changing significance for those who experienced them. In the Black Sea flood we would have a more distant source that might account for the existence of flood stories throughout the ancient world. If only we could prove the theory true.

Of course, Ryan and Pitman's theory is not without chronological difficulties. The Mesopotamian finds of Woolley and Mallowan seem to be the better fit in terms of both the region and the chronology. By contrast, the vast time lapse and geographical disconnect for the Black Sea flood appear to make it the less likely candidate, if any single flood is really behind the tales. Perhaps we will never know for certain.

Flood Geology or Textual Abuse?

Eating from the fruit of the tree of scientific knowledge has led to a loss of innocence for many believers. The sort of literalism demanded by so many fundamentalists today does not ring true to those who take the geological and evolutionary sciences seriously. Yet is there a place for religion at the table of the sciences? The culture war that creationists are waging has pushed many scientifically minded people away from interest in religion.[111] Many secular scientists join the creationists in thinking that religion and science must ever be in conflict with one another. While rightly wishing to keep creation science out of the biology classroom, those who erect a barrier between modern science and religion run the risk of throwing the baby out with the bath water. Believers in the Bible have not always had a siege mentality when it comes to the sciences. In fact, the popularity of flood geology and creation science serves to conceal the many and varied attempts to bring religious realism and a scientific sensibility to the interpretation of scriptures. Since these more creative efforts, rather than fundamentalism, have dominated the Jewish and Christian centuries, the alternative approaches deserve separate treatment. I turn now to consider a very different world of biblical interpretation, one that is more hopeful about the exchange between religion and science without being ensnared in a hyper-literalism about the biblical text.

5

From Sarcophagus to Ship

Traditional and Early Scientific Visions of the Flood

Long before the fundamentalists linked the flood story to "creation science," others were trying to make logical sense out of the story of Noah's ark. Imaginations equally energetic as the French ark seeker Navarra have over the centuries tried to paint a picture of the world of Noah and those dreary days aboard the ark. Jewish and Christian interpreters alike embellished the tale in order to find spiritual insight and moral guidance. Increasingly a kind of realism came to dominate their presentations. While not scientifically motivated, these fairly graphic depictions set the stage for early modern scientific thinkers who during the sixteenth and seventeenth centuries attempted to rationalize the stories in terms of mechanical theories of the earth's physical processes and history. Eventually this trend would come to fruition in the eighteenth and nineteenth centuries with attempts to read the flood story in light of the newly emerging geological sciences and the study of fossils. While the nineteenth century ultimately sounded the death knell over the flood story as a historical event, the encounter between the Bible and science began to reveal new ways to read the Bible as a work of humanistic importance. I will begin this discussion with the early Jewish and Christian readings of the flood story.

Where Did Noah Put the Garbage?

We have seen that the early medieval rabbis regularly embellished the tale.[1] Sometimes this embellishment appears to arise out of a concern to render the fantastic flood story more natural and realistic. We are not surprised to find the rabbis puzzling over where the garbage was kept in the ark. Some thought it was kept in the lowest level, while Noah and the clean animals inhabited the second level, and the unclean took the upper level. Other rabbis put the garbage at the top. Those who imagined the garbage to be on the top level also had to speculate about trapdoors and Noah's shoveling activities.[2]

Likewise, the rabbis speculated about the numbers of compartments required for such a vessel, with one saying there were 330 and another 900. Such rabbis see the Torah as teaching "practical knowledge," having to do with construction techniques and styles that one might find valuable when building other structures. Presumably arks would not be called for in the future but the skills learned in the ark's construction would come in handy long after the flood.[3]

Christian interpreters during the early centuries of the church and throughout its medieval period also sought to address all the questions the pious imagination might ask about the realities of the flood story. What, for example, did the ark look like? Over the course of the Christian centuries the ark was conceived of in many sizes, shapes, and forms: a pyramid, a chest or box, a sarcophagus, a ship with sails, a houseboat or castle at sea, a cube or rectangular vessel, and even a masterpiece of precision architecture (typically shown under construction with its structural framework exposed).[4]

Did the ark have three, four, or five decks? There were advocates for each of these options.[5]

What about windows? Did Noah have only the one window mentioned in the Bible, or were there many little ones?

How long did it take to build the ark? Was it 100 or 120 years?

Did Noah have assistants? This possibility creates a bit of a moral dilemma. Imagine the horror of those who had for so long labored on "Noah's Folly," only to find that the boat they had been building for decades was really needed and that they were locked out as the waters began to rise. Not a pretty picture. To avoid the moral repugnance of Noah relying on workers who must then be abandoned to their fate, other interpreters contended that Noah built the ark all by himself. He did, after all, have over a century to complete the task.

What about the animals? How many animals would Noah have to take into the ark to ensure that all the basic species were covered? Did he take mosquitoes?

Did the carnivorous animals eat meat during the voyage, or did they become vegetarians for the duration? One interpreter, Augustine Torniellus, imagined that Noah fed the carnivores from an extensive stock of sheep and that "as the carnivores devoured the sheep, the Ark would get roomier."[6] Doubtless there were also fewer stalls to clean as a result, much to Noah's relief.

Did Noah take fish on the ark? If not, then how were they able to survive in seas that many thought had been turned into boiling cauldrons by God's wrath?[7]

How did Noah manage to feed the venomous snakes and fearsome lions without being bitten?

What about the manure? The commentator Tostado imagined a key divine provision that allowed "the odour of the dung" to be "miraculously carried off so that the air was not corrupted and men and animals were not slain by the pest."[8] Daily interventions of this sort must have brought joy to the nostrils of Noah and his kin.

Finally, was there sex on the ark? Some thought that the people abstained out of grief for their world, but the animals probably were not so aggrieved. Others imagined the animals breeding on the ark. Some even thought that this is how Noah's son Ham got into trouble on the ark, having had sex (presumably with the animals) during the voyage.[9]

All these and their infinite variations represent efforts by pious Jews and Christians over the centuries to understand how it was done: How did God turn Noah into the greatest escape artist the world has ever known? Even though the Jewish and Christian interpreters carried their speculations to great lengths, one has to admire the freedom with which they played with the story. They focused on details not out of modern historical curiosity but out of a sense of spiritual connectedness to Noah and his trials—trials that for the Christian prefigure those of Jesus' followers at the end of time (Matthew 24:37–39; Luke 17:26–30). That sense of connectedness hints that the story works on more levels than merely the historical. However, since belief somehow seems easier when it is underscored by fact, over time the effort to make logical sense out of the story will begin to dog religious interpreters. Quaint medieval realism will be challenged by the harder realism of world exploration and modern science.

Did Noah Vacation in Brazil?

As Europeans navigated the world and explored the vast Western Hemisphere, their encounters with the variety of animal life, flora, and human cultures in these quarters raised serious questions about the Bible, even as the New World was conquered in the name of Christ. Science and exploration would soon come to complicate the easy acceptance of the Bible as a historical and scientific record, pressing readers beyond medieval pietistic fantasies.

Exploration, for example, raised curious questions about the capacity of the ark. Strange animals were encountered in other parts of the world, many more than one would have thought Noah could carry aboard his boat. And how did they get transported to the New World after the flood, leaving no trace in the Old World?[10] Were the New World animals also on the ark? Did Noah's descendants transport them to Asia, Africa, and the Americas after the flood? The new global reality sat uneasily next to the time-honored tale.

The link between the New World and the flood story seemed less and less plausible. Renaissance specialist Don Cameron Allen draws our attention to Justus Lipsius (1547–1606), who "does not think that the animals could have been carried to America by boat, because men would hardly transport rattle-snakes." Why not be rid of snakes instead of taking them along? Why have them aboard? So if not by boat, Lipsius "concludes that Africa was once connected with America by the land bridge of Atlantis."[11] The suggestion, however mis-taken, had the virtue of somehow keeping the Bible and global discovery together. Yet when one has to rely on Atlantean fictions for an explanation, we can sus-pect that science will soon be ready to offer a more credible account based on even better "evidence" and sounder "reasoning."

Allen also points to Jean de Lery (1534–1613), a "voyager" who "insisted that most of the Indians were the descendants of Canaanites who fled before Joshua," and to Marc Lescarbot (1570–1642), who believed that the New World was originally "settled by Noah who led a personal expedition to Brazil."[12] Such assertions were clearly designed to reconcile the fact of a Native American population with the story of Noah. European writers were beginning to sense the tension between traditional readings of the Bible and the new horizons they were encountering.

Unfortunately, no amount of supposed parallels between Native American and Jewish customs or efforts to claim Native Americans as the Lost Tribes of Israel could overcome the hurdles faced by such claims. Doubts began to sur-face. John Woodward (1665–1728) was clearly worried about how flood survi-vors from the Old World came to settle in the New. When and how did they make the trip? Especially troublesome was the fact that the New World inhabit-ants were so vastly different in terms of language, diet, dress, customs, and politics as to confound any connection to the Old World survivors of the flood. He was even more puzzled that the New World peoples should have forgotten their origins in the Old World. Woodward has no solution to such oddities.[13]

The more one pondered the problem, the less likely was the connection between Noah and the New World. Seeking to put an end to the absurdities, German naturalist Johann Friedrich Blumenbach (1752–1840) wrote, "I find it incomprehensible how the sloth could have made the pilgrimage from Mt. Ararat to South America since it requires an hour to crawl 6 feet."[14] New data and new perspectives were forcing a reevaluation of the biblical flood story.

Mathematical Meteorology: Calculating the Waters

The dilemma of New World ancestry was not the only conundrum posed by the encounter of the Bible and emerging facts. Science was beginning to find other points of contact and conflict with the sacred text. For a time, however, a num-ber of clever early modern scientists and thinkers found the flood story suscep-tible to a positive scientific assessment. In the sixteenth and seventeenth centuries, scientifically minded Christians focused more closely on figuring out the true size, shape, and cargo of the ark: mathematically speaking, how could the ark hold all those animals? What types of animals were brought aboard, and could they be identified according to their scientific classifications? One interpreter, Bishop Wilkins, thought that if taxonomically minded people "would stop calling every animal by five names . . . there would be plenty of room on the Ark."[15] They also wanted to know how the process of the flood happened. What natural mechanisms did God employ to pull off such a massive catastrophe?

With this era of interpretation we see a fundamental shift taking place even as the details are pored over in good medieval fashion. In this period of expanding intellectual horizons, believers were trying to reconcile traditional understandings of Genesis with what for their day were the newer scientific ideas of Copernicus (1473–1543), Galileo (1564–1642), and Newton (1642–1727). The new tools of biblical interpretation would now include telescopes, world maps, mathematical computations, and razor-sharp minds. Medieval musings about the text would be replaced by hard data and historical analysis.

Many thinkers in the early scientific era attempted to determine where all that flood water came from. This appears to have been largely a Protestant enterprise. As Cohn explains, "For Catholic theologians this was no great problem: for them the Flood was a miracle, for which a rational explanation was neither possible nor desirable. Protestants, on the other hand, were concerned to show that Scripture and reason were at one, here as elsewhere. And a few audacious spirits went so far as to argue that the Flood must have been only a local catastrophe."[16] While, as we shall see, Cohn is not entirely correct in this judgment about Catholics, it is true that many Protestants jumped at the chance to comb the scriptures with scientific principles at the ready to demonstrate the Bible's veracity in all spheres.

A case in point is the renowned Elizabethan explorer of the Americas, Sir Walter Raleigh (1554–1618).[17] Formerly one of Queen Elizabeth's favorites, Raleigh found that his fortunes changed for the worse after his secret marriage to Elizabeth Throckmorton. Those fortunes further declined under James I, who condemned Raleigh to death in 1603 on the charge that he had been an agent of Spain. Popular outrage at the accusations forced James to delay the execution some thirteen years. In the meantime, imprisoned in the Tower of London, Raleigh remained active, writing, among other things, his five-volume *History of the World*, a work whose preface alone has been termed "the culminating document of Renaissance historiography in England."[18] He had plenty of time, in other words, to think about the flood.

In the course of these volumes, Raleigh offers a "scientific" analysis of the flood. He was very concerned to present scientific support for the biblical account of a worldwide flood and took great pains to insist that interpreters not confuse the biblical universal flood with later stories of more localized events. According to Raleigh, "soothsayers" in America still told tales of this global flood. He also asserts that at the time of the flood certain astrological signals, such as the conjunction of Jupiter and Saturn in the "watery sign" of Cancer, would have foretold this global event.[19] Yet Raleigh's main interest was to account for the vast amount of water required for the flood, seeking to present a more mathematically plausible picture of the ark itself.

For Raleigh the requisite water came from two different sources. He envisioned deep reserves of water contained under the earth. He also postulated that the atmosphere, to its highest points, was capable of condensing all at once (through a miracle) to produce torrential downpours. Of the terrestrial depths Raleigh writes, "It is not then impossible, answering reason with reason, that all those waters mixed within the earth three thousand five hundred miles deep should not well help to cover the space of thirty miles in height."[20] Of the air, he says, "It pleased God to condense but so much of this air."[21] Apparently it was also God's delight to send these waters sweeping over the whole of the earth. We must imagine Raleigh's God smiling as the corrupt peoples of the earth are annihilated by a flood that follows scientifically plausible principles.

Having placed the Bible's account of the water on a scientific footing, Raleigh sought to do the same for the ark. Given that the ark had no mast or sails, thought Raleigh, it simply floated in one spot to ride out the flood. To calculate the size of the ark, having wrestled with five different definitions of cubit, Raleigh settles on a cubit of "one foot and a half" and suggests the boat was roughly "600 feet in length, and 100 feet in breadth, and 60 feet in depth."[22] He endorses the calculations of the French mathematician and monk Johannes Buteo (1492–1570) concerning the cubic capacity of the ark, which he estimated to be 450,000 square cubits. Johannes Buteo's minute calculations of the required cubits updated the views of earlier rabbinic and Christian interpreters concerning the size and shape of the ark.[23] Buteo's "ovens that used smokeless wood" solved other obvious problems for the premodern, scientifically minded literal believer.[24] Raleigh was taking those concerns many steps forward. Building on Buteo's figures, he estimated that only about 100 distinct species of animals would be required to account for all the animals of the earth. The vessel had sufficient capacity to repopulate the planet, provided one excluded the "needless curiosity" of speculating about sea cows, sea horses, and the like.[25]

As for the ark's resting place, Raleigh could not endorse the Armenian "Mount Ararat" connection made by traditional Christianity. He opted instead for some other point in the east, perhaps elsewhere in the Caucasus, although he was attracted to possibilities much farther east such as India or even Japan, since they were known to be sources of ancient wisdom and culture probably stemming from Noah's descendants.[26] In any event, this more easterly resting point seemed to Raleigh to be consistent with the fact that Noah disappears from biblical history, leaving one to imagine that he may have lived out his final days in an exotic land where he gave himself over to a life of worship and divine contemplation.[27]

Raleigh's history charts the interplay between divine will and human action from the time of the creation of the world and Abraham, through the destruction of the Jewish temple, down to the conquests of Philip of Macedon, Alexander the Great, and the Romans. The flood, although an event of cosmic proportions, is but one moment in that divine drama.

Reaction to Raleigh's history was mixed. James I sought to suppress the volumes, "for diverse exceptions, but specially for being too saucy in censuring princes," explained John Chamberlain to Sir Dudley Carleton in 1615, three years before Raleigh's execution.[28] One wonders where the censors were. Yet the writings survived in the hands of sympathetic admirers. The volumes went through ten editions and many reprintings throughout the seventeenth century, garnering praises even of Oliver Cromwell, who instructed his son, "Recreate yourself with Sir Walter Raleigh's history: it's a body of history, and will add much more to your understanding than fragments of story."[29] Obviously, Raleigh influenced the ideas of many about the flood story, casting it in mathematical, geographic, and geological terms.

In the end, Raleigh's Herculean attempt to bring biblical truth into the realm of reasoned historical discourse justifies David Lloyd's 1665 assessment of him as both a "great soldier" and a "bookish man."[30] His work was a stellar example of the Protestant scientific mind fully engaged with the currents of history and the speculative powers of science. Just as Raleigh's contemporary Galileo was showing people how to read the heavens, earning Raleigh's praise, Raleigh himself showed the realm how to read the Bible in this scientific age.[31] Needless to say, though, these intricate calculations by Raleigh and others began subtly to undermine the Bible's straightforward portrait of forty days and forty nights of *rain*. The emphasis fell on the twists and turns of their quasi-scientific speculations rather than on the story itself. Strangely, Raleigh's mathematical labors seem to have ended up subtracting from the Bible rather than adding to it.

Noah's Apartments: The Jesuitical Vision of Athanasius Kircher

Probably the grandest vision of them all, belying Cohn's assertion that Protestants cornered ark mathematics, comes from the German Jesuit Athanasius Kircher, whose work *Arca Noe* (1675) includes line drawings that detail every last compartment of the ark, deck by deck.[32] In this monumental scheme, the ark is a massive rectangular craft that required a host of laborers to construct. Noah's role in this deluge drama is to play "a sort of presiding architect" over the entire ark construction process.[33]

Kircher elaborates on the working of the ship's three decks. The upper deck, for Noah's family and the birds, boasted first-class amenities: "The apartments designed for the humans were ventilated with special air vents which kept the atmosphere quite fresh."[34] Beneath them was the second deck, which served as the storage level for food and tools. The first deck harbored the animals. The underlayer of the ark constituted the "sentina" for waste materials. In Kircher's mind's eye, the ark was a world unto itself, on the order of a floating Arizona "Biosphere."

One senses with Kircher that the premodern "scientific" ark has already reached its zenith. The very moment that pious whimsy can envision the ark in all its splendor is the same moment that reason stands ready to consign blueprints for the ark onto the ash heap of discarded protoscientific imaginings.

Perhaps Kircher lived at the wrong time. This Jesuit polymath also claimed to have deciphered Egyptian hieroglyphs. Unfortunately, the finding of the Rosetta stone at the end of the eighteenth century would reveal that despite his profound intellect, Kircher lived in an era that denied him the firsthand data and well-honed theories needed to comprehend the course of ancient and biblical history. An overactive imagination is no substitute for good science. As we shall now see, "scientific" constructions will continue to gain the upper hand, if not for the ark itself, at least for the flood as an event of global geological significance.

Flood Mechanics: Sacred Theories of the Earth

If the budding scientific mind had finally exhausted its need to calibrate the inner workings of the ark, could science at least salvage the flood as a credible historical event? All manner of natural causes and mechanical details were supplied by clever interpreters to reconcile the observed processes of nature with the flood story of the Bible. Late in the seventeenth century, for example, Thomas Burnet's landmark book on geology, *The Sacred Theory of the Earth* (1681), offered a clever, comprehensive, and enduringly influential attempt to put human reason to work making sense of the Bible's creation and flood stories.[35] Gone was the need to invoke a miraculous explanation for these events. The spirit of the age, as epitomized by Burnet's Cambridge colleague Sir Isaac Newton, was to discover the greater miracle in the natural mechanisms that God employs to govern the universe. Burnet sought to discern the mathematical machinery that operated to bring about the great flood. He argued that the flood had to be a universal one. More than 10 billion people (Burnet's calculation) would have been born between the creation of humans and the time of the flood. It would take a monumental deluge for God to destroy all those who had scattered about the earth by that time. Anyone who thinks about the problem realizes that the amount of water required to cover the widespread land masses and mountains of today would be enormous indeed. Rains alone could not do the job. Was there another explanation?

Burnet was in a bit of a mental quandary. What mechanism, he wondered, caused the destruction of the people of the antediluvian world? Burnet relied on reason to challenge the picture that most might have had in mind.[36] He suggested that the original earth was much flatter. As the earth's crust was continually heated by the blazing sun and as the waters beneath the crust turned into pressurized vapors, it eventually cracked and collapsed, forcing the waters underneath to rush forth over the relatively flat earth. Here was the missing mechanism. The same natural processes that brought about the flood left the world in the state of mountainous upheaval we find today. For Burnet, the flood was more a geological than a theological catastrophe. Perhaps God had anticipated humanity's sins and set up a clockwork mechanism to deal with those ills when the time was right.[37]

The same clockwork mechanism that brought about the flood is at work in the world today, according to Burnet, carrying us inexorably forward to the time of the fiery upheaval that will restore the smooth skin of the earth, ultimately bringing it to its final state as a star in the heavens. Burnet's *Sacred Theory of the Earth* is a tale of an earth that is now pitched between the former flood and the coming fire, between paradise lost and paradise restored, between ancient chaos and future cosmos.

Once this door was open, there was no end to the "scientific" explanations that might be dreamed up. While some like Erasmus Warren thought that Burnet's theorizing "strikes at the roots of religion," others felt compelled to improve on such theories from within the constraints of scientific reasoning and nature's mechanics.[38]

William Whiston, for example, the successor in mathematics to Sir Isaac Newton at Cambridge and noted translator of the works of the ancient Jewish historian Josephus, extended astronomer Edmund Halley's work by suggesting that the Great Comet of 1680 previously tangled with the earth in 2349 B.C.E., the year that Archbishop Ussher calculated for Noah's flood. As the earth passed through the comet, the comet's head and tail sparked periods of tumultuous rains that swept over the entire planet. The natural processes behind the Bible's flood could now be understood.[39] Fortunately, Noah's ark was located east of the collision point, permitting him a few hours to finalize his preparations.[40] Such is the scope of Whiston's "scientific vision" in his *New Theory of the Earth* (1696).[41]

John Keill's subsequent critique of Burnet, in Allen's words, revealed "the utter futility of supporting Genesis by laboratory data," but it would be decades before the split between Genesis and geological science would be complete.[42] Complete, that is, until Ryan and Pitman.

Did the Flood Make a Lasting Impression?

During the eighteenth century, an odd state of affairs began to emerge. With no clear or singular orthodox interpretation of Genesis to stem the tide, a variety of attempts were made to account for the flood story in the light of the mounting geological finds.[43] Scientific opinion eventually split. Some argued that the flood was one of a series of major geological disruptions that have catastrophically shaped the world. Others, such as de Maillet, regarded the flood as simply an isolated occurrence that had no lasting geological significance.

The divergent interpretations had compelling supporting arguments. For those who were puzzled, as was Bishop Robert Clayton, about the unique plant life of the Americas, the only answer could be that the flood was an event local to the Middle East.[44] Those who regarded the flood as one of the major geological events of the past could nonetheless argue that it was not the sole explanation of the world as we know it. As Rappaport observes, for example, "For Lehmann and Wallerius the flood was unique in its universality and in its having deposited much of the sedimentary crust; but earlier and later revolutions had also played some role in producing the present arrangement of the strata."[45]

While dividing somewhat over the precise details of the flood's action, most natural scientists of the time believed that the standard processes of nature, such as earthquakes, floods, and volcanic activity, generated the flood of Genesis and to a greater or lesser extent gave shape to the world as we know it. In this we see continued movement in the direction established by Burnet and Whiston, namely, an effort to place the biblical record on a rational basis. Unlike Burnet and Whiston's rather fanciful schemes, however, eighteenth-century thinkers were increasingly taking into account actual data from geological observation. As Rappaport explains, one key factor was "that such upheavals, however great and unpredictable, could be explained by using the known laws of physics and chemistry."[46] The application of these laws was rooted in a thorough estimate of the geological record.

By turning attention toward geological layers rather than the pages of Holy Writ, such interpreters had unwittingly shaken loose the realm of geological research from any slavish reliance on the Bible for the basic data of the natural sciences. Unlike those who in the preceding two centuries tried to correlate the Bible with new finds and theories of the earth—to rationalize the Bible, as it were—these eighteenth-century thinkers inaugurated a new trend that continues in our own day with the researches of Ryan, Pitman, and Ballard. What Rappaport observes for the eighteenth century remains true of the recent Black Sea explorations: "In this range of views, one feature is common to all descriptions of the flood: departures from a literal interpretation of Genesis."[47] Even the fundamentalists Whitcomb and Morris, though they would no doubt vehemently protest, are really products of the eighteenth-century Enlightenment's demand that the Bible be rationalized to prevail in the court of scientific opinion. However, in the case of Whitcomb and Morris's reading, the judges in that court must first obtain credentials in creation science to counter the fact that modern science has moved so far afield from the biblical text.

As the nineteenth century rolled into view, the geological data began to outstrip the biblical record. Many researchers were simply concerned about unlocking the mechanisms of geology and applying them to the past, without putting the Bible at the center stage. During this period, the Neptunists were pitted against the Vulcanists and Plutonists. On the one hand, the Neptunists (named after the Roman god of the sea, Neptune) followed A. G. Werner (1750–1817) in arguing that ancient geological developments were governed by the shaping power of a vast primeval ocean that had deposited the minerals found in the earth's lowest strata. Noah's flood had no place in Werner's scheme. On the other hand, the Vulcanists and Plutonists, named for gods of the earth's fiery lower depths, believed that the volatile forces at work in the earth's crust constituted the essential mechanism behind geological processes. The Vulcanists, following Nicholas Desmarest (1725–1815) and J. C. W. Voigt (1752–1821), focused primarily on the disruptive power of volcanic activity, especially in basalt formation. The Plutonist James Hutton (1726–97), focusing on gradual processes such as erosion and sedimentary deposition, imagined the strata of the earth churning throughout all eternity like a vast steam engine. Noah's flood, likewise, played no role in Voigt's Vulcanism or in Hutton's Plutonism. Whether one adopted the Neptunist, Vulcanist, or Plutonist view, the Bible's conceptions and stories were left by the wayside.[48]

One figure, however, who is to be credited with keeping the Bible's flood solidly within the context of geological upheavals was George Cuvier, although it was not Cuvier himself but his English translator Robert Jameson who stamped Cuvier's *Essay on the Theory of the Earth* (1817) with a *supernatural* flood.

Cuvier himself was aware of the tensions between the writers of the past, who had only the biblical stories of creation and flood to work with, and modern scholars, who had at their disposal numerous schemes and systems for studying the geological history of the earth.[49] Could the Bible and geological science be put together in any sort of meaningful way? Cuvier suggested that the flood of Genesis was the "last grand *cataclysma*."[50] He could not deny the flood event as such, since he found that Moses' catastrophe was known throughout the world, in writings from Assyria, India, China, and the folk traditions of Africa and the Native Americans: "Thus all the nations which possess any records or ancient traditions, uniformly declare that they have been recently renewed, after a grand revolution in nature."[51]

By making this flood the last in a series of geological upheavals that have shaped nature and human civilization over the centuries, Cuvier provides a twist on the biblical story even as he diminishes its ultimate importance as a geological event. The flood, that "great and sudden revolution," "buried all the countries which were before inhabited by men and by the other animals that are now best known."[52] There was much of significance to study with regard to the earth's geological history beyond the Bible's flood, and Cuvier turns his attention away from the flood for the rest of his book. Though neatly accounted for, the flood's waters continued to recede into the background for most geologists as other revolutions and ancient geological eras came into focus.

Onto these unsettled soils stepped the ingenious Charles Lyell, whose arguments for a uniformity of causes both in the past and in the present effectively set aside the biblical flood as a necessary explanatory device for understanding the earth's geological history. In a system first presented in 1830 and refined many times subsequently, the Oxford-educated Lyell combined four sorts of uniformity: uniformity of natural laws, uniformity of processes between present and past, uniformity of rate of geological development, and uniformity of geological states.[53] Essentially, according to Lyell's "actualism," the geological processes of the past must be understood in terms of processes that we also see at work in the present. While, as we have seen, few geologists were as strict about uniformitarianism as was Lyell, preferring to invoke both uniform processes and catastrophic events as part of a progressivist scheme, nonetheless global floods of universal proportions are not on the program for serious geologists after Lyell.

Lyell said that premodern theologians and geologists had wasted a great deal of time trying to account for the burial of fossils by invoking the biblical flood. Reviewing the history he laments

> more than a hundred years having been lost, in writing down the
> dogma that organized fossils were mere sports of nature. An
> additional century and a half was now destined to be consumed in
> exploding the hypothesis, that organized fossils had all been buried
> in the solid strata by Noah's flood. Never did a theoretical fallacy, in
> any branch of science, interfere more seriously with accurate
> observation and the systematic classification of facts. . . . But the
> old diluvialists were induced by their system to confound all the
> groups of strata together instead of discriminating,—to refer all
> appearances to one cause and to one brief period, not to a variety of
> causes acting throughout a long succession of epochs. They saw
> the phenomena only as they desired to see them, sometimes
> misrepresenting facts, and at other times deducing false conclu-
> sions from correct data. Under the influences of such prejudices,
> three centuries were of as little avail as a few years in our own
> times, when we are no longer required to propel the vessel against
> the force of an adverse current.[54]

Lyell came to think (wrongly) of the history of geology as a great intellectual battle of science against medieval ignorance. On the one side he saw arrayed several generations of unsound speculative schemes that had been built on the shifting sands of faulty faith. On the other side were pitched sound geological investigations that offered informed views rooted in the bedrock of sensible scientific inquiry. In point of fact, there was more in common between Burnet's massive world machine and Lyell's uniform system than might first meet the eye, in terms of both the rational character of their mechanisms and the extent to which both bolstered their systems with speculative theorizing.[55] Nonetheless, Lyell's belief that science was battling biblical ignorance caused many to back away from traditional biblical religion and move toward the systems that science had to offer.

Although a few rejectionists such as Eleazar Lord (see later discussion) fought valiantly against "uniformitarianism" and other gradualist notions—a battle still waged today by Whitcomb and Morris—most scientifically minded religionists of the nineteenth century felt constrained by the evidence to make room for a more rationally grounded, progressive scheme. The geological record ruled out a global biblical flood in the past and dictated that any local flood would not have had lasting consequences. While Lyell is not to be held entirely accountable for the shift in thinking, he helped shape the trend against using the Bible as a source of geological information. What Lyell did, however, was to bring a critique of diluvial thinking, long stirred up by the Edinburgh crowd, right into the heart of the Oxford and Cambridge world, where it could no longer be ignored.[56] Noah's flood had reached a geological dead end.

With so much upheaval in geological thought occurring in the early 1830s, we are not surprised to find a key figure such as the Reverend Adam Sedgwick of Cambridge disavowing flood geology in his presidential address before the Geological Society of London in 1831. Regardless of whether one followed Werner, Desmarest, Voigt, Hutton, Cuvier, Lyell, or some other modern theorist, a new assessment of the Bible was in order. Sedgwick's confession may seem startling to us, but it reflects the trends of his day. Nearing the end of his farewell address, he proclaims:

> Bearing upon this difficult question, there is, I think, one great
> negative conclusion now incontestably established—that the vast
> masses of diluvial gravel, scattered almost over the surface of the
> earth, do not belong to one violent and transitory period. . . . We saw
> the clearest traces of diluvial action, and we had, in our sacred histo-
> ries, the record of a general deluge. . . . Having been myself a believer,
> and, to the best of my power, a propagator of what I now regard as a
> philosophic heresy, and having more than once been quoted for
> opinions I do not now maintain, I think it right, as one of my last acts
> before I quit this Chair, thus publicly to read my recantation.[57]

A lengthy and rather tedious speech draws to a stark conclusion. No religionist could ignore the significance of these words for future biblical interpretation. No geologist could miss in this statement the door that had been flung open for continued scientific investigation. The era of writing biblical theories of the earth was over.

Likewise, in 1836 the Reverend William Buckland (1784–1856) of Oxford distanced himself from his previous belief in a universal flood, an outmoded conviction that he had initially outlined in his *Vindiciae Geologicae* (1820) and buttressed with more detailed evidence in his well-known *Reliquiae Diluvianae* (1823). The *Vindiciae Geologicae*, a lecture given by Buckland at Oxford University in 1819 on the occasion of a royal endowment of a readership in geology at that institution, takes us into the formative thinking of this gifted scientist and theologian regarding a "universal flood." The early Buckland is awash in the theories of Cuvier.[58] He heartily endorses the view that the earth is quite ancient and that creatures now long extinct once roamed the earth's landscape and seas. Yet Buckland is not committed only to geology in the *Vindiciae Geologicae*; he is equally dedicated to his Bible: "The facts developed by it [geology] are consistent with the accounts of the creation and deluge recorded in the Mosaic writings."[59] He embraced Cuvier's view that a fairly recent universal flood, perhaps some 6,000 years ago, had left its distinctive mark the world over.[60] Buckland's judgment on geology's vindication of scripture was firm: "The Mosaic account is in perfect harmony with the discoveries of modern science."[61] He goes so far as to claim that even without the Bible geologists would be forced by the evidence to conclude that a worldwide flood occurred in the recent past. His *Reliquiae Diluvianae* presented a vivid portrait of pre-flood England. An ancient hyena den in Yorkshire yielded hippos, rhinos, and elephants from before the flood, tropical remains covered by mud from the deluge. Beyond Yorkshire, the universal flood supplied Buckland with the means to explain particular strata stresses, peculiar gravel deposits, various valley formations, and specific fossil remains around the globe.[62] The theological lessons of geology were clear to Buckland. Far from being simply a manifestation of divine wrath, the flood was an example of "the finger of an Omnipotent Architect" at work.[63] Each ancient catastrophe, including the remarkable recent disruption of Noah's flood, represented an event through which the biblical God refashioned the earth to meet the needs of its current human occupants.

A decade and a half on in his thriving career, Buckland made a dramatic reversal of his view of the flood and the meaning of the Book of Genesis. He adopted the position that the Bible's flood left no lasting mark. The confidence of relative youth gave way to a more considered view. In his Bridgewater Treatise, *Geology and Mineralogy Considered with Reference to Natural Theology* (1836), Buckland hardly mentions the flood, arguing that those who link the biblical flood to the world's geological strata fail to grasp the "enormous thickness" of those strata with their "infinite subdivisions."[64] The lack of human remains in these layers tipped the balance for Buckland and others.[65] Geology's catastrophes and extinctions could hardly be attributed to Noah's flood, which the Bible tells us involved the deaths of the earth's human inhabitants, the descendants of Adam. The accumulating data had forced Buckland in a new direction.[66] The advances in geology made in the half century prior to this Bridgewater Treatise led Buckland to conclude that geologists were finally in a very good position to reconstruct the history of life on earth. The 1830s allowed for a stocktaking not possible in the prior two decades when Buckland's Mosaic diluvialism flourished. Finds of such ancient creatures as plesiosaurs, ichthyosaurs, megalosaurs, and iguanodons impressed Buckland with a growing vision of a lost world before the time of humans. If not the Bible's flood, then what mechanism drove geological change in that era? Encounters with Swiss naturalist Louis Agassiz (1807–73) convinced Buckland that massive glaciers had once shaped and re-shaped the landscape. The earth had known ages long before Noah's time and had experienced a series of catastrophes before the Bible's flood.

Of course, the religionist who reads Buckland's later writings might be alarmed to find that the earth's story was no longer simply Noah's flood story.[67] Yet by branching out beyond the Bible, Buckland sensed that religionists could make real gains. He admitted that his views did call for "some little concession from the literal interpreters of scripture," but if literalists could learn to be open to geology, they would be rewarded by serious advances in "natural theology," as geology gives evidence of the "stupendous Intelligence and Power" that has designed the world.[68] For Buckland, it was this awareness of design, not the flood story, that was the true hallmark of Genesis.

Buckland hoped for concessions from fellow geologists who might come to recognize in the Bible the key to unlocking the significance of intelligent design in nature. Thus, later in his career, Buckland carried on the spirit of William Paley. Paley's classic statement of divine design had been spelled out in *Natural Theology* whose title captures well his unique blending of geology and God.[69] If we were to find a watch lying on the ground, says Paley, we would have no trouble imagining that there was a watchmaker behind the watch. So also, he argues, we should have no trouble finding the divine maker in the evidence of design that nature supplies. These were ideas that stamped Buckland's thinking from the start, an awareness of design in nature that stayed with him long after he abandoned the flood story as a geological construct.[70] Needless to say, for the later Buckland, greater scientific openness did not mean that the Bible was to be abandoned in favor of a fully naturalistic theology. Scripture and geology remained compatible partners at least on the broad scale. Careful biblical interpretation, for example, told him that geology's great ages were already written into the first chapter of Genesis. All one had to do was to realize that when the Bible says "In the Beginning," it means that the universe was created long ago and that this world was much later "fitted up . . . for the reception of mankind."[71] In other words, the world that we know was refurbished out of materials that might have already existed "millions of millions of years."[72] This ancient world of "wreck and ruins" was restored during Genesis's week of creation, a week of relatively recent vintage when compared with the antiquity of geology's ages.[73] Such considerations paved the way for Buckland's extensive discussions of vast geological time periods and long-extinct life-forms. Still, one cannot help but notice that Noah's flood is nowhere to be seen in Buckland's later writings, except as a model to be rejected. Buckland chose to swim along new intellectual currents, changing how he and many others would view the Bible.

The stones and strata might speak of ancient mysteries, but no longer did they speak in harmony with the traditional reading of the flood story for

Buckland, Sedgwick, and many others. Various religionists predictably reacted as Bishop Shuttleworth did: "Some doubts were once expressed about the Flood; Buckland arose, and all was clear as mud."[74] Yet believers such as Sedgwick and Buckland thought of themselves as not having in the least rejected scripture. Sedgwick asked, "Are then the facts of our science opposed to the sacred records? and do we deny the reality of a historic deluge? I utterly reject such an inference."[75] The failure to recover evidence of the Bible's flood was not an occasion to dismiss it entirely. Obviously, however, the Bible had to be put on a new basis if it was to continue to play a meaningful religious or historical role. Sedgwick and Buckland came to think that the Bible's flood probably had occurred but that it left no trace in the geological record. A decisive moment in biblical interpretation had been reached. The old readings had to make room for new accommodations between scripture and science.

If These Fossils Could Cry Out

When confronted by the uncertainties of faith in an age of science, believers were no doubt reassured by the systems that ingeniously balanced faith's hopes with nature's reasons, such as those concocted since the sixteenth century. Yet history tells us that all the clever theories of the natural scientists would soon be outstripped by the stark realities of a world that was groaning in travail to reveal its long-held and woefully misunderstood secrets. The stones, strata, and fossils were not to be so easily accounted for. The more they reared their curious heads (and bodies and tails), the more clear it became that the stone relics of sea creatures and other oddities were not simply "sports of nature" mimicking living creatures but were in fact the once-animate remnants of a world far older than any Bible reader might have imagined.

As fossils began to more clearly come into focus, there were efforts to reconcile the Bible with the newly understood finds. Allen identifies Sir Matthew Hale, author of *The Primitive Origination of Mankind* (1677), as "the first Englishman to use the evidence of fossils as arguments for the universality of the Flood."[76] Hale remarked, "I am satisfied that many of them are but Relicks of Fish-shells left by the Sea, and there in length of time actually Petrified."[77]

Perhaps the most noteworthy of the early fossil inspectors was Niels "Steno" Stensen (1638–86). Scientists love puzzles. Steno was long puzzled by sharks' teeth. Why, he asked, were so many such teeth found on the island of Malta? Did nature produce them on some sort of whim? So many teeth had been found on the island that one could well doubt they were real. Yet they looked for all the world like authentic sharks' teeth. How did they get there? Did the biblical flood story hold the key?[78]

Imagine trying to figure out what such objects, dug out of the ground, actually were in the absence of substantive knowledge of the earth's age, strata formation, or the processes of fossilization. Steno was working on a puzzle with a lot of missing pieces. Rather than shying away from the difficulties, however, he tackled the problem of fossils head-on. He especially sought to understand how deposits of animal shells, bones, and plants came to their final resting place on mountaintops far from the sea.[79]

Part of Steno's labors, described in his *Prodromus* (1669), was directed at unlocking the secret of how once-living objects came to be embedded in rocks. By meticulous observation and logic, Steno argued that fossils were not naturalistic imitations shaped out of clay by Nature's hands but were in fact the genuine article: remains of animals and plants stuck inside the rocks that developed around them.[80] Their final state, he argued, can be studied to discern their origins and entrapment, since the "present condition of any thing discloses the past condition."[81] To know that once-living objects had become trapped marked a great advance in the understanding of fossils. But when did that fossilization originally take place?

Steno makes an insightful leap here, and yet he has taken us only part of the way. He must also somehow account for the presence of these fossils on mountaintops. How did they get there? The only answer, according to Steno, was Noah's flood.[82] No other flooding is known in world history or literature to explain these oddities.[83] When one pieces together the data, the fossils became evidence for the truth of the biblical flood story. In Steno's own estimation, his study revealed "nothing opposed to Scripture, or reason, or daily experience."[84] The Bible's flood was key. The flood shaped a world of fossils and mountains— the world as we know it.

Likewise, Abraham de la Pryme (1671–1704), reporting to the Royal Society of London, the premier scientific organization of England, spoke confidently of shellfish fossils: "From all this it sufficiently appears, that there was a time when the water overflowed all our earth, which could be none but the Noachian deluge."[85]

Others joined the chorus. For John Woodward, the fossils tell one unmistakable story: "The whole Terrestrial Globe was taken all to pieces and dissolved at the Deluge."[86] In his book entitled *An Essay towards a Natural History of the Earth and Terrestrial Bodies* (1695), Woodward defends the view that fossilized shells, bones, and plants were the leftovers of a pre-flood paradise that underwent a drastic remodeling by a God who knew that after Adam and Eve ate the sinful fruit humans needed a world fitted to their lower natures.

The flood, for Woodward, was not just about punishment for sin, although it did serve that purpose. Before the flood, too much of a good thing led humans into temptation, sin, greed, violence, and murder. The world had become, in Woodward's words, "little better than a common fold of Phrenticks and Bedlams"; it had become one big madhouse.[87] How was God going to make the world a place where fallen humans could live? Big changes were needed. The flood solved the problems posed by the temptations of paradise. The flood is

God's great redesign of the world to fit it to humans and their flawed natures, or, as Woodward writes, "to *retrench* and abridge the *Luxury* and Superabundance of the Productions of the Earth, which had been so ingratefully and scandalously abused by its former Inhabitants."[88] Far from being an act of divine vengeance, the flood turns out to be another example of God's great compassion for lapsed humanity.[89] The reshuffled earth would yield minerals and gems only as required and not in overabundance. The ground would need to be plowed more often, thereby keeping our minds off evil and our time given over to productive labors rather than wicked deeds. Finally, humans would live only to 120 years, giving them far fewer years in which to sin than before the flood.[90]

What concrete proof did Woodward have for his theories? Geologically speaking, he thought that science was now in a position to make sense of the evidence, proving that the Bible's picture is historical truth. Working with "Observations" and "Fact," Woodward imagined that "each particular Pit, Quarry, or Mine" in England contained evidence for his hypothesis about the flood.[91] Arguing against those who thought of fossils as simply "sportings of active Nature," that is, nature's playful imitations of living creatures, Woodward finds in fossils the remains of creatures who lived before the flood.[92] In this, he shows knowledge of Steno's writings.[93] The existence of fossils that are spread worldwide led Woodward to one conclusion: the "most horrible and portentous Catastrophe that Nature ever yet saw" really did happen as the Bible says.[94]

Science also can explain the mechanism of the flood. Arguing against Burnet's scheme, Woodward suggested that the center of the earth contained a vast cavity that formed the abyss where the floodwaters were stored, waters that connect to the ocean above and provide equilibrium around the globe even today.[95] Between this core abyss and the earth's crust are strata that have fires and heat inside them, producing volcanoes and underground vapors.[96] The flood that emerged from the great abyss reshaped the entire surface of the pre-flood world by means of a "universal deluge" that redeposited in layers of sediment the dead remains of pre-flood creatures, with the heavier ones descending lower in the strata and the lighter coming to rest toward the top according to gravity (an idea that lives on in Whitcomb and Morris's writings).[97] Trees managed to stay upright, and many were replanted, explaining the ease with which Noah's dove found an olive branch and also why unusual trees are found in far-flung locations (offering needed wood to the inhabitants as a gift of God).[98] This, in short, is Woodward's scientific reconstruction based on what seemed to him the obvious meaning of the fossil evidence and geological processes. Throughout his study, the writings of Moses are shown to be "punctually true."[99]

For Woodward, geology and fossils offer a living record of the flood. Science put theorists in a position to decipher that record. One might wonder why the ancients lost the memory of so momentous an event. On the one hand, Woodward reminds us that garbled tales of the flood are numerous.[100] Those tales were the "loud Rumour" of ancient storytellers.[101] Yet there is a practical reason why most ancients simply forgot about the flood: they were far too busy with the difficulties of survival after the flood to bother keeping the precise details of the catastrophe in order.[102] Gradually the memory became distorted and even lost. It is left to science to bring that distant memory to light once again and to confirm the words of the Bible: "In a word, that the *whole terraqueous Globe* was, by this means, at the time of the Deluge, put into the Condition that we now behold."[103]

The Swiss naturalist Johann Scheuchzer (1672–1733) went beyond Steno, de la Pryme, and Woodward to claim that one of his fossil finds most certainly represented the very bones of a person who had perished in the flood. For flood geologists this had always been a knotty problem, since only marine fossils had been found in these flood layers. One wondered what happened to all the people who supposedly perished in Noah's day. Scheuchzer was sure he had on his hands the remains of one of that wicked generation. We now know that Scheuchzer's wicked man was really a Jurassic period dinosaur.[104]

The connection of the fossils with Noah's flood persisted late into the eighteenth century. In 1799, Richard Kirwan defended the view that fossils were "the most unequivocal geologic proofs of a general deluge."[105] For Kirwan the universal flood written about by Moses was "the most horrible catastrophe to which the human and all animal species, and even the terraqueous globe itself, had at any period since its origin been exposed."[106] The flood, on this scientific reading, was a traumatic event that left deep marks on the world. It was the flood, for example, that produced the split between a once-connected Asia and America.[107] According to Kirwan, the advances that had been made in geology during the twenty-five years prior to the writing of his book put biblical readers in the position to "prove it [the flood] by geological facts."[108]

What was the evidence? Animal remains discovered by geologists in various strata the world over constituted indisputable facts. Only the flood could explain the hurly-burly nature of the fossil record. How else, apart from Noah's flood, could one account for the seashells that had been found high up on various mountains? While the earth's original ocean may have been higher than it is today, it was never high enough to set shells on a mountain in Peru at a level of 14,220 feet.[109] Only the flood could do that. Likewise, bones of elephants and rhinos found in Siberia could not have made their way there except by the flood.[110] According to Kirwan, there was no other way to explain how these creatures could have traveled from their homes in south Asia, crossing treacherous mountains to reach the Siberian wasteland. It made more sense to say that a universal flood first surged out of the Southern Hemisphere and then crashed into the mountains of Ararat, sweeping these hapless animals away from their homelands to deposit them in far-off lands.[111] One need not, however, scour the globe for clues. The teeth of arctic bears found in Europe were just one sign that animals had been torn from their native habitats by the flood. The fossils give prime evidence of the biblical flood.

Needless to say, Kirwan believed that his reading of scripture was rooted in its "plain literal sense."[112] His conjectures may seem anything but literal, but let us pause and linger over that notion. With Kirwan we are at the cusp of the older eras of scripture reading. Allegory and metaphor have always been a part of biblical interpretation. Still, the belief that such interpretation always somehow rested on a more literal foundation kept the interpreters from straying too radically beyond fundamental theological tenets. After Kirwan, literalism will increasingly yield to science. Yet in some circles the impression that a geological reading of scripture is truly the literal and more correct interpretation of the text will linger well into the nineteenth century.

That Kirwan's reading is not as literal as he imagined is evident in some of his more fanciful interpretations of Genesis. He suggested that prior to the flood only vegetarian animals roamed the earth, which meant that fewer animals boarded the ark since extras were not needed for meals. Conveniently, meat eaters were created by God after the flood to devour the carcasses of the animals that were drowned.[113] While hardly literal, Kirwan's reading is certainly clever. Apparently those carcasses could not be eaten quickly enough, however, because Kirwan also believed that they polluted the once pure pre-flood air, a factor that caused humans to live shorter lives after the flood. Again, cleverness trumps true literalism. As a final example, Kirwan indicates that the family troubles Noah experienced after the flood led him to pick up and move with some of his kin to China. This, for Kirwan, explains the origin of the Chinese monarchy.[114] Kirwan seems not to sense the growing tension between a literal reading of the Bible and a scientific assessment of the text.

Much more will need to happen in the world of biblical interpretation before the tension becomes critical and new accommodations are sought. The decade after 1814 would become pivotal as Buckland and others introduce into the picture ichthyosaurs and iguanodons, incontrovertible evidence of a lost world that existed before the creation of humans. The 1820s and 1830s further churned the theological waters as geology and paleontology made even greater strides, revealing the life-forms that inhabited each stage of the earth's geological past. The next step required seeing in the fossil record not only evidence of ancient life but also a progression in terms of their development over the millennia. We have seen that Lyell resisted the idea of progression in the geological record, but even before Darwin many others could not help seeing signs of development in the strata and the fossils.[115] Some, like Buckland, saw in the strata a succession of eras on earth but posited no genetic link between them. Others, like Étienne Geoffroy Saint-Hilaire (1772–1844) and the anonymous author (Robert Chambers) of the *Vestiges of the Natural History of Creation* (1844), went so far as to see in the fossils evidence for "progressive development," setting the stage for Darwin. Once Darwin turned the evolutionary corner in 1859, with "natural selection" as a mechanism linking the eras of earth's past, there could be no going back. Would the Bible keep up with science?

The Incredible Shrinking Flood:
Smith and Hitchcock Redefine Scripture and Science

Throughout the nineteenth century the realization grew that the world was vastly
older than Bible-based calculations allowed and that fossils present us with a
record of life far more exotic than previously believed. Religionists promoted a
series of carefully crafted accommodations to keep the geological findings and
the believer's Book together.[116] R. L. Numbers points out that there were two
major options for the nineteenth-century Bible believer, namely, the "day-age"
theory and the "gap" theory.[117]

The first option, the day-age theory, held that the Bible's seven "days" of
creation actually meant God's immortal days and not twenty-four-hour human
days. If one of God's days could be centuries in human terms, the Bible's time
scale could be extended to include deep geological time.

The second option, popularized by Buckland, was the so-called gap theory.
This view held that the initial act of creation in Genesis 1:1 was separated (perhaps by millions of years) from the six days outlined in the rest of the first chapter of Genesis. On this view, God created the world long ago. After a time it fell
into disrepair. At some point in the more recent past (somewhere during the
last 6,000 to 10,000 years), God took six days (each twenty-four hours long) to
spruce things up a bit and to create humans. The gap view, like the day-age view,
neatly accommodated the entire geological column to a seemingly strict reading of the biblical creation story.

Of course, each of these views created problems on a second front, namely,
the flood story. If the earth is very old and has undergone vast periods of geological development, what are we to make of the flood? The idea that a universal flood
was responsible for shaping the planet and for the production of fossils was obviously in trouble. Sedgwick and Buckland had reduced the biblical flood to little
more than a phantom. Were there not other possibilities for religionists?

Into the breach stepped the clever cleric John Pye Smith, who delineated
the "partial flood" theory in his classic *Scripture and Geology, on the Relation
between the Holy Scriptures and Some Parts of Geological Science* (1840). Smith
held that there was no contradiction between science and scripture. The real
problem was that careless critics were interpreting incorrectly when they insisted
that the Bible told of a global flood that shaped all of the strata of the earth in
one fell swoop. Smith repeats over and over that reason and sense-knowledge
must be taken seriously. That the earth was very old and the earth's strata had
built up over countless millennia was plain for all observers to see. To that extent, the believer was constrained to accept the truth that science had brought
to light.

What, then, of scripture? Smith admits and even seems to relish the fact that
on the surface scripture seems to stand in contradiction to the findings of science.

We catch him ending a lecture with the cliff-hanger statement "I seem to be taking the part of an enemy."[118] He carefully sets out the apparent contradictions. If the earth's strata have grown up over millennia, this appears to contradict Genesis, which makes it look as if one great catastrophe in the not-too-distant past altered the world forever. The world's numerous species and diverse animal habitats would seem to contradict the Bible's story of a man saving the world by taking a relatively few representative "kinds" aboard a boat. The lack of sufficient water reserves to cover the great mountains of the earth flies in the face of the claim that the entire world was destroyed by the flood. Smith acknowledges that such contradictions must cause "alarm and anxiety" in the disquieted believer.[119] Was there no antidote for this hydrological headache?

Smith's solution is both elegant and effective. He suggests that when the Bible says that the entire earth was flooded, it only means that the limited territory in which humans lived in the Middle East and the Caspian Sea region was destroyed. The Bible's view was a restricted one. Likewise, the extent of the flood was rather limited.[120]

In Smith's hands, the Bible becomes a "faithful description of the facts that did occur," but now in a very modest sphere of influence.[121] This partial flood was Smith's way of putting the findings of geology together with a more sensible reading of scripture. The Bible need not be dismissed as mythical, nor need it be embraced as entirely literal. Smith's middle way opened the doors for further scientific exploration and deeper biblical investigation.[122] "It is not the word of God, but the expositions and deductions of men, from which I am compelled to dissent."[123] Smith was convinced that he had the key to reading the Bible in a way that fit quite well with the findings of modern geology. He was appalled that some "tortured the book of life out of its proper meaning" by creating a "Mosaic geology."[124] A Mosaic geology would falter on two fronts: such a concoction would represent an amalgam of bad science and bad biblical interpretation. Still, the Bible is scientifically true when "correctly" interpreted.

For his day, Smith's achievement was impressive. He sought to interpret scripture in light of good science. He knew it was "a fearful thing to array science and religion against each other."[125] Consequently, he refused to think that solid biblical understanding and good science could stand in conflict:

> The study of revealed religion, thus pursued, cannot but be in perfect harmony with all true science. The works and the word of God are streams from the same source, and, though they flow in different directions, they necessarily partake of the same qualities of truth, wisdom, and goodness.[126]

Smith captures the concord between science and religion in a crisp analogy: "Nature and Revelation are both beams of light from the same Sun of eternal truth." As such it is "impossible that any real discordance should exist."[127] In practical terms, Smith links faith more closely to science by allowing new insights about scripture and geology to arise from their close encounter. Smith reminds us that progress is possible in religious knowledge, not simply in the natural sciences.

The appeal of Smith's theory to the thinking believer is obvious. Neither solid science nor belief in the Bible has to be sacrificed. This understanding of the close kinship of religion and science is best summarized by one of the modern "heroes" identified by Smith as voices of good sense in matters of science and faith, the American Edward Hitchcock (1793–1864).[128] Hitchcock, who has been described as "one of the country's oracles on Genesis and geology," believed that when science teaches us how to read scripture, it becomes a matter of "illustration and not collision."[129] Hitchcock, like Smith, had struck a constructive compromise that allowed scripture to be seen in a new light rather than compel science to adhere to the dictates of scripture.

The evolution of Hitchcock's own views of the flood before his encounter with Smith reflects the changing fads and fashions among biblical geologists in the early nineteenth century.[130] Initially embracing Cuvier's series of revolutions, Hitchcock thought of Noah's flood as global in scope and visible in its lasting effects, though with human remains left at the bottom of the world's oceans, since land and sea had literally switched places in the cataclysmic upheaval. Then, converted by Buckland's diluvialism, he adopted the position that the flood had indeed swept the world but left land and sea in the places they always had been. Human remains simply had not yet been recovered. The lack of human remains led Hitchcock and others to take up the view that Noah's flood did occur, but since the flood was a relatively brief occurrence, its effects could not be sorted out from the numerous diluvial events of the past, though the evidence of such events did make Noah's flood geologically plausible. Finally, before Noah's flood was swept completely from sight, Hitchcock was saved by Smith's partial-flood theory.

In fact, the two men formed something of a transatlantic mutual admiration society. Smith, who was connected with Homerton College near London, wrote a brief unsolicited letter that became the "Introductory Notice" to Hitchcock's third edition of his *Elementary Geology* in 1841.[131] Smith praises Hitchcock for producing a volume that is "more comprehensive with regard to the various relations and aspects of the science than any one book with which I am acquainted." He also notes the practical benefits of such geological knowledge for choosing "the best localities for missionary stations" around the world.[132] Smith specifically recalls the direct influence of Hitchcock's earlier writings on his own theological reflections concerning geology, considering this interaction a collaboration with a "fellow-laborer in the gospel of Christ."[133]

Hitchcock, in turn, pats Smith on the back by relying on his reinterpretation of the Bible to give theological legitimacy to Hitchcock's own thoroughly modern geological investigations.[134] Hitchcock's position as professor of natural theology and geology at Amherst College represents a mixing of disciplines that would be unthinkable today. However, the fruitful interchange of ideas between Smith and Hitchcock demonstrates the vital possibilities for dialogue between geological science and biblical interpretation at that time. Smith's impact on Hitchcock was so strong that later in his career Hitchcock looked back with gratitude for his meeting with Smith in London: "I am thankful that I was permitted to see the man, whom, of all others in Europe, I most desired to see."[135] Reflecting on that visit, which took place just one year before Smith's death, Hitchcock writes fondly of Smith as "a man of eminent piety as well as learning."[136]

There was no conflict in either of their minds between serious science and bold biblical interpretation. For Hitchcock, this meant taking full account of both geology's ancient age for the earth and theology's reinterpretation of the Bible, which allowed for these great ages and proposed a more limited biblical flood. Explaining the new trends that moved researchers beyond the past attempts of theologians to explain all global geological phenomena by reference to a universal flood, Hitchcock writes: "One after another have these extravagancies of hypothesis been given up, and nearly all geologists have come to the conclusion, though without denying the occurrence of the Noachian deluge, that no certain marks of that event are now to be discovered on the globe."[137] Thus, long before fundamentalists latched on to Morris and Whitcomb's flood geology as the only way to read scripture, we find committed evangelical Christians presenting a very different view of the relationship between geology and faith.

Smith and Hitchcock's case is hardly an isolated one. Most scientifically minded believers in the nineteenth century were inclined to forge new links between geology and the Bible.[138] Hitchcock heartily endorsed Denis Crofton's *Genesis and Geology; or, An Investigation into the Reconciliation of the Modern Doctrines of Geology with the Declarations of Scripture*, and urged an American publisher to reprint it and bring the word "within reach of American Christians."[139]

In a preface to the American edition of this slender volume, Hitchcock elevated Crofton to a lofty position above Buckland, Sedgwick, and even John Pye Smith, professing that "this author seems to me to have treated the subject with great candor; so that if his conclusions do not seem satisfactory to any, they will at least be saved from irritation and disgust."[140] This hermeneutical sage, who would apparently preserve American Christians from intellectual indigestion, had in turn endorsed the work of Smith and Hitchcock in the pages of his book. The three were at work forging a new consensus among nineteenth-century religionists regarding the relation between the scriptures and the strata.

Crofton's little book succinctly places ten "propositions" before the reader in defense of the position that the Bible and the new geology were made for one another. For Crofton, when science conflicts with scripture, the interpreter must impartially judge "whether the difference between the two be real, or only apparent, and whether the seeming discrepancies admit of a sound reconciliation."[141]

Crofton finds reconciling elements everywhere. In his reading of the Bible's creation story, he discerns a long interval of time between the original creation of the universe in Genesis 1:1 and the rebuilding of that universe that commences with Genesis 1:2. The gap between the verses is now filled in by geology.

Crofton thinks of the days of the first chapter of Genesis as literal twenty-four-hour days, since he claims that any effort to read them as "epochs" will not square with geological history. The progression of geological and animal development does not fit neatly with the seven days of Genesis 1. As a result, Crofton remains content to see the Genesis week as a slice in the not-too-distant past when God set to work "mending" a very old and rather dilapidated earth.[142]

Crofton reassesses the meaning of the creation week. The so-called first day of Genesis 1 is not to be understood as the very first day in the life of the universe but merely the first day of the universe's "re-creation." The "light" spoken of in Genesis 1:4 was not created on this first day. Indeed, light had existed for millennia untold; this light is simply "called into action" by God on the first day of re-creation week.[143] Similar arguments are put forward for the other days. Day four, for example, is when the sun, moon, and stars finally appear to earthly view, not the day when they were first created.[144] Geology aids us in making sense out of the story.

What about the flood tale? Obviously on Crofton's reading the earth may have been quite old by the time of its "re-creation." The flood would have been an event of merely recent geological impact and significance. But even here Crofton calls for careful interpretation of the Bible. He opts, as Smith did, for a limited flood, arguing that the word translated "earth" in Hebrew can simply refer to a "part" of the earth. The flood of Noah was probably regional and not global. The character of the fossil finds suggests that different periods are in question. Fossils do not give evidence of one major world catastrophe.[145] Once again, geology saves us from misunderstanding the Bible.

Crusaders for Catastrophism: Defending the Bible

There were certainly those who took exception to this easy blending of science and scripture.[146] The Reverend William Kirby resisted accommodating scripture to the new geology, defending the view that the flood was responsible for the fashioning of the earth's strata. Smith recognized Kirby as "a respectable clergyman" but excoriated him for "having wandered out of his proper province to introduce some of the wildest speculations upon geological subjects that ever germinated in the brain of men, while in the same work, he generously relieves our astounded minds by acknowledging that he has not studied geology."[147] Bad science, in other words, was not to be used to salvage scripture.

On the American scene, one of the more strident attacks on those who sought to forge a link between modern geology and the Bible came from Eleazar Lord, better known as the president and founder of the Erie Railroad. His book

The Epoch of Creation (1851) constituted a frontal assault on the scientific and theological compromises of Hitchcock and Smith.

Lord took issue with geological estimates of the age of the earth. In his view, the science of geology dealt with natural phenomena in the context of the historical present. Only divine revelation can tell us where, when, and how it all began. Those opening words of Genesis, "In the beginning . . . ," confirmed for Lord that the sequence started with seven actual days during an era not too long ago, certainly not the myriad of years that geologists liked to imagine.

Lord also took issue with the view of God implied by the "developmental hypothesis," his phrase for geological and animal evolution. Lord bitterly denies that the perfect God would muck about for millions of years trying to improve an imperfect creation.[148] The whole idea struck him as preposterous. He much preferred the biblical picture of a dignified God employing a whole series of miracles (his "supernatural interpositions") to fashion the world in a short span of time. Lord opposed any attempt to use the findings of geology to guide a reinterpretation of the biblical passages regarding creation: "If they [biblical miracles] did not occur, the whole history must be a fable."[149]

One miracle stood out above all others: the flood of Noah. Lord insisted that only the flood could make sense out of the geological record. Since the fossils do not form a simple sequence as the geologists pretend (Lord here anticipates Price, Whitcomb, and Morris), then the flood must be invoked to explain the mixed-up characters of those materials.[150] In other words, the animals that had died between Adam's sin and the time of the flood not only were buried after their deaths but their bone deposits were churned up along with the bones of those that died at the time of the flood. The fossil record reflects this great mishmash of remains.[151] This, Lord claims, is the situation geologists have found, not the neat patterns of the science textbooks. As for extinct animals (ones similar to those in existence today—he ignores anything that we would now term a dinosaur), he says that God must have had some moral reason for letting them perish in the changed environment of the post-flood world.[152] He saw the trend among theologians and Christian geologists to engage in natural speculation and biblical reinterpretation on this matter as an unambiguous rejection of the Bible.[153]

Against Hitchcock, Lord argued that putting science first means placing scripture in an inferior position. If scripture comes from God, then scripture ought to be taken more seriously than the "assumptions, hypotheses, and inferences of the geologists."[154] In plain English, such a person should "feel embarrassed at every step."[155]

Against Smith, Lord argued that the "local flood" theory played right into the hands of the "infidels" who have trouble with the miraculous element of the Bible: "Infidelity, driven forth from the fields of metaphysics and philosophy, has taken refuge in the dark recesses and labyrinths of physical nature," so why try to please them?[156] Why limit the flood to a tiny district that has never been discovered by geologists, when the entire globe gives evidence of the turmoil of the great flood?[157] For Lord, the choice was clear: a global flood is both geological fact and biblical truth.

Despite exceptions like Kirby and Lord, there were many clerics and believing scientists who chose to stand on the cutting edge of geological, biological, and theological studies while maintaining faith in their scriptures. This may come as a surprise to those today who prefer to imagine that religion has always sided with ignorance in the face of science's obvious truths. It will also come as a surprise to contemporary fundamentalists who think that serious believers have always defended the universal Genesis flood story against the devilish theories of Darwin's minions. While it is true that the universal flood theory still had a few defenders in the late nineteenth and early twentieth centuries, this view has gained the upper hand among fundamentalists only in more recent decades. Flood universalists such as Eleazar Lord and George McCready Price were truly voices crying in the wilderness until Whitcomb and Morris came along. Hitchcock and Smith take us into much more progressive territory, although still remaining squarely among those whom we would today term fundamentalists and evangelicals rather than liberal readers of the Bible.

Thus, although we should not fault earlier researchers like Hale, Steno, or Scheuchzer for their lack of understanding, it became increasingly obvious to many religionists in the first half of the nineteenth century that such theorists were terribly wrong. The flood of the Bible was not the reason that fossils of sea creatures were ensnared in rocks and scattered on mountaintops the world over. The flood was not the reason behind the fracturing of the continents and the eruption of the mountainous elevations of the earth. Neither was the flood behind the petrified remains of ancient dinosaurs. Yet to account for all this evidence, the idols that had been made of the Bible's foreshortened chronology of the earth and the universal flood had to be lifted off their sacred altar and dashed on the ground of better science. A new paradigm was badly needed if believers were to stay on top of the game. Fortunately, people like John Pye Smith and Edward Hitchcock were able to see beyond biblical blinders to craft another view that linked Genesis with geology.

Behind the Story or Beyond?

While building on much that came before, a new chapter was about to be written concerning the relation between science and scripture with Darwin's *Origin of Species* (1859).[158] Although many were predisposed by their familiarity with the geological discussions to envision close links between evolutionary science and scripture, others, such as T. H. Huxley and Herbert Spencer, insisted on driving a wedge between science and the Bible.[159] Darwin's success in religious circles may be surprising to those who are disposed to think that religionists fought Darwin at every turn. What they fought was the view that no God had a hand in the geological and evolutionary processes. Remembered today as "Darwin's forgotten defenders," evangelicals like Asa Gray, G. F. Wright, and James Dwight Dana did not shun the new vistas that science had opened before the watching world.[160] Such believers carried on Smith and Hitchcock's view that scripture and science could not stand in genuine contradiction because the same God was the author of both the book of nature and the book of belief.

Eventually, with the active support of many pioneering theologians and Christian scientists, our understanding of space and time was liberated from the Bible's much narrower "world" and limited "generations" of some 6,000 years. The stones and fossils were freed to speak of events and times far removed from Archbishop Ussher's seventeenth-century calculations by which he determined with calendrical precision that the world's creation took place on Sunday, October 23, 4004 B.C.E., and the flood occurred Sunday, December 7, 2349 B.C.E.[161] Believers managed to stay on board even as the groundwork was laid by Darwin and others to set aside the Bible as a significant source for historical information regarding human origins. Scientifically minded believers might still turn to the Bible to gain insight into the "why" of our origins, but science would gain preeminence when it came to the "how" part of the equation—even among people of faith.

A word of caution is in order, however, regarding pseudoscientific and scientific speculation about Noah's flood. As tantalizing as these approaches may have been—whether the study of ark architecture, the fashioning of "theories of the earth," calculations of the waters, talk of limited floods, the invention of creationist "flood geology," Mesopotamian tell digs, and even Black Sea archaeological soundings—it seems that each and every attempt to recast the flood tales as hydrological history or in terms of "theological geology" ends up shearing away elements that are essential to the tales themselves. Refracted in the fundamentalist's "canopy of the firmament" or the surging waters of the secular archaeologist's lakes and rivers, the long-lived tales begin to look rather flimsy by comparison. Yet the flood traditions appear to come from hardier literary stock than our natural theologians and scientists would have us believe. Ancient flood tales insist on matters both human *and* divine. Discoveries of water, fossils, or ruins alone will not unlock the deeper wells of the flood tale. To move below the surface of the story, we must turn to grapple with the myth as such. We ask, then, the question Joseph Campbell asked of all such stories, namely, wherein lies the power of this myth?[162]

6

Weather Reports?

Adopting the Mythic View

Every semester, on the first day of my course on ancient mythology, before I hand out the syllabus, before I give out the initial readings, and even before I say much more than my name, I begin by handing my students a sheet of paper on which they are asked, "Please write in one or two sentences your definition of mythology." As the semester proceeds and the students gain a greater sophistication regarding the varieties of ways that scholars think about mythology, these initial definitions come to look fairly rudimentary, if not downright embarrassing. At that point I often ask them to tear up their outgrown definitions, consigning them to the trash.

Typically when students take their first stab at a definition, they characterize myths as stories that are not true. The usual explanation they arrive with from their high school days is that myths are stories that were designed to explain the workings of nature to an unscientific mind. Such stories may have been clever for the times, but today most of us see right through them and can live without them. Myths were white lies about the world that the ancients told themselves to feel in control of nature's elements.

Myths as Nonsense: T. H. Huxley on Fiction

No one has wielded a sharper sword against claims for the historical truth of the biblical flood story or of mythic tales in general than the ardent defender of Darwinism T. H. Huxley (1825–95). In a spate of essays over the years, Huxley hacked apart the flimsy armor of his religionist opponents, especially Samuel Wilberforce (1805–73) and William Gladstone (1809–98). Huxley's 1860 debate on evolution against Wilberforce, bishop of Oxford, has become the stuff of legend. His writings against Gladstone, the pious prime minister of Great Britain, skewer and roast Gladstone's beloved Bible, destroying any hope that the secularist scientist will find anything of worth in the biblical flood story.[1] For Huxley, "the Deluge story is a pure fiction."[2] How did he arrive at this stark conclusion?

Four pillars undergird his views. In the first place, Huxley's reasoning rests on evolutionary theory and geological investigation. So much progress had been made in this regard that by the 1880s and 1890s, the period of his key essays on Genesis, Huxley saw no reason for scientists to spend any time mulling over possible connections between the Bible and the results of the scientific analysis of earth's development and human origins. To the suggestion that they seriously ponder the flood, Huxley writes, scientists will "look at you with a smile and a shrug, and say they have more important matters to attend to than mere anti-quarianism."[3] For the secular scientist, both the Genesis story of creation and the story of the flood are of no historical or scientific value. The biblical baby is thrown out with the bath water; Huxley envisions no turning back.

Second, Huxley's view is a function of his understanding of literature in general. For Huxley, there are essentially three sorts of stories: those that are perfectly true, those that are partially true, and those that are completely ficti-tious.[4] The newly born science of historical criticism had made scholars aware that even the best of the ancient Greek and Roman writers mixed fiction into every batch of history they cooked up. It only stood to reason that the Bible was at best a blend of fact and fantasy.[5] Huxley avows having a great regard for fic-tion, such as Shakespeare's plays. Yet he points out that he would never think of turning to Hamlet or Macbeth for accurate information about the periods in question. Nor, one presumes, would he turn to the Bible for anything more than general moral guidance.[6]

In the third place, Huxley's argument derives from comparisons with re-cently excavated ancient Near Eastern texts. With the discovery of other ancient flood stories, Huxley felt free to ask if any of those stories carried historical weight. He sensed that the Mesopotamian flood tale had greater claim to his-torical accuracy insofar as it referred to river floods rather than a universal ca-tastrophe as in the biblical version.[7] On that score, the scientist can make sense out of flood stories outside of the Bible. However, Huxley finds the polytheism of the ancient Mesopotamian story patently absurd.[8] Contending that the poly-theistic elements are too entwined with the more believable aspects of the story, Huxley concludes the whole thing is historically worthless.[9] If the more logical-sounding Mesopotamian story cannot pass muster, then the Bible, which has commandeered and expanded the Mesopotamian story beyond all measure, will certainly fare no better. Since Huxley refuses to take refuge in the "allegorical method" to save any of these stories, he can only conclude that "the story of the

Flood in Genesis is merely a Bowdlerised version of one of the oldest pieces of purely fictitious literature extant."[10] Taking note of the Roman poet Ovid's version of the flood, the story of Deucalion, Huxley insists, "The Noachian Deluge has no more claim to credit than has that of Deucalion; . . . it is utterly devoid of historical truth."[11]

Finally, Huxley plays to great advantage the card passed to him by theologians of the day who were questioning the authorship of the Bible. If the flood story was not from Moses but was a mix of two stories from authors who lived at a much later date than Moses, then surely no one could believe that it had been passed on by "the mother of Moses," who "was told the story of the Flood by Jacob; who had it straight from Shem; who was on friendly terms with Methusaleh; who knew Adam quite well."[12] For Huxley, the late date and mixed authorship of the flood story cast a cloud over any possible historical value to the text.

Before we begin to think that Huxley was converting to the progressive theological camp, however, we must also observe that he rather deftly played his historical card not only against the biblical literalists of his day but also against the progressive theologians who had handed it to him in the first place. Huxley chided their attempts to blend science and faith by hypothesizing that the flood was really a partial flood that actually occurred sometime during the glacial epoch in the not-too-distant past, a view not unlike that of Ryan and Pitman.[13] He argued that these attempts led to geological absurdities, contradicting what is known about the immense period of time required for the development of the Jordan River valley and the Dead Sea.[14] Huxley's impatience with these muddy theological efforts is summed up succinctly when he says, "A child may see the folly of it."[15] Huxley thought of himself living in a "day of compromises" in which there was still a struggle over the historical character of the Bible, but he thought that the future belonged to those who not only dismissed the pre-Abrahamic stories of creation and flood but also moved beyond the post-Abrahamic parts as well.[16]

Taken together, Huxley's four-pronged attack appears unanswerable. The secularist who questions the historicity of the Bible would seem to have the upper hand.

While I will seek to move beyond Huxley's confident dismissal of mythological texts, there is much to be gained from a serious encounter with his ideas. Prior to the nineteenth century, naive readings of Genesis dominated the discussion. With the nineteenth century, the advent of secular evolutionary science changed the rules of the game for all biblical interpreters, including the biblical literalist. The fundamentalist, as much as anyone else, has come to adopt historical and scientific strategies to save the text, unconsciously admitting that this is the predominant path to truth for moderns, even theological truth. As a result, anyone who wishes to recover the truth of myth and the Bible, whether fundamentalist or liberal, is forced to rely on scientifically inflected channels by which that truth can be transmitted to the tough analytic mind of the present. This is the legacy of Huxley.

Unfortunately, the rationalist grid that clues us in to the fictional character of myth also serves to distance us from the literature that once sustained our ancestors. The myth has been unmasked and, like the wizard in the land of Oz, at once loses its power over us. Huxley's secularized evaluation of myth leads us to see that the more immediate truth of myth was directly available only to the ancient peoples who actually lived their lives around such tales. For Huxley, this shift away from myth is all to the good. The mythic age was a time of ignorance from which we have been liberated by science. Science gives us the better truths. Yet, as we shall see, there are other ways to read the old myths. Bridging the broad gap that separates us from the mythmakers, those who treat myths as the "literature of the spirit" find in these ancient traditions a rich heritage that continues to stir the mind and enliven the heart with transcendent tales of natural wonder, spiritual mystery, and humanistic truth. The narrow secularist approach need not have the last word. Yet to be successful we need to build a reasonably well-grounded bridge to the past.

Literary Excavation as an Alternative

If the biblical tales of creation and the flood offer us neither a science lab manual nor merely a collection of fraudulent fables, what are we to make of these stories? Is there no way to avoid fundamentalist science fictions? Is there no escaping the nineteenth-century secularist stalemate regarding the value of myth? Perhaps the answer lies not behind, above, or beyond the text but in the text itself. A study of the rhetoric of the text can help us track down stylistic clues that will enable us to read the old tales in a new light. A close reading of the creation story in the first chapter of Genesis points the way here.

Notice that creation takes seven days. The very word "day" has proven to be an obstacle in the interpretation of the text for both secularists and religionists. For the secularist, seven literal days for the development of the entire universe has been shown to be preposterous by modern science. For the fundamentalist who still clings to literal twenty-four-hour days, the scientific findings have to be swept under the biblical rug. Bible believers who try to interpret the days to mean "eras" still run into the problem that the sequence in which things happen in the Bible does not precisely parallel what science has found to be true for either the development of the universe or the evolution of life on earth. Talk of literal days flies in the face of the scientific facts, while reliance on elongated eras gives us a Bible that only superficially resembles science. Is there no alternative to endlessly manipulating the Bible and science?

The biblical detective will dust the text in search of its compositional fingerprints, literary signs that might give away the meaning of the text. Many will sense that seven is a symbolic number. Maybe there is something about the way that the text is arranged according to the number seven that betrays its deeper meaning. Perhaps there is a message to be gleaned from the way in which the seven days unfold.

One oddity that leaps out at us is the fact that light is created on the first day, but the celestial bodies that give off light are not created until day four. What is going on here?

The creationist, as always, has an immediate "scientific" answer. Whitcomb and Morris, for example, argue that a canopy of vaporous haze covered the earth for several days before the appearance of the sun, moon, and stars on day four. This approach treats Genesis 1 as if it had been written from the perspective of an observer on earth, for whom the dispersal of the vapor makes it seem as if the lights were created on day four. This reading plays fast and loose with a text, all the while claiming to be reading it literally.

The more progressive evangelical Christian might say that Genesis 1:1 represents the big bang, whereas day four represents the settling out of our solar system billions of years later. This is clever, but it makes Genesis 1 relevant only to twenty-first-century people.

Of course, the Huxleyan secularist does not offer us much help here either. Dispensing with the text in the name of a superior science avoids any dilemma about days one and four in Genesis. The Bible's seven-day saga, the secularist would say, is nothing more than misguided speculation about the origins of the world. Science tells the better story. Unfortunately, this quick fix by the Huxleyan misses some big literary fish that are easily caught in the net of anyone who cares to do a little bit of patient textual fishing.

The observant reader will note that days one, two, and three have a common theme; they set the stage for what occurs on days four, five, and six. In fact, the cycles of three balance each other exactly.[17] Thus day one gives us the luminous backdrop for the specific brilliance of the sun, moon, and stars of day four. The sky expanse and the waters of day two serve as the stage for the birds and sea creatures of day five. Finally, the dry land with its vegetation and trees that appears on day three forms the appropriate setting for the cattle, wild beasts, creeping things, and humans that arrive on the earth on day six. The first three days, in other words, offer the larger landscape for the second cycle of days four, five, and six. We are obviously not looking at science, even creationist science, but at artfully structured language. Genesis 1 is, in other words, a kind of poetry.

The stylized structure of the creation story in Genesis 1 presents us with heightened language that might best be considered a poetic myth, one that is designed to inspire an awe before nature through the balanced beauty of its language. The story is cloaked with ancient mythic trappings, but it nonetheless carries a timeless message about the divine wonder woven into every layer of nature. The Bible's own truth about the depths of creation is relevant to all people in all places. While it is not science, the text encourages the ardent secularist not to become complacent before the marvels of nature. While it is not creation science, the text calls creationists to move beyond cold creationist facts to see in poetry a mode of transcendent truth. The Genesis story reminds us all that poetic language is required to evoke realities that are only hinted at by science and are obscured when creationists treat the biblical text as a photographic record of the past. The attempt to read the Bible through scientific lenses did not unlock this truth. A close reading without any scientific blinders seems to be the most productive way to read such a text. Its character as a meaningful myth then emerges as a compelling story to be taken seriously regardless of our scientific scruples.

In the Genesis story, then, we discover the poetic truth that moved the ancient Israelites. This is what they have passed on to us, not science. Perhaps such poetry is the language of a God whose truth is not captured by the mundane prose of the creationist or the sanitized formulas of secular science. In any event, we are led by this investigation of the creation story to ponder whether the flood story is also to be read as a serious poetical myth rather than as either science or creation science.

Beyond Flash Flood Warnings

Those who, unlike T. H. Huxley, have a sense of the vital role of mythology for the shaping of human life and culture will understand why I have my students rip up the simplistic definitions of myth that they handed in on the first day of the semester. The act of shredding is symbolic of the need to move beyond their high-schoolish views. Many students, for example, think of ancient myths as nothing more than primitive explanations for the operations of nature, especially thunderstorms, earthquakes, and volcanic activity. But ancient myths were much more than weather reports about the sun god, storm warnings about the wind god, or the daily *Babylonian Gazette*'s flash-flood bulletin about the doings of the water god. Entire societies were built up around these myths, and ancient peoples did not build their societies on weather reports alone; they also turned—to keep to our newspaper analogy—to the front-page news, the sports page, the variety section, and the religion column.

For the ancients, the front-page news announced the king's economic successes and excesses. The sports stories were the tales of the king's triumphs in war, all of which were credited to the gods who fashioned and sustained the universe, and put the king in power. The variety section covers all the doings of the elite whose ostentatious monuments record their noble contributions to the building up of the empire in the name of the gods. And, of course, the religion column takes us into the life of the temples, where the gods of the myths ate, drank, slept, and had their tête-à-têtes with their fellow divinities.

Where are the myths in all of that?

They are found on every page.

Myth bound the whole of society together. Kings, the elite, the temple complex, and the numerous workers and farmers beneath them—mythical stories cemented the ancient social pyramid in its place.

Another Mesopotamian myth, the Babylonian story of creation, offers a good example of the socially binding power of myth. In this tale the children of the gods come to be locked in fierce combat with the mother goddess, Tiamat. Only the intervention of the god Marduk saves the gods from utter destruction. The victorious Marduk creates the universe out of the carcass of Tiamat and uses the blood of her fallen general, Qingu, to create humankind. The creation of the city of Babylon and its rich temple complex rounds out Marduk's labors.

This powerful myth was read, or perhaps reenacted, each year as part of the Babylonian New Year's festival. This eleven-day event held great social importance for the people, for this was the time that the "destinies" were fixed and the prosperity of the land was assured for the coming year. The festival was also of great political significance, for during the rites the king was brought before the high priest and forced to kneel and was even slapped across the face in order to demonstrate his humility before the gods. His tears in that moment were a sign of the king's great devotion to the most high god. Clearly the myth worked to shore up the king's position as the chosen of the gods.[18]

Such myths, then, were like America's constitution, undergirding the king and the populace by thrusting a divine foundation beneath their commonwealth. These myths were like a corporation's mission statement, setting out national dreams and goals.

If we think of myths in this way, the meaning of the creation and flood stories is found not in their possible historical origins but in their continued ritual use, their enduring social significance, and their powerful political import. What the great translator P. Lal has said of the Sanskrit epic, the *Mahabharata,* also holds true of the Bible: "The hold the *Mahabharata* has on the Hindu—indeed, the Indian—imagination is difficult to describe to a person who does not belong to a myth-culture."[19] The *Mahabharata,* that great epic that tells of the trials of Pandu's five noble sons as they vie against the evil Duryodhana and his kin, has shaped Hindu culture in profound and subtle ways. Whether in ancient India or ancient Israel, myths live because, like rich computer software, they encode all the lessons, values, and ideals needed by their societies. They store the megabytes of mythical beliefs people need to endure the hard times, to make sense of their particular historical circumstance, and to chart a path into the future without losing a symbolic foothold in the past.

The essential belief underscored by myth was that the natural world, however chaotic it may seem, provides a way of escape and that this way of escape is for people to keep rebuilding civilization, even after great disasters. The gods (or God) order and reorder the cosmic powers in heaven and the social apparatus on earth. Of course, the implication is that the keepers of the stories—the palace and the priests—are the ones chosen to guard and nourish that rebuilt world. This, too, is encoded in the story, in which sacrifices by obedient priests are required to appease the gods and a divinely elected human sovereign must govern the land beneath a sometimes hostile sky.

The Earliest Mesopotamian Flood Tales

By far the most ancient of the extant Mesopotamian flood tales is the Sumerian story of Ziusudra, whose name literally means "Life of Long Days." Preserved only in fragments, this text, which dates from sometime before 2000 B.C.E., still yields the basic outline of its story.[20] The flood, we learn, is a key event in the Sumerian past. The devastation sent by the gods is detailed in an account closely tied to other fragmentary narratives that depict the major events of Sumer's legendary history. The record begins with the creation of the Sumerians, called the "black-headed" people. There follows an account of the descent of kingship from heaven to earth. The text goes on to relate the establishment of the five great cult centers of lower Mesopotamia, namely, Eridu, Badtibira, Larak, Sippar, and Shuruppak. The fifth city is hailed in the later Epic of Gilgamesh as the hometown of the flood hero Utnapishtim. At this point in the story, the focus turns to the tale of King Ziusudra and the account of the flood.

This pious ruler is carrying out his sacrifices when a god informs him of the impending catastrophe. The text is severely damaged at this point, and it is not clear why the gods have decided to send a flood. In any event, Ziusudra is spared after enduring a massive flood that lasts seven days and nights. Through his boat's survival the world's vegetation and the "seed of mankind" are preserved and renewed. After the flood, Ziusudra opens the window of the boat, receiving the rays of the sun god, Utu. Ziusudra is probably blessed by Utu at this juncture, but the text is too damaged to be certain of the god's action. After offering up an ox and a sheep to the gods, Ziusudra is rewarded with immortality by the sky god Anu and the wind god Enlil, who give Ziusudra a place of residence in the idyllic land of Dilmun.

The Ziusudra tale establishes the basic pattern of the flood story. Over the centuries, many other written versions would follow in its wake. An important successor to the Ziusudra story is the legend of Atrahasis.

The Atrahasis tale, dating from roughly 1700 B.C.E., though also found in copies as late as the time of King Ashurbanipal (668–627 B.C.E.), is better preserved than the Ziusudra story. It gives us a reason for the flood.[21] It seems that the gods felt overburdened by all their labors and staged the first "strike" in history, burning their tools and refusing to work. Humans were made from clay to serve as replacement workers. The problem was that the humans multiplied, and their noisy antics kept the gods awake. In response, the gods tried out a series of population reduction measures, including plague, drought, and, when all else failed, a flood. Fortunately for the humans, Enki, the god of wisdom and water, warned the hero Atrahasis (Mr. "Exceedingly Wise") to build a boat and ride out the flood. Although the wind god Enlil was angry at Atrahasis's escape, the others accepted his offerings. The fragmentary state of the text leaves Atrahasis's later fate unclear.

The Atrahasis flood story, which effectively adapted and extended the Ziusudra tale, found new life as a scene in a major composition, the Epic of Gilgamesh. Insofar as Gilgamesh is a key player in Mesopotamian myth, I must linger a bit over the traditions surrounding this cultural icon.

Bilgames: The Hearty Hale Hero?

The Epic of Gilgamesh represents an updating and amalgamation of tales of the heroic Gilgamesh, a king who may very well have been a real personage living roughly 2600 B.C.E. but attained the status of a legend on the order of a King Arthur. Individual tales of Gilgamesh survive in texts from the eighteenth century B.C.E. that are doubtless copies of stories going back to the Sumerian golden age in southern Iraq, namely, the time of the Third Dynasty of the city of Ur (twenty-first century B.C.E.). While the Bible makes Ur the home of the great patriarch Abraham, the city is better known among Mesopotamian scholars for fostering the traditions of Gilgamesh (known in the early texts as Bilgames), a hero who was remembered in his own way for as long as Jesus has been talked about in the Christian world. The figure of Gilgamesh is far older than the epic that bears his name, and it is worthwhile to examine the oldest of his tales to see how the tradition grew.[22]

In one Sumerian legend, Bilgames of Uruk faces down the rebellious King Agga of neighboring Kish. Agga's forces besiege Uruk. The Urukians send out hero after hero against this raging Goliath, to no avail. Their first hero is captured and beaten mercilessly. The second is laughed off the wall as a weakling. But then King Bilgames ascends the wall, throwing terror into the invading soldiers. Agga wisely sues for peace and discovers that Bilgames is a true hero who balances strength with compassion. They become allies.

Something of the darker quality of the Bilgames legends can be gleaned from another of these early tales. This story opens with Bilgames distraught over death, a theme that is central to the later Epic of Gilgamesh. His distress leads him on a venture to cut down a choice cedar tree in the forest that is guarded by the fierce creature Huwawa (later known as Humbaba). In fear, Huwawa casts a spell over Bilgames, putting him into a deep sleep. Later aroused, Bilgames cautiously but with grim determination chops his way through Huwawa's forest into the presence of the creature, all the while pretending to be bearing gifts for Huwawa. The guardian of the forest is ambushed by Bilgames and his side-kick, Enkidu. Huwawa pleads for mercy, and Bilgames nearly relents. However, Enkidu counsels him to slay the creature. They bring the head of the murdered Huwawa before the gods, who are horrified at this misdeed. The story ends with Bilgames and Enkidu cursed by the gods. The theme of the pair's arrogance in killing Huwawa also finds its way into the later epic.

Another early tale tells of Bilgames's encounter with the goddess Inanna (the later Ishtar). In this story, the goddess finds a tree that has been uprooted by the wind. She takes the tree back to her abode, hoping to grow it and get wood for furniture, only to find that it bears no branch or leaf. To make matters worse, a snake makes its nest in the tree's base, a vulture takes over its top, and a notorious demon-maiden commandeers its trunk. In her disappointment, Inanna calls on Bilgames for assistance. The heroic Bilgames is up to the challenge. Striking at the snake, he sends the squatters packing. As a reward, Inanna fashions what seem to be a drum and a drumstick (or perhaps a ball and a bat) for Bilgames out of the wood of the tree. Bilgames uses these to oppress the populace, perhaps using the drum to send the young men off to their deaths in war. In any event, the objects fall into the netherworld. To recover them for Bilgames, his faithful companion Enkidu volunteers, against Bilgames's counsel, to descend to that land from which none may return. Enkidu finds himself trapped in the underworld, unsuccessful in his effort to recover the lost objects. Bilgames begs for his release, but to no avail. He is only permitted to visit with his lost companion's ghost at the edge of the netherworld. Bilgames learns from him that the fate of the dead is a murky one indeed. In the later Epic of Gilgamesh, the death of Enkidu is made a central feature of the story. Striking, too, is the later portrayal of the goddess. Whereas in the early tale Bilgames assists her, in the later epic we find Gilgamesh insulting her because of her ill-treatment of her lovers. The later Gilgamesh wisely refuses her amorous advances in the hope of avoiding their evil fate.

The themes of death and loss appear in yet another of the early tales, which begins with Bilgames on his deathbed. In a dream, he learns that the gods are uncertain what to do with this hero who is part god and part human. The text summarizes Bilgames's great adventures, fully recounted in the later Epic of Gilgamesh. Included among his great deeds is his successful visit to Ziusudra, the survivor of the flood. This visit is mentioned, in part, to show to Bilgames that Ziusudra was the only human ever granted immortality. Bilgames would have to settle for a consolation prize, serving as the lord of the Netherworld. His name would, however, be revered forever among earthlings through annual festivals where great wrestling matches would be held in his honor. Heartened by these promises, Bilgames has the Euphrates diverted and his tomb hidden beneath the river. He and his entire entourage are said to have entered their final rest at that time, echoing in myth the very sort of gruesome finds that Sir Leonard Woolley made in the royal tombs of ancient Sumerian Ur, which contained not only the king and queen but also a number of devoted attendants who joined them in death.

Rescued from 2,000 Years of Oblivion

These early tales of Bilgames/Gilgamesh pave the way for their adaptation and retelling in the larger Epic of Gilgamesh, which took shape in the Old Babylonian period (2017–1595 B.C.E.) and was later expanded to include a full retelling of the flood story.[23] This more complete version of the epic dates roughly from the thirteenth century B.C.E. and is credited to the now famous scribe and scholar Sin-liqe-unninni. The standard translations of this epic, it should be noted, are largely based on later copies of the epic found as part of the library of the Assyrian king Ashurbanipal (668–627 B.C.E.). While the detailed account of the flood story seems not to have been a part of the Old Babylonian version of the epic, even its earliest form apparently included mention of the mysterious visit that Gilgamesh makes to speak to the survivor of the flood, the faraway figure of Utnapishtim. In other words, from a very early time the tales of Gilgamesh came to be associated with the flood story.

The rediscovery of the Epic of Gilgamesh is one of the high points of Middle Eastern archaeology. It was recovered in the mid–nineteenth century through the bold archaeological adventures of the British explorer Austen Henry Layard. Layard's efforts led to the recovery of the palaces of the Assyrian kings. Those palaces brought the biblical world to life in ways that Layard's predecessors could not have imagined. Gone were the days when Moses, Jesus, and the others were depicted as if they were hanging out in Renaissance Italian inns. Now the biblical imagination of the Victorians, who packed the galleries of the British Museum in London to catch glimpses of archaeology's latest marvels, would swim with visions of eagle-headed genies standing in the halls of ancient Iraq's royal potentates. The carved reliefs of Assyrian kings hunting lions or at war with Lachish in southern Judah would bring a realism to the reading of the Bible that was impossible before the large-scale digs of ancient Mesopotamian cities. But the numerous writings of ancient Assyria held their secrets a bit longer. Their decipherment would bring still further insights into the Bible's lore.

The report of the recovery of an ancient Mesopotamian flood story created something of a sensation. In the early 1870s, George Smith employed his skilled engraver's eyes in deciphering Layard's Nineveh texts. Working first only in his spare time, and later as a cuneiform document restorer at the British Museum, Smith made the find of the century amid the stacks and stacks of broken tablets. Recognizing the significance of a fragment of the Gilgamesh flood tale, the awestruck Smith exclaimed, "I am the first man to read that after two thousand years of oblivion." E. A. Wallis Budge tells of Smith's exuberance in that moment of discovery: "Setting the tablet on the table, he jumped up and rushed about the room in a great state of excitement and, to the astonishment of those present, began to undress himself!"[24]

Sometime later, Smith presented his findings in a more scholarly fashion (and proper attire) in an address to the Society of Biblical Archaeology in London entitled "The Chaldean Account of the Deluge," suggesting by the title the extensive links between the Mesopotamian story and the biblical account. For Smith, "this [Chaldean] account of the Deluge opens to us a new field of inquiry in the early part of the Bible history."[25] The implication was clear: the search for the origins of the various ancient flood legends need go no further than their point of "common origin in the Plains of Chaldea."[26]

As it turned out, the flood story formed just one frame in the larger Epic of Gilgamesh as edited by Sin-liqe-unninni and later preserved in the library of King Ashurbanipal and elsewhere.

At the start of the epic, we find the part-human and part-divine King Gilgamesh tyrannizing the people of his city. Young women and brides were being ravished, while the young men were oppressed and left downcast. The townspeople cry out to the gods for relief from their oppression. That relief comes in the form of the mighty opponent and alter ego of Gilgamesh, Enkidu, who is born as a wild human residing in the animal kingdom. A shepherd who spies this curious figure requests assistance from Gilgamesh in the hope that the outlandish man might be subdued. Selecting a prostitute as the tool of entrapment, Gilgamesh aids in the domestication of Enkidu. Seven days of torrid sex serve to distance Enkidu from his natural ties to the animals, driving him out of the wilds and onward to the city of Uruk. At Uruk, he and Gilgamesh engage in a fierce battle that ends in a draw, leaving the two as brothers.

Moving on to the field of adventure, the pair tangle with the keeper of the cedar forest, Humbaba. After subduing Humbaba, Gilgamesh seeks to show compassion, but Enkidu counsels a sterner course. Humbaba is slain. The dangerous encounters are multiplied when the goddess of love and war, Ishtar, seeks to seduce Gilgamesh. The king's rebuke of this heavenly femme fatale stirs up Ishtar's rage. Our heroes also slay the Bull of Heaven, a figure dear to Ishtar. Enkidu answers Ishtar's anger over the loss of the bull by pulling off a shoulder piece of the carcass and slapping the goddess in the face! For this transgression, the gods order Enkidu killed. Having challenged the gods, going so far as to insult the goddess of love and war, the dynamic duo are torn asunder by divine judgment. The death of the devoted Enkidu leaves a distraught and disheveled Gilgamesh to traverse the lethal sea. He risks sailing into the presence of Utnapishtim, the survivor of the flood who had been made an immortal by the gods, in order to find the key to eternal life.

At this point in the epic, Gilgamesh has suffered severe setbacks, but he still harbors the illusion that he will find a way to escape his own mortality. Hoping to somehow obtain the elixir of life, Gilgamesh asks Utnapishtim, whose name means "he found life," how he became an immortal. Utnapishtim's response takes the form of the flood story, a tale of such epic proportions that even the somewhat obtuse King Gilgamesh realizes that his quest for immortality is doomed to failure.

Utnapishtim recounts that when the gods decided to send the flood, the water god Ea warned Utnapishtim to build a boat. Completed in seven days, Utnapishtim's six-decked cube carried secure inside its hull those people and animals who would ride out the seven-day storm. While all on earth perished, after seven days the land reappeared and the boat came to rest on a mountain. Utnapishtim sent out a series of birds to see when it might be safe to disembark. When one of the birds found a resting place, Utnapishtim left the boat and offered up sacrifices that drew the gods "like flies." Although the wind god Enlil was angry, the rest of the gods sustained Utnapishtim's successes, causing even Enlil to bless Utnapishtim and his wife with the immortality that Gilgamesh so desired but could not have.

Subsequent events seal Gilgamesh's fate. Utnapishtim suggests that if Gilgamesh were to stay awake for a week he might obtain eternal life. Needless to say, Gilgamesh falls promptly asleep, while Utnapishtim's wife marks each day with a loaf of bread that hardens into stone as the days wear on. When Gilgamesh awakes, he realizes this approach will not work. Finally, Utnapishtim directs Gilgamesh to a magical life-giving plant in a nearby river. The struggle to uproot the plant from the river is so difficult that Gilgamesh finds his hands bloodied from the rocks. Setting aside the plant as he washes his hands, Gilgamesh finds that he has lost his last hope for eternal life to a snake, which has stolen this elusive treasure. For humans, there is no escaping mortality.

The epic represents a quest for wisdom and life. In coming to grips with life's limitations, Gilgamesh found a kind of wisdom, even if his dreams of full divinity were shattered. At the end of the epic, he boasts about his city's mighty walls, recognizing that human "immortality" can only be found in what lives on after we shuffle off this mortal coil.

Cannibalizing Atrahasis: Theology beyond the Bible

The scope of the Epic of Gilgamesh is breathtaking in comparison with the earlier Gilgamesh tales and the isolated rendition of the flood scene in the Ziusudra story. While the author and later editors of the Gilgamesh epic pieced together a variety of tales, the process was not entirely without originality and creativity. Jeffrey Tigay, in his insightful study *The Evolution of the Gilgamesh Epic*, observes a number of developments that have theological significance.

Tigay compares the flood account of the Gilgamesh epic with that of the Atrahasis story, the source of the epic's flood story. The epic's expansions and deletions of the Atrahasis story provide clues to the views of the epic's editor. The editor, for example, "adds the important command to take animals on board."[27] Also, the editor "has the god instruct the hero in a ruse to fool the towns-people."[28] Tigay also notes that the sun god Shamash is given a more critical role in the epic than in the earlier tales, "having him tell Utnapishtim when to board his ship."[29] Likewise, Tigay observes that the Gilgamesh epic "exempts [the sky god] Anu from blame for the flood."[30]

These additions may simply reflect an attempt to make the tale seem fuller and more thematically consistent. Yet the epic also exhibits several key omissions. In the first place, whereas the Atrahasis story has the mother goddess offering a lament over the destruction of those humans she had created, the Gilgamesh epic knows no such event. Tigay thinks the omission may simply reflect the epic editor's differing interests.[31] This is possible, although one readily observes that the omission serves to bolster the male gods at the expense of the female, which also seems to be an interest to those who composed and edited the epic. The negative portrayal of Ishtar in the epic finds no counterbalance in a lament by the mother goddess. The omission of any reference to the mother goddess suggests that an antifeminine bias has crept into the epic.

Perhaps more theologically noteworthy is the fact that "every passage in the *Atrahasis* version which mentioned or implied divine hunger has been dropped or modified in *GE* [Gilgamesh epic tablet] XI."[32] This splicing is too consistent and extensive to have been done without a purpose. As Tigay observes, "These omissions and modifications add up to a systematic elimination of implications that the gods starved and thirsted during the flood."[33] While the sacrificial system might seem to create a relationship of mutual dependence between humans and the gods, the editor of the epic underscores the chasm between the gods and Gilgamesh: staring into that chasm, Gilgamesh finds the wisdom of what it means to be human. The gods inhabit a realm that humans might touch while alive but which death inevitably steals from all but the flood hero.

Another theologically significant omission is seen in the epic's silence on the cause of the flood.[34] We saw that the Atrahasis epic blamed the noisy behavior of the growing human population for provoking the gods to send the flood. The Gilgamesh epic knows no cause. The author may intend for us to think that the gods were as capricious in this regard as they seem to have been in many other places in the epic. Of course, the arbitrary character of the flood is a logical counterpart to the gods' capricious slaying of Enkidu. From the perspective of King Gilgamesh, at least, the trials sent by the gods appear to have no rhyme or reason. It is the human task to muddle through these challenges to find a clearer path in this death-dealing world. The insight of the Gilgamesh cycle is that life, not the gods, teaches wisdom to those who have ears to hear the truth. The omission of a specific cause for the flood helps to set the parameters of the human search for wisdom.

Of Magic Boats and Scattered Bones

With the recovery of the Ziusudra, Atrahasis, and Gilgamesh stories, we are now in a better position to understand the cryptic last stage of this tradition as known from later Greek and Roman records. A late retelling of the flood story by the Babylonian priest Berossus in the early third century B.C.E. shows us just how long-lived this tradition was in Mesopotamian circles and beyond. The tale of Berossus then passed into other hands through such writers as the Jewish historian Josephus, the early church historian Eusebius (third–fourth centuries C.E.), and Georgius Syncellus (flourished late eighth century C.E.), who himself drew on the historian Alexander Polyhistor (105–35 B.C.E.).[35] In its own modest way, Berossus's version is nearly as long-lived as that of the biblical flood story, even longer if we tie it back to its source in Sumerian tradition.

In Berossus's version, the Sumerian hero Ziusudra shows up as "Xisothros," who is warned by the god Kronos that the flood is being sent to destroy the world. Already in early Christian times we find Saint Cyrillus writing "a little essay to prove that Noah was not Xisuthrus, the Babylonian demigod," but the links between the tales are readily apparent.[36] Instructed to bury all the major writings of the time, Xisothros is also told to build a boat to preserve family, friends, and animals. The purpose of the boat building was to be kept secret: "If asked where he was going, he was to reply, 'to the gods, to pray that all good things will come to man.'"[37] The boat is huge, measuring 1,000 by 400 yards. After the flood, Xisothros sends out a series of birds to determine when it would be safe to leave the boat, which had come to rest on a mountain. Upon disembarking, Xisothros makes a sacrifice that pleases the gods so much that he and his family are drawn into the invisible dimension of the gods, while other survivors go on to rebuild Babylon, guided by Xisothros's buried writings. The tale relates that people still find remnants of the vessel in Armenia and use its bitumen for various magical purposes.[38] The story of Xisothros was as old in Berossus's day as the stories of Jesus are to us. If one of the measures of the power of the myth is its longevity, then the flood story wins the prize as a tale of enduring mythic power.

Other renditions of the flood story turn up in ancient Greco-Roman writings. Ovid's *Metamorphoses* includes the tale of the flood endured by Deucalion and Pyrrha. This story strongly hints that Western culture has been touched by the Mesopotamian flood tradition. Ovid (43 B.C.E.–17 C.E.) writes that the world declined from the idyllic Golden Age to the bestial Iron Age, a time of unprecedented violence with humans attacking each other and giants building a stairway to heaven to challenge Jove's throne. The last straw comes when Jove, disguised as a human, visits the earth for himself, a scene reminiscent of the Bible's story of the Tower of Babel where God visits the earth to see how well things were going. On his visit, Jove is given a dinner by Lycaon only to find out that Lycaon intends to kill his guest. In response to this heinous act and the rest of the world's evil, Jove decides in his anger to wipe out the human race. He prepares to destroy the entire world with his lightning bolt but is reminded that the Fates have reserved such a conflagration for the end of time and so elects to send a flood. Fortunately for humankind, the pious Deucalion and his wife, Pyrrha, are spared. Yet despair nearly overcomes them as they survey the desolate land after the waters subside. At the flood-wracked shrine of Themis, the goddess hears their importunate prayers and gives them oracular advice to cast the bones of their great mother behind them. Pyrrha refuses this sacrilegious command, but her husband suggests that stones are the bones of their great mother earth. The couple does as the oracle suggested, and out of the stones emerge the people who would repopulate the world.

A similar story is narrated by other Greco-Roman writers, though preserving more ancient details. In a second-century c.e. text attributed to Lucian, *De Dea Syria*, most of Ovid's elements are repeated.[39] The era is a time of violence, and the flood is sent by an unnamed god as recompense for these misdeeds. Deucalion is spared because of his piety and boards the boat (literally "chest" like the Bible's "ark," which means "box"). Here, however, Lucian parts company with Ovid and relates details that are more reminiscent of the Mesopotamian and biblical stories. Deucalion is joined by his children, wives, and every kind of animal, which enter in pairs. By a miracle all the animals get along during the voyage. After the earth swallows up the water and the boat comes to rest in Lebanon, Deucalion disembarks and sets up altars and a temple to Hera. Unlike Ovid, who gives a major role to Pyrrha, this version highlights only the male figure, paralleling the Mesopotamian and biblical traditions.

Another version of the Deucalion story with its own unique slant is found in a collection of Greco-Roman myths attributed to Apollodorus, written perhaps in the second century c.e.[40] In this collection, Deucalion is the son of Prometheus, the god who molded people out of water and earth and gave them fire. Pyrrha is equally highborn, the daughter of Pandora, the first woman made by Prometheus. When Zeus decides to destroy the people of the Bronze Age, Prometheus warns his son, who builds a boat (literally "chest") to save himself, his wife, and some nameless "provisions." Zeus floods Greece, the scene of this story, the heavy rains killing all except those who fled to the tops of the tallest mountains. Deucalion floats for nine days and nights and lands in Parnassus, where he sacrifices to Zeus, the "god of escape." As a reward, Deucalion gets to choose whatever he wishes and elects to have more people created. As in Ovid, the survivors are told to throw stones that turn into people, men from Deucalion's rocks and women from Pyrrha's.

The flood story in Greco-Roman circles is of hardy literary stock. While the precise lines of transmission are obscure, the story manages to survive in a recognizable form with key details intact, especially references to divine wrath, a pious male hero, the saving of relatives and animals, the altar, and the birth of a new world. We are led to see in these stories not merely an assortment of isolated tales but a continuous storytelling tradition that runs from Ziusudra through Gilgamesh and the Bible down to the Greco-Roman age. The flood story in both its general outline and its specific details inscribed itself on the consciousness of ancient Middle Eastern and Mediterranean peoples. While the tale may not be of an actual historical event, one wonders why so many peoples felt compelled to keep this particular story alive for so many centuries.

Flood Fables or Psychic Artifacts?

This long-lived tradition of heroes and floods is ancient and widespread. We can readily see that these myths are more than weather reports. They are tales that have spoken in various and sundry ways to centuries of communities that have cherished the story's noble ideals, enduring insights, difficult questions, and capacity to rekindle the spiritual imagination in the face of many disasters. Whereas the children of Enlightenment philosophy, such as Voltaire, or of Enlightenment science, such as T. H. Huxley, might regard these flood stories as fabulous folktales or ignorant fables to be dismissed as scientifically unsupportable, the late nineteenth-century and early twentieth-century researches of mythographers like J. G. Frazer offer another possibility.[41] Regardless of whether the tales represent divine revelation, Frazer and others turned the tables to ask what these tales reveal about ourselves.

In his 1916 Huxley lecture, Frazer acknowledged that by the modern standards of geological science the flood stories ought to be considered fables just as Huxley claimed. He went on to speculate, however, about the prevalence of the tale in so many parts of the world. Frazer saw two distinct processes at work in this vast diffusion of flood legends: genetic transmission and independent development. Certainly the story circulates and is reproduced within given regions, such as the Middle East in the case of the Bible and the Americas in the case of Native American flood tales. But for Frazer genetic transmission alone could not account for the worldwide spread of these stories. Frazer thus abandons the idea that all flood tales ultimately stem from one Noachian event, a view that had misled many others into defensively assuming that the biblical version preserves the best record of some ancient cataclysm. Instead, he argues that the global existence of such myths requires, in anthropological terms, that they are the independent products of the "similar working of the human mind under similar circumstances."[42] In so saying, Frazer takes us well beyond Voltaire's and Huxley's dismissal of Genesis as a collection of misguided prescientific fables. For the anthropologist and the modern mythographer, these tales may reveal precious little about the world's geological history, but they are immensely valuable as psychic artifacts that the excavator of the human mind can ill afford to overlook.

French structural anthropologist Claude Lévi-Strauss thought that myths worked with a mathematical precision.[43] He observed that myths are often pre-occupied with resolving simple oppositions such as heaven and earth, life and death, mortality and divinity, savage and domesticated, and nature and culture. Focusing on a related series of tales from a given region, he came to see that seemingly dreamlike and irrational myths actually function in an almost com-puter-like fashion to sort out the disparities between the extremes of life's op-posites. In the movement of related myths Lévi-Strauss could hear the rhythms of the human mind at work seeking to resolve the binary oppositions. Those who thought mythically were able to come to grips with their own assertion of civilization over against the dangers of nature and the perceived encroachments of the divine.

The Gilgamesh tales and Middle Eastern flood stories present us musiclike mythical variations on an enduring medley of psychic questions and social chal-lenges faced by the peoples of that region over the centuries. Their themes and progressions represent a rather repetitive symphonic chorus of elemental mythic relations: heaven and earth, humanity and divinity, male and female, clean and unclean, wicked and just.

M. Casalis offers one such analysis of the biblical and related ancient Near Eastern flood stories.[44] For Casalis the flood story reflects a bipolar continuum in which "dry" stands at one end and "wet" stands at the other. At the middle of the continuum stands "life," which arises where wet and dry cancel each other out, or where the dangers of extreme dryness or extreme wetness balance each other.

This bipolar structure is true of both the P and J versions of the story ac-cording to Casalis, though with different emphases (on P and J, see chapter 3). For P, which depicts the created order arising out of chaos in Genesis 1, the flood represents a return to the watery chaos out of which heaven and earth emerged, thereby allowing for the possibility of a new creation. For J, for whom in Genesis 2–4 life arises out of the combination of rivers and dry land (and human life out of the conjunction of that clay with the breath of God), the flood represents a restoration of life to a land corrupted by evil (an element that Casalis omits). P and J, in other words, move in different directions on the wet-dry continuum, yet they share the same midpoint of "life," which is the situation to which the world returns after the flood event. The flood myth mediates wet and dry, providing a revitalized ground after the earth had been violated by sin and rebellion.

The deep logic uncovered by Casalis shows us how subtly myths sort out those factors that threaten life and civilization. Beneath the myth lies a world of meaning no less important than the surface tale. In fact, this deep structure may represent the meat of the myth, for such an analysis reveals to Casalis (quoting Lévi-Strauss) not "how men think in myths, but how myths think themselves out in men without their being aware of it."[45] The psychic and social solutions achieved through myth remain valuable for us to heed today: in the face of disruptive "acts of God" in the natural, social, and moral spheres, our individual and collective efforts can provide us with at least a temporary bastion against the storms of life. Lévi-Strauss and Casalis enable us to see beyond flood geology and the surface tale to unearth the subterranean layers of the mythmaking language of the flood texts.

Another student of myth and the mind, C. G. Jung, would point us in other directions.[46] Sensing that dreams, psychological images, and myths are tied to psychic processes hidden from the conscious mind, Jung perceived in mythic patterns and their attendant symbols the concrete manifestations of powerful underlying psychic elements. If we could pull back the mythic curtain, after the fashion of Dorothy in The Wizard of Oz, we would finally spy the features of the ghost that runs the machine. Short of that, we can work with the mythic elements to begin a first encounter with our common human psychological system, what Jung calls our collective unconscious. While each of us adds an important personal dimension to this unconscious, according to Jung it is the collective side that reveals to us the underlying urges and dark drives that press us at every turn in our lives.

Much like Frazer, Jung suggests we can see in myth not the geological past but the coded radio transmissions of the hidden psychic self to the conscious mind. This theory of the encounter with the unconscious can be puzzling. Many criticize Jung for his arbitrary readings of mythic images. He deems these "archetypal images" because they supposedly correspond to underlying psychological propensities and states that are inaccessible to the conscious mind in a direct way. Despite the criticisms, it is valuable to inspect the flood stories for images that may speak to our common psychological depths. The rage of the gods at mortal arrogance, the secret warnings of the gods to the hero, the fury of the storm that wipes out the world, the utter dependence of the gods on human sacrifice, and the vision of the ancient sage who survives the flood all seem to illuminate psychic imbalances in ourselves that demand our attention.

That the flood is so vehemently defended in fundamentalist circles or is so derided in secular spheres may suggest, to a Jungian at least, that Jung's ideal of psychological individuation—mental and spiritual wholeness—has yet to be achieved by either camp. Why should the fundamentalist fear new knowledge? Why should the secularist debase our collective mythic inheritance in favor of pinning all hopes on unending future progress? The flood story may not be a great geological tool, but it appears to function quite well as a sensitive psychological barometer, both for the past and for today. Perhaps if we are willing to treat the stories as narrative Rorschach inkblots, we will find in them a reflection of our collective psyche. Contrast Ryan and Pitman for whom "the myth lives" only because "it is surely a true story of the permanent destruction of a land and its people and a culture suddenly and catastrophically inundated."[47] However compelling their theory may be, this explanation does not do justice to the anthropological and psychological reasons for myth's longevity.

Every picture tells a story. Perhaps there is a lesson in Michelangelo's de-piction of Noah's flood in the Sistine Chapel. Michelangelo's version of the story was ahead of its time. Of the human drama, D. C. Allen observes that "no painter before Michelangelo had dared to push the Ark to the rear of the scene and make the intense sufferings of the doomed the essential artistic focus. This is a hu-manization of the story which is in keeping with the rational abandonment of the Genesis text."[48] The changing fads and fashions in the depiction of the Noah story over the centuries, as Allen observes, are really a measure of the history of belief and its rejection: "So in time the Deluge, which was once the story of the salvation of mankind by one God-fearing man, comes to be a symbol of human suffering and the eternal woes of men before the power of an angry Creator. We begin with Moses and we end with Kafka."[49]

Allen is quite right in all this. The advent of rational scientific speculation has humanized the story but not merely for the painter. For the archaeologist, the focus must now be on the origins of the flood legend in human history. On that side of the story, Ryan and Pitman serve as provocative guides. Yet the mythographer also has a human tale to tell, the story of the myth's power in the lives of individuals and societies over the centuries and today. The scientific story or historical news flash from the past is not the only story a myth can tell. Myths are perhaps best understood as mirrors of their societies and windows into our souls. Spade or marine archaeology cannot have the last word in realms where psychic archaeology is also needed.

7

Diverting the Stream
of Tradition:

Reinventing the Flood Myth

Having ridden the rapids of history and tradition, it is time to put the Bible's particular version of the flood story into perspective. To what extent is the Bible indebted to the surrounding Middle Eastern cultures, and to what extent does the Bible offer a new turning in human thought? The image of diverting the stream of tradition captures both the Bible's connectedness and its uniqueness. How does the Genesis flood story reflect its wider literary environment even as the biblical writers reinvent the mythic tradition for their own ideological and theological purposes?

We can easily observe that all the key Mesopotamian literary elements remain in focus in the Bible. Thus we find Noah being warned by his protecting deity to build a boat, as were Ziusudra, Atrahasis, and Utnapishtim. Only those who are in the boat manage to ride out the flood, while those left behind perish. After the waters disperse, the Bible's hero emerges like his counterparts to repopulate the earth and receive divine blessings.

The Bible retains, in other words, all the central elements that made the myth memorable. Any ancient bard would know these features, passing on a complete tale even as the details might be embellished to suit new needs and changing audiences. But focusing on similar plot lines hardly begins to do justice to the ways the Mesopotamian and Israelite mythmakers felt free to play with and share the flood tradition.

The Atrahasis Story as a Theological Precursor

In a previous chapter, I characterized the Atrahasis tale as a successor to the Sumerian Ziusudra tale and a precursor to the Gilgamesh epic's telling of the flood tale. The Atrahasis tale, like the Ziusudra tale before it, places the flood story in the context of the story of creation. Indeed, both the larger Ziusudra narrative and the Atrahasis tale roughly parallel the movement of the first chapters of Genesis, insofar as all three narratives link the themes of creation and flood. They offer what we might call a narrative theology, that is, an understanding of divine things spelled out in story form. There are many other similarities between Genesis and the Atrahasis legend that illuminate the very strong ties between the Bible and Mesopotamian culture. What do the biblical writers accept from Mesopotamian culture, and what do they reject or modify?

Both traditions share a deep sense of the subordinate status of humanity: we are put on earth as stewards and servants of the gods. The Atrahasis tale begins with the gods suffering under labors imposed by the highest gods, the Anunnaki. The lesser gods "set fire to their tools" and stage a protest before the god Enlil.[1] In turn, the god Ea orders that humans be created to bear the burden of the labors: "Let him bear the yoke assigned by Enlil; Let man carry the toil of the gods."[2]

Drawing on the view that Genesis was compiled from different sources, as discussed in chapter 3, we find that both the P (Priestly) and J (Yahwist) segments of the early chapters of Genesis incorporate this idea of servitude, even as each writer envisions the outworking of that idea in distinctive ways. For P, the great commandment from God to "Be fruitful! Increase! Fill the earth and subdue it!" (Genesis 1:28) can also be read as a command to do the work of God in the world. More explicitly, the J writer makes Adam the caretaker of the garden (Genesis 2:15). Adam names all the animals and tends the garden, again doing the work of God. Labor as such is not the curse that God hurls at Adam after he partakes of the forbidden fruit. Rather, Adam finds that his once-joyous labors have now become a heavy burden: "God said to Adam, 'Since you obeyed your wife and ate from the tree that I explicitly put off limits, the soil is cursed because of you. With misery you will eat from it throughout your life. Thorns and thistles will spring forth for you. You will eat the plants of the open countryside. With sweat on your brow, you will eat your meals until you return to the soil, for you were taken from it. Since you are dust, you shall return to dust'" (Genesis 3:17–19).

Despite their differences, P and J share with the Atrahasis story a clear sense of the "natural" ordering of things and the servitude of humanity. There are main gods and there are subordinate gods; then there are humans propping up the entire cosmos.

Atrahasis and the Bible also share a profound recognition of the divine side of our fragile human natures. The human who is created in the Atrahasis story, though a servant, nonetheless bears the unique stamp of the gods. Humans are a mix of the clay of the ground and the dead remains of a god. In one sense the clay speaks to the mortal side of humanity: in our frailness, we must die. Yet the divine glue that holds us together emblemizes that side of us that is not simply of this material world. For the ancient Mesopotamians, we humans bear the image of the divine in mortal clay.

Needless to say, both J and P play with this very idea that we are a mix of elements from two worlds. For the P writer, this is captured in that hallmark phrase of the biblical tradition, "Let us make man in our image, according to our likeness" (Genesis 1:26). If the "us" is the ancient pantheon of gods, we may have here a fragment of an epic from a time when Israel's religion was more polytheistic. In any event, humanity's divine aspect is front and center in this passage. The J writer, likewise, finds a divine stamp in the humans whom God has fashioned. In creating Adam from the dust of the ground, God also found it necessary to blow into his nostrils the "breath of life" (Genesis 2:7). The Mesopotamian and biblical recipe for baking a human was exactly the same: one part clay or dust mixed with a generous dose of the divine.

This brings us to a third shared factor, the notion of divine "rest." Having created humans, the gods can take a break from their labors. In the Atrahasis story, after creating humans, the goddess Mami tells the gods: "I have removed your heavy work; I have imposed your toil on man."[3] In the Bible, P places great emphasis on the seventh day of creation as a time in which God finally finds rest: "The sky, the earth, and the starry array were completed. On the seventh day God completed God's labor, resting on the seventh day from all the labor that God had done. God blessed the seventh day, sanctifying it, since on it God rested from all God's labor, namely all God's creative doings" (Genesis 2:1–3).

In J, God's labors include the initial planting of the garden and the creation of Adam. After that, it appears that God is sitting on the sidelines. When the going gets tough for Adam, God simply creates another worker to help out, namely, the woman Eve (Genesis 2:18). After the curse, there is a division of labor for the humans: the woman's job is to bear the children and serve her husband, while his task is to till the stubborn ground (Genesis 3:16–19). The Lord's last garden labor is to make "garments of skins" for the human couple, who now know that they are naked (Genesis 3:21).

Both Atrahasis and the early Genesis tales are also caught up with the question of human procreation. In the Atrahasis epic this takes the form of an acknowledgment that after the flood there are women who can give birth and there are women who cannot:

> "In addition let there be a third category among the peoples,
> (Let there be) among the peoples women who bear and women
>   who do not bear.
> Let there be among the peoples the *Pāšittu*-demon
> To snatch the baby from the lap of her who bore it."[4]

This concern with procreation and its challenges is shared by Genesis. We have already seen that P enjoins human reproduction with a divine command to be fruitful and multiply. J is also concerned about reproduction but recognizes its painful difficulties for women. In issuing the curse on Eve, God says: "I will most surely increase your childbearing misery. You will give birth to your children in pain. Your desire will be toward your husband, and he will rule over you" (Genesis 3:16).

Furthermore, both P and J attest the growth of the human race. For P, lengthy lists of genealogies intersperse the narratives about creation and the flood. For J, this growth takes a more individual form as we watch the arrival of Cain and Abel. That same emphasis on reproduction immediately follows the story of humankind's creation in Atrahasis. Fourteen birth goddesses create fourteen humans, seven males and seven females.

The positive side of all this is that more and more people were born who could do the work of the gods. For the Bible, likewise, more and more humans could service God's world. The downside, however, becomes immediately apparent, and the Mesopotamian and biblical traditions both recognize the dangers. For the Atrahasis tale the issue becomes that of an exploding population. In very practical terms, the humans are just making far too much noise such that the gods cannot get a good night's rest. In response, the gods send plagues, drought, and, when all else fails, the flood—a disaster that Atrahasis survives only with the aid of the god Enki.

Here one senses that the Bible parts company with its Mesopotamian counterpart. Whereas the Atrahasis tale worries about an expanding population and the humans' noisemaking, the Bible adopts a legal tone. For the Bible, the issue is moral, not acoustic. Both J and P take the sin line. The J writer is the most dramatic. For J, the divine giants known as the "sons of God" have been having sex with human daughters (Genesis 6:1–4). Moreover, human beings are simply credited with being generally "wicked," thinking "only evil all the time" (Genesis 6:5). For this, J's Lord vows to wipe all living things from earth in an act of righteous indignation. The P writer is a bit less dramatic but no less clear about the moral character of God's action. For P's God, the earth has become "corrupt," being "full of lawlessness" (Genesis 6:11). The witless humans merit the same punishment in P as they do in J, destruction through the flood. The Mesopotamian gods gave the humans several chances to shape up; the biblical God makes the punishment fit the crime with greater exactitude and swiftness.

As a final comparison between the Atrahasis tale and the Bible, we may also note the obvious fact that both traditions provide a means of redemption in the shape of a divinely aided hero. Less obvious but no less important is the effect this choice has on the gods. In the case of Atrahasis, the selection of a flood hero is a sign that the gods are divided against themselves. On the one hand, the god "Enlil did an evil deed on the peoples," whereas "Enki opened his mouth and addressed his slave."[5] One god sends destruction, while another god risks saving one of the humans. When this conflict between the gods is transferred to the Bible's monotheistic tradition, the consistency is maintained by having the one God be both the author of the flood and the savior of the human race. How can the one God be both a destroyer and a savior? It is the Bible's insistence on the moral justification of the flood that allows God to both send the flood and rescue the righteous Noah. Without a moral component to the flood equation, the Atrahasis tale falls back on a conception of the gods that made sense to many ancients, a pantheon that is at odds with itself. Zeus's battles with his wife, Hera, and the rest of the gods are just a later version of this age-old conception. Biblical monotheism avoids divine schizophrenia by inserting a moral logic into God's actions.

We find numerous points of similarity between Genesis and the Atrahasis story. It is easy to see that the biblical writers stand squarely within the Middle Eastern mythic tradition when they compose their tales. Yet we can also see that the Bible's writers are taking those traditions in new directions, particularly with regard to law and morality. It is not surprising, then, to find this same moral canopy hanging over the rest of the Bible, for Bible's myths serve social purposes very different from the Atrahasis story's more limited concerns for overpopulation and divine insomnia.

Not a Story Told but a Lived Reality

Do stories of the flood in the Bible act as some sort of moral social glue, binding the ancient Israelites together? The noted anthropologist Bronislaw Malinowski offers a useful construct. Malinowski thinks that we cannot really appreciate myths by simply reading them in the comfort of our easy chairs before the fireplace in a classic American three-bedroom ranch house. To truly understand a myth, Malinowski insists, we must immerse ourselves in the myth's home culture and watch how the story lives and breathes in that setting. For Malinowski, a myth "is not merely a story told but a reality lived."[6] A living myth shapes people's daily habits and informs their social interactions. A living myth, in short, acts as a "social charter" governing the whole of a society in both obvious and subtle ways. As Malinowski puts it, "Myth fulfils in primitive culture an indispensable function: it expresses, enhances, and codifies belief; it safeguards and enforces morality; it vouches for the efficiency of ritual and contains practical rules for the guidance of man."[7] If we read the biblical flood narrative as a social charter, its mythic purposes are clear.

The social charter governs the family. The flood story encourages family life and baby-making. The survivors are repeatedly told in the priestly version to repopulate the land (Genesis 8:16–17; 9:1, 7).

The social charter regulates worship. The P version of the flood story supports the sacrificial ritual system that was so dear to the priests: Noah builds an altar for burnt offerings and thus secures God's mercy (Genesis 8:20–21). Similarly, the purity and dietary laws that are central to later Judaism receive their divine stamp of approval in the flood story (Genesis 9:4).

The social charter governs human action in society and the world. Notions about justice and God's response to murder are grounded in the charter (Genesis 9:5–6). The governance of the entire animal kingdom is put squarely on the shoulders of humankind (Genesis 9:2–3).

This social charter is given a name in the Bible. Called the "covenant," it is a solemn agreement between God and God's people in which God promises divine protection to a people who are recognized to be "evil from their youth" (Genesis 9:21). The bow that is put in the sky is the weapon of God now at rest, the effect of which is to allow humans to survive and flourish, provided they enact the laws that are needed to sustain a viable community. This charter is written in the clouds so that both God and God's people can continue to read its terms (Genesis 9:9–17).

When the tales are treated as a cultural charter, we see that no amount of hydrological or geological speculation can diminish their powerful social undertow. When we understand that the flood story functions as a veritable constitution of the people, we see that it is far more than appears on the surface. The story is laden with the beliefs and values of those who shaped and reshaped this story to speak to changing historical moments in the ongoing Jewish experience of God.

Monotheistic Deity or Water Warrior?

That experience led to a key intellectual development, which Ryan and Pitman term the "radical departure" of the Bible from the Mesopotamian and other traditions: the biblical allegiance to monotheism.[8] The First Commandment—"You shall not have other gods except me" (Exodus 20:3)—is the theological line in the sand drawn between ancient Israel and the surrounding cultures. Yet even here the Bible flows from the region's mythic traditions even as it tries to move in its own direction.

We know both from the Bible and from ancient inscriptions that not all in Israel adhered strictly to the monotheistic creed. In fact, at Kuntillet Ajrud, a traveler's way station in the deep south where the Negev Desert borders the Sinai, votive images have been found that appear to depict an ominous-looking deity and his companions, accompanied by the inscription "To YHWH and his Asherah."[9] This Asherah was the main female goddess and wife of the chief Canaanite god El, who headed the pagan pantheon of the region. Clearly, some believers in ancient Israel were not taking any chances with their religious destinies, deciding to play both sides of the theological fence by worshiping the God of Israel and this God's pagan counterparts.

Nevertheless, through the Bible, the monotheistic vision won the day. Monotheism is the hallmark of the three world faiths that emerged from these Middle Eastern sands: Judaism, Christianity, and Islam. But is the Bible's monotheism entirely unique to the ancient Middle East?

A corollary to monotheism is the idea that God is the sole Creator of the world. It is true that the idea of a singular creator God is peculiar in the Near East, except perhaps for the Egyptian heresy of Pharaoh Akhenaten, who worshiped only the sun disk Aten. But it is also the case that many ancient Middle Eastern myths elevate the creative action of one god above all the others, even when the belief system admitted many gods into the pantheon. In this is a valuable clue to the origins of biblical monotheism.

The Babylonian creation epic is a prime example.[10] In that tale, the children of the dominant deities, the father Apsu and the mother Tiamat, found themselves at war with their willful parents. The younger gods slew Apsu, doubtless much to the delight of Freudians, who view religion as appeasement for an early act of patricide. Then, just when all may have seemed settled, the divine children fell into deeper conflict with the mother goddess Tiamat. Here the myth upsets the Freudian analytic applecart; a conflict with the mother hardly conforms to the Freudian scheme, which prefers to discover maternal incest wishes in ancient myths. The threat of war leads the children to call on Marduk, son of the water god Ea, to serve as their champion. Marduk agrees to fight provided he is acclaimed supreme above all the gods when his victory is celebrated. The gods really have no choice and so assent to Marduk's demands.

The scene turns to the battle itself. Marduk wields great demonic weapons, ensnaring and then killing Tiamat. With her defeat, the act of creation can take place, for it is out of her carcass that the entire universe is made. From her pierced eyes the Tigris and Euphrates emerge, and out of the blood of her defeated commander humans are created. The gods are put in charge of the various parts of heaven and earth. Babylon itself is made the gateway of the gods, and its temple serves as the focus of the Babylonian world. Finally, with great feasting and the chanting of the fifty names of Marduk, the epic, which lauds Marduk's fierce creative powers, comes to a fitting conclusion.

Certainly there are strong parallels between Marduk as supreme deity and the Bible's creator God. The elevation of a single deity is shared between the cultures. Undoubtedly this is the process by which Israel's monotheism emerged, first making Israel's God the chief of all the gods and then demoting the other gods to angelic status even as the biblical God's prominence increased. In the official ancient Israelite religion, then, this one God stands without peer. Yet throughout the Bible vestiges of an ancient pantheon can be seen. The Psalms, ancient Israel's hymns and prayers, contain oblique references to the triumph of God over the gods.[11] The Book of Kings contains the famous story of God's defeat of the pagan Baal in a trial by fire, wherein only the Bible's God proves potent enough to send the fire from heaven that destroys the false prophets of Baal (1 Kings 18). Thus, even though biblical religion puts all its philosophic stock in monotheism, the process by which this idea emerged probably mirrors the ancient Mesopotamian elevation of Marduk. Biblical religion simply takes the idea of elevation to its logical conclusion.

In the context of our interest in the flood story, one parallel between Marduk and the Bible's creator God stands out: each god shows power over water. If the measure of Marduk's supremacy is his defeat of the sea goddess Tiamat, the Bible's God is certainly not to be outdone in this arena. Throughout the Bible there is something of an obsession with God's power over the waters. When the people cross from Edom and Moab into the Holy Land, following their commander Joshua to attack the Canaanites, the river Jordan miraculously parts (Joshua 3–4). Earlier, when the Israelites wandered the barren Sinai, on several occasions God provided water from the desert rocks (Exodus 17:1–7; Numbers 20:1–13). Of course, the big water diversion that started the whole journey, the parting of the Red Sea, was a divine triumph of mythic proportions:

> Then Moses and the children of Israel sang this song to YHWH,
>   saying:
> I will sing to YHWH,
> For he is exalted.
> Horse and rider,
> He threw into the sea.
> YHWH is a warrior.
> YHWH is his name.
> Pharaoh's chariots and his army,
> He threw into the sea.
> Eminent officers
> Drowned in the Red Sea.
> Deep water covered them;
> They sank into the abyss like a stone" (Exodus 15:1, 3–5)

Israel's bards and poets celebrated God's sea victory over Pharaoh precisely because the ancients saw in such a hydrological contest a decisive demonstration of their own God's power. God's defeat of Pharaoh is no less a creative act than Marduk's defeat of Tiamat. The watery triumph elevates each god.

Farther north in ancient Syria, in 1400 B.C.E. the people of the town of Ugarit had their own myths about divine sea battles.[12] Here we find original tales about the grand deeds and loves of the Canaanite god Baal. This god is known to us from much later stories in the Bible, where he is depicted as a weak rival to the God of Israel. With the discoveries at Ugarit, however, we have the genuine article, Baal as his believers conceived of him. In those tales Baal is praised for having defeated Mot, the god of death. Baal also is credited with receiving his great "house" (temple) from the main god El. Most significant for our present discussion, Baal is said to have fought and defeated the sea god Yam, an act that brought stability and renewed prosperity to the land.

With these Syrian archaeological discoveries of the 1920s, the ancient Canaanite bards have finally been allowed to speak for themselves. In their tales, Baal's powers are equal to the powers of Israel's God or Babylon's Marduk. Each is a god who can tame the waters, creating new worlds and constructing entire nations.

Modern believers might want to turn the biblical god into a nonanthropomorphic universal force. However, the ancient Israelites thought of their God as a "water warrior" in much the same way that the ancient Canaanites and Babylonians thought of their chief deities. The Bible aims to rival its competition in the philosophic fighting ring by showing Israel's God as equally effective in victories over the forces of nature. The flood story is yet another example of the power of Israel's God over unruly waters. While other gods might be able to fight the sea, Israel's God is no less powerful than they. When it comes to water, monotheism can hold its own against any pagan pantheon.

Diverting the stream of ancient Middle Eastern mythic tradition, ancient Israel taps into myths that are refashioned to nourish different but not altogether unrelated religious beliefs and practices. Ancient Israel's monotheism is connected to the surrounding cultures, however much the tradition sought to distance itself from its neighbors.

If the Bible's God is a water warrior, have we returned to affirming the idea that myths are "weather reports," a view that was expressly denied previously? Let us split the difference. In a sense, the combat stories of Marduk, Baal, and Israel's God have as their special focus water. The natural component cannot be denied to any of the flood traditions. However, such stories point beyond the natural world to a greater divine order. Each battle myth underscores the main deity's ability to create the very societies that preserve these traditions. Marduk creates Babylon, Baal builds his holy house at Ugarit, and Israel's God leads a people out of Egypt to conquer the Holy Land. In each case, the story of the watery triumph is not an end in itself but the ideological foundation upon which solemn temples, lofty palaces, and entire societies were built.

The story, therefore, is not about the weather but about the political aspirations and social fears of those who carried on the ancient mythic traditions. For each culture, this story of watery survival and divine protection served to highlight the precarious nature of human society and the need for deeper roots in the divine if the survivors hoped to flourish beyond catastrophe. These myths exhibit a vision and a power that appear only as we take the stories seriously as human stories, lingering over the literary details to tease out their social and religious significance to our ancient forebears. The enduring meaning of the tales is revealed only as we take stock of their human dimensions. It is at this level that we discover our ancestors passing on wisdom about life and death, hope and defeat, survival and inevitable catastrophe.

Splitting the Stream of Biblical Tradition

This is not to say that the Bible has nothing new to add to the discussion. The comparison between Genesis and the Atrahasis story identified formidable points of tension with the surrounding cultures. But we can take this a step further: there are also tensions between the Bible's own two flood stories that should not be overlooked. It is as if the biblical writers are further splitting the stream of tradition that they had diverted from the wider Middle East.

As we have seen, the Genesis flood story appears to be an amalgam of two different versions.[13] Readers who fail to divide the stories between the J (Yahwist) and P (Priestly) versions miss the diverse richness of the ancient Israelite debates about the nature of God and of God's relation to the world.

The divisions between J and P go to the heart of what it meant to be an ancient Israelite. The Israelites were struggling with tough theological questions: What kind of God is Israel's God? How does this God interact with the world? What is the reason for the world's evil ways? What does God demand of God's people? What is the nature of God's justice? Does God have a plan for the world? We may not be able to answer the question Who wrote the Bible? (to quote the title of an important book by Richard Eliot Friedman), but we can certainly say that each ancient writer or school of writers had definite opinions about the nature of the God of Israel and about the human predicament.

The best way to gauge these conflicting opinions is to draw and quarter the text, isolating the two different flood stories to observe the diverging views put forward by these writers. Reading the stories as separate and complete units helps us to make sense of the distinctive contributions of J and P to the ancient Israelite tradition (see the appendix).

J, for example, has a particular understanding of the cause of the flood and of YHWH's actions (YHWH being the predominant name for God employed in the J writings). In J, divine beings have mated with human women to produce wicked offspring. Moreover, the people in general are engaged in all manner of evil. Their evildoing is a follow-up to the betrayal of YHWH by Adam and Eve in J's Garden of Eden story. Apparently the world had gone downhill ever since, and YHWH felt compelled to do something about the situation. Roused like a temperamental Zeus, YHWH decides to fight back.

While YHWH's reaction might seem impulsive, J has been at pains in the earlier chapters of Genesis to show that YHWH's brand of justice demands a concrete judgment of evil. With Adam and Eve the sanction was banishment from the garden. For Cain it was the wandering that was decreed as punishment for his murder of his brother Abel. After the flood J will have the arrogant builders of the Tower of Babel scattered to the four winds and their language mixed up. In each case a clear misdeed is countered by a forceful divine response. However, each judgment is also accompanied by a sign of grace. In the case of

Adam and Eve, YHWH sews animal skins to clothe the sinful pair. For Cain, a distinguishing physical mark is to serve as a warning to others not to touch Cain to harm him. In the case of the scattered tower builders, YHWH comes down and speaks clearly to one man who will bring true belief into the world, namely, Abraham. The flood story, likewise, witnesses this same balance of just judgment and compassion: the world is destroyed because of evil, but YHWH intervenes to ensure that one family survives.

Clearly J is up to something theologically. If we knew where to put J on a time line, we would have some very real insights into the growth of Israel's religion. The trouble is that scholars are divided over the date of J, suggesting three different scenarios for the writing and compiling of the material.

The first option puts the writer of J in the court of King David and his son Solomon in the tenth century B.C.E. If so, then perhaps the message is that David's God is a God of wrath against evil adversaries. David's elevation of YHWH's ark-shrine (2 Samuel 6) and Solomon's construction of the Temple in Jerusalem (1 Kings 5–8) both serve to concretize the noble ideals of this judging YHWH. The provision of David as the divinely chosen king and the granting of wisdom to Solomon would be signs of YHWH's compassion toward the chosen people.

The second option for the dating of J would put the writings well into the time of the monarchy, perhaps under Hezekiah (727–698 B.C.E.). Under the divided monarchies of Israel and Judah, civil war and foreign invasions took their toll. How were the people to understand the troubles that beset YHWH's beloved Judah? The J flood story might tell us that the kingdom of Judah deserved the attacks of the Assyrians because the people of God had been corrupt and worshiped false gods. J might also be hinting that YHWH is willing to forgive, provided the king clean up the realm—which Hezekiah did by wiping out the "high places" of pagan worship, striking down the sacred pillars, and cleansing the temple in Jerusalem (2 Kings 18).

The third option is to treat J as an introduction to the longish history of Israel and Judah compiled either during the time of Josiah (640–609 B.C.E.) or very early in the exilic period (587–539 B.C.E.). This account, is known to scholars as the Deuteronomistic History, comprises the books of Joshua, Judges, 1 and 2 Samuel, and 1 and 2 Kings.[14] If so, we need to look at the *end* of the story to see what the beginning might mean. The story ends with the destruction of Judah and the exile of the people to Babylon. The prologue of J in Genesis might suggest that the exile was a just punishment at the hands of an angry God. Does the story of Israel have to stop there? Definitely not! J may be hinting that YHWH will take care of the exiles just as YHWH took care of Noah through the raging waters. If YHWH is so disposed, the people will want to rebuild the destroyed Temple after the exile to offer sacrifices in the same way that Noah did at the end of J's flood tale. There is a further hint regarding those who survive the exile. Just as "only Noah and those with him in the ark remained" (Genesis 7:23), so also for the Deuteronomistic History only Judah and its exiles seem to matter in YHWH's plan. We know that after the exile, with the return from Babylon, there were great conflicts between those who were exiled and those who had been left behind. J and the Deuteronomistic History side with the exiles as the ones on whom YHWH's favor rests.

If J is caught up with ideas of justice, judgment, sacrifice, and survival, what is P up to?

The cause of the flood and God's actions in P are quite different from the portrayal in J. P's God is above the fray. There is certainly corruption. Yet rather than smolder as J's YHWH does, P's God has a plan of action. P's God has such a plan because P's God is a god of order and planned growth. Remember that the P writers are the ones who also gave us the God we first meet in Genesis 1 who shaped all of creation in an orderly and sustained way, giving the command to "Be fruitful! Increase! Fill the earth and subdue it" (Genesis 1:28). No amount of corruption could thwart God's productive plans. Through very detailed instructions to Noah, God provided a way forward through the stormy waters. This is the same God who not only gave creation its original design but also will later give detailed commands about circumcision (Genesis 17:3–14) and mandate a myriad of additional sacrificial practices in the Book of Leviticus to keep the world on the straight and narrow. Where J accents justice and survival, P strikes a chord for purposiveness and prosperity.

If we could put P on a time line, we would, as with J, have a very real insight into the development of Israel's faith and religious practice. Most scholars place P after the exile, during the time of the nation's revival and rebuilding of its temple. Scholars further suggest that the P writers are among the architects of the Priestly commonwealth that flourished during the early Second Temple period (fifth–fourth centuries B.C.E.). If this reconstruction is correct, then we can see in the flood story a striking example of the way that the P writers breathe confidence into Israel's faith, making J look arbitrary and punitive by comparison. P's flood story is forward-looking, anticipating a time when the people live out what Noah and his family are encouraged to do: "Bring out every animal—the birds, the cattle, and the crawlers that crawl on the land—so that they can swarm throughout the land, and be fruitful, and increase throughout the land" (Genesis 8:17). P's message reaffirms Genesis 1 and stands in stark contrast to the obsession in J and the Deuteronomistic History with having to demonstrate the just basis of God's judgment of evildoers (in J) or grapple with the dangers that thwart Judah's very survival (in the Deuteronomistic History).

The contrasts between P and J are striking. By isolating the two stories and exploring their respective views, we come to see that the two versions do not simply differ in the details, such as how many days the flood lasted, how many pairs of animals were taken aboard the ark, or whether it was a raven or a dove that was sent out. Rather, the two tales represent different visions of God and of God's relationship to God's people. The two theological traditions were equally treasured, stimulating ancient Judaeans to think in diverse ways about the nature of God and about God's actions in the world.

Yet the observant reader will insist on asking why it is that the Bible gives us not two separate stories but a unified amalgamation of the two. Does the combination simply represent a melding of the two strands?

It is curious that the tradition did not discard one vision in favor of the other. Nor did it set the two tales in sequence, one right after the other, as the final editors do with the two creation stories in Genesis. Rather, the flood stories were merged. Perhaps the final editor, who has the last theological word, wanted posterity to see that one narrow view of God would be insufficient for getting the community through the hard times, that even conflicting visions of God are valuable for facing the variety of challenges that history will throw in the way of God's people. Rather than advancing one image over the other, the biblical compilers understood that a belief in God as a just judge must be tempered with a vision of a forward-looking God. J's upright YHWH might teach moral awareness, but only P's planning God can point the way toward the construction of a flourishing society. The biblical record as a whole is more than the sum of its theological parts.

Despite these differences between J and P, we should not lose sight of the fact that by comparison with the Atrahasis epic both J and P have stepped decisively out of the surrounding Middle Eastern theological waters. Neither is simply a rehearsal of the old tale. The Yahwist version explores the moral side of the story, the question of divine retribution, and the possibility of divine compassion. This is not simply another ancient tale about gods who go on strike or who are upset that human noise is disturbing their divine slumber. Rather, amid the cesspool of human sin, J takes to the moral high ground. YHWH, in other words, may be depicted as an Enlil or a Zeus but an Enlil or a Zeus who happens to have some moral standards. The Priestly writer certainly shares the ancient Middle Eastern concern over the fracturing of the order of the universe, but P's constructive vision of the fruitfulness of the future is a far cry from the dire straits and narrow escape that the Atrahasis story presents.

The Israelites joined their ancient counterparts in affirming that the human realm stands in absolute dependence on the terrifying power of the divine. The Bible thereby preserves for us the wisdom of the bygone Middle East. Yet the biblical flood stories also stand apart from their immediate world, offering new insights and alternate theological views that take the concepts of the ancient world into virgin territory. If we are to fully appreciate the biblical contribution, we must bear in mind both the Bible's connectedness to its world and its uniqueness in that world.

The lesson here is that the Bible itself is an elastic text that is unafraid to have its stories stretched by the challenges of new ideas and the needs of changing political circumstances. Who would have thought that the old story was continually reinventing itself? The biblical lesson is clear: traditions remain alive to the extent that they are rooted in the past but also speak in a vital way to the emerging vistas of human history. Living as we are today in a world where many still go to war to defend their one narrow view of God, the complexity of the Bible's grand pair of contrasting visions of the flood God remains a breath of fresh air.

8

Race, Sex, and the Curse

When Myths Go Wrong

There is one section of the Noah story that is definitely left out of the Children's Bible. Evidently certain parts of scripture are considered too seamy for young readers. This particular story has long been exploited by those who focus on racism and sex in the Bible for a variety of unsavory purposes. Whether or not we like the passage, we cannot overlook the sordid side of the story if we wish to know the full scope of the Genesis flood tale. I am referring to the tale of Noah's naked drunkenness and his curse upon Ham's son Canaan.

Since many have offered definitive interpretations of this text, which actually presents many ambiguities, it is best to have the entire story before us, warts and all:

> Noah began acting like a man of the soil by planting a vineyard. He drank some of the wine and became drunk. Then he exposed himself inside the tent. Ham, the father of Canaan, saw the nakedness of his father and told his two brothers who were outside. Shem and Japheth took a garment and, putting it on their shoulders, walked backward to cover the nakedness of their father. Their faces were turned backward; they did not look at the nakedness of their father. When Noah woke up from his wine drinking, he realized what his youngest [or "littlest"] son had done to him. He exclaimed, "Canaan be damned! He will become the lowest of slaves to his brothers!" Then he said, "YHWH, the God of Shem, is blessed! May Canaan be a

slave to them. May God enlarge Japheth. May he dwell in
Shem's tent. Let Canaan be their slave!" (Genesis 9:20–27)

It is a strange tale, and unexpected behavior from a man who was earlier said to
be a "righteous" soul (Genesis 6:9). What can this story mean?

Sexual Sleuthing and the Potency of Alcohol

A clever, if ultimately dissatisfying, reading is given to us by H. Hirsch Cohen
in *The Drunkenness of Noah*. Cohen's is the sort of mind that revels in finding
connections. He is very excited, for example, about his "discovery" that the volcanic explosion in the Aegean Sea at Thera around 1500 B.C.E. stands behind
the biblical flood story. Of course, he has to backtrack somewhat when he realizes that the original Mesopotamian flood story and the related flood layers of
Sir Leonard Woolley are far older than that. Not surprisingly, Cohen then "finds"
two sets of historical events combined in the biblical tale.[1] He conveniently makes
the connections, and the biblical story's essential background is revealed. Or so
he thinks. When it comes to the drunkenness scene, Cohen offers some tantalizing insights based on connections he discerns.

Cohen wonders "why a man worthy enough to be saved from the waters of
the flood should be portrayed later as lying naked in a drunken stupor."[2] Why,
indeed? He engages in a bit of what he calls "philological sleuthing."[3] Taking
his lead from erotic paintings and sexually suggestive poetry of the ancient world,
especially Greece and Egypt, and from the biblical Song of Songs, Cohen observes that ancient cultures frequently linked wine, fire, and the male genitalia.
Alcohol, he argues, was understood to contain those fiery procreative juices that
were needed, especially by older people, to ensure successful sexual intercourse.
Wine was for the ancients what Viagra has become for us.[4]

If Cohen is right, this bit of information changes dramatically how we read
the Noah scene. Noah was not some postdiluvian delinquent, morally no better
than those who perished in the flood. Rather, by quaffing his viticultural Viagra,
Noah was hard at work trying to follow God's command "Be fruitful and multiply! Swarm throughout the world! Increase in it!" (Genesis 9:7). At age 600,
Noah needed whatever help he could get to carry out those orders.[5] In Cohen's
words, "Noah's determination to maintain his procreative ability at full strength
resulted in drinking himself into a state of helpless intoxication."[6] With alcohol placed in its proper procreative perspective, Noah reclaims his image as
an obedient servant of God. The story even has humorous overtones.

Essentially, then, for Cohen, Noah is to be seen as a good guy both at the
beginning of the story and at the end.[7] Sounding like counsel for the defense,
Cohen seeks to clear the name of Noah from centuries of libelous associations:

Noah's intoxication resulted from his need to increase his procreative power and not from a weakness for alcohol or from any ignorance of the effects of alcohol. How ironic that he who hastened to obey the divine command calling for a replenishment of the earth's population should have to suffer the opprobrium attached to drunkenness. Noah deserves not censure but acclaim for having played so well the role of God's devoted servant."[8]

Sadly, however, the morally upright Noah became the undeserving victim of Ham's wiles. Here, too, Cohen thinks interpreters have failed to grasp the import of the story. Cohen tells us to stick closely to the text, which tells us that Ham was gazing at Noah and then boasted of it. Perhaps we need look no further than the act of gazing to discern the crime.

For Cohen, to look is to acquire. If Noah had artificially boosted his sexual powers and was engaged in the very act of sexual intercourse at the moment Ham barged in, then Ham through his gazing stole away the magical potency of Noah. If so, Ham left Noah's tent a very powerful man indeed, especially if Noah had drunk enough alcohol to stoke procreative fires that would enable him to fill the earth with great numbers of children. Ham's act of gazing was not simply some sordid act of voyeurism. His deed amounted to a usurpation of Noah's place in the divine scheme of things after the flood, for Ham robbed Noah of his procreative potential. The other sons, by contrast, refused to look and thereby avoided the taint of encroaching on the place of their father. Upon waking, Noah recognizes that something has gone terribly wrong, presumably having sensed, like Superman in the presence of kryptonite, that his vital energies had dissipated.[9] Strangely, though, he curses Ham's son Canaan and not the perpetrator himself. This leaves Cohen one last conundrum to crack.

According to Cohen, Ham's successful appropriation of Noah's procreative powers explains why Noah could not curse Ham. Having lost his potency, Noah could not retrieve it from Ham. Before it was too late, however, Noah cursed Ham's descendant Canaan so that any effort made by Ham to pass that potency on to his son would be thwarted by Noah's curse.[10] That curse, as Cohen notes, constitutes Noah's "only words in the entire flood story."[11] The significance of these words has been lost on generations of interpreters. If we adopt Cohen's understanding, we unlock the meaning of a number of details, including the true implication of this seemingly displaced curse.

Cohen's clever commentary seeks to make sense out of aspects of the story that have confounded generations of Bible readers. One cannot but feel, however, that Cohen uses so many keys in so many far-flung locks in an effort to open up the story that the essential meaning of the text has slipped through his fingers. The tale seems to have become a victim of too much free association of cultural ideas.

Cohen's primary mistake is to overlook the ways in which ancient flood sto-ries typically usher their central characters into the realities of the post-flood world. In the Epic of Gilgamesh, the survivor of the flood is granted everlasting life, a reality that dogs Gilgamesh as he is thereby reminded of his own postdiluvian mortality.[12] Ovid's survivors, the husband and wife Deucalion and Pyrrha, heed the goddess's command to "scatter your great mother's bones" by tossing rocks that grew into statues that suddenly became human as the world moved on.[13] The biblical writer may simply be situating Noah amid the realities of the post-flood world, suggesting that Noah's pre-flood uprightness is no longer the guarantor of future survival. Rather, the rock on which a post-flood world will be built is God's promise never again to destroy the world—human sinfulness notwithstanding. To the Jewish exiles in Babylon for whom this story may well have been penned, this would have been a word of hope in a world of tragedy. Cohen's clever recon-struction obscures the obvious moral message of the text.

There are other ways to read this tale, proving that scholars are not the only ones eager to fill in the blanks in a text that resists easy explication. We may never discern this passage's true meaning, but by tangling with some outland-ish theories, we will receive an education in how *not* to read a text. Interpreting the Bible, as we shall now see, can be a dangerous sport.

Noah, Racism, and African-American Enslavement: The "Curse of Ham"

If fools rush in where angels fear to tread, it is no surprise to find prejudiced commentators producing dubious theological certitudes from this odd episode in Noah's story. The worst offenders have given the passage a racist tinge. Afrikaners in South Africa made use of the Ham story to justify apartheid and resist democratic elections in that country.[14] However, perhaps most notorious is the use of this passage by slaveholders and preachers in the pre–Civil War Southern United States to justify the enslavement of African-Americans.

In tract after tract and book after book, pro-slavery writers in nineteenth-century America invoked this very passage to defend the view that African-American slavery was a legitimate product of the "curse of Ham." Ham was seen to be the ancestor of the Africans, and the curse of Noah was thought to have come to fruition in the institution of slavery. T. Stringfellow wrote in his *Scrip-tural and Statistical Views in Favor of Slavery* (1856), "God decreed this institu-tion before it existed" and has "connected its *existence* with Prophetic tokens of special favor, to those who should be slave owners or masters."[15] Stringfellow sees nothing short of a divine mandate behind slavery in America: "The first recorded language which was ever uttered in relation to slavery, is the inspired language of Noah."[16] The Ham story plays a foundational role in pro-slavery thinking.

We already sense that by labeling it the "curse of Ham" rather than the "curse of Canaan," which in actuality it is, such interpreters operate with their own unique brand of literalism. They are neither exact nor loose literalists but "cheap literalists"; the basic features of the story are distorted such that even the name of the figure who is cursed is framed inaccurately. In their counterarguments abolitionists were fond of pointing out that pro-slavery interpreters could barely keep Ham and Canaan separate, much less properly interpret the rest of the passage. Sadly, the facts of the case do not deter the cheap literalist, whose agenda overrides the plain reading of the text. Cheap literalism is literalism of the most dangerous sort precisely because deadly institutions like slavery can be claimed to reflect God's revealed will for the world. Scripture is distorted for sinister purposes, a fact that is all the more disturbing when one realizes that such interpreters do not recognize the damage they are doing in the name of God. How did the pro-slavery argument work?

Pre–Civil War slavery advocates constructed their interpretation in a curious fashion.[17] Where we might have expected the Southern writers to accent the sexual side of the story, given their lurid prejudices about African sexual prowess, they instead focus on the question of Noah's paternal honor.[18] Rather than speculate on matters of rape or incest in relation to the text as other interpreters both past and present have done, the Southern reading tended to center on the dishonorable character of Ham's deed, his disrespectful treatment of his drunken father. That it was Noah who was drunk in the first place was beside the point for Southern writers; what mattered was that Ham acted with dishonor against his father. Stephen Haynes points to numerous examples of this sort of reading in his book *Noah's Curse: The Biblical Justification of Slavery*. This selection from the tract *African Servitude* (1860) is typical:

> Noah became a husbandman, planted a vineyard, and partaking too
> freely of the fruit of the vine, exposed himself to shame. . . . A true
> spirit of filial regard, love, honor and obedience moved Shem and
> Japheth to protect their father; just the reverse of that which
> influenced their brother Ham to dishonor him. . . . In consequence
> of his [i.e., Ham's] lack of faith . . . the Judge of all the earth . . .
> determines that they shall be made subject to, or become servants to,
> the rest of the families of the earth.[19]

This statement brings together a trio of values that Haynes finds regularly in such writings: filial obedience, dishonor, and slavery. Here and in other texts, Haynes discerns evidence that pro-slavery writers conceived of slavery not simply as a necessary economic institution but one that was religiously justifiable as a punishment for violating the patriarchal ordering of God's world, whether at the time of Noah or on the plantations of their own day. The image of Noah as a planter who deserved respect resonated well with the social world of the nineteenth-century South. For example, in Samuel Davies Baldwin's book *Do-*

minion; or, the Unity and Trinity of the Human Race, Noah's utterance is treated as a "divine political constitution of the world."[20] In other words, the Bible was seen as the place "where agricultural life, the patriarchal family, and the imposition of slavery were believed to originate."[21]

Haynes shows us that by papering over the profligate behavior of the patriarch Noah, pro-slavery writers played fast and loose with the text, ignoring those story elements that inconvenienced their argument. We might, for example, say that the text is conscious of the patriarch's faults, in that the supposedly noble Noah is depicted as unthinkingly blurting out a curse while in an abject state of drunkenness. However, in the South of the nineteenth century, the emphasis fell on the question of honor. Haynes draws attention to the observation of fellow historian Kenneth Greenberg that in the South "when a man of honor is told that he smells, he does not draw a bath—he draws his pistol! The man of honor does not care if he stinks, but he does care that someone has accused him of stinking."[22] When the issue is framed in terms of honor, the focus is on the reaction of the one offended (the patriarch or plantation owner) and not on any circumstance that may have initially occasioned the altercation (the son or slave). African-Americans were caught in the crosshairs of the religion, economics, and social values of the South that ensnared them through a code of honor that found a kindred spirit in the Bible.

Haynes has unquestionably latched on to a key perspective, but some vital aspects of the social function of the Ham story in the South are downplayed in his discussion. Fortunately, Peterson's study of the Ham tale, *Ham and Japheth: The Mythic World of Whites in the Antebellum South,* clarifies the wider web of societal connections between the Ham myth and the nineteenth-century South. Peterson does not overlook the honor factor but casts his net more broadly.[23] His analysis deserves closer inspection.

Peterson observes that white Southerners, for all practical purposes, had donned the Puritan utopian mantle. He argues that Southern Christians were seeking to construct a commonwealth grounded in a literal reading of the Bible.[24] A central biblical text in that social project was the story of Noah's curse of Ham. Stringfellow, for example, kicks off his defense of slavery with a reading of the Ham story.[25] For Southerners, the tale justified not only slavery in general but black enslavement in particular. It placed a divine seal of approval on the social order, economic structures, and theological mind-set of the South. White Southerners saw themselves as the heirs of Noah's son Japheth, carrying out God's eternal plan by enslaving African-Americans (the descendants of Ham) in a land once dominated by the Indians (the descendants of Noah's son Shem).[26] As Peterson explains,

> The Southern versions of the Ham myth were rooted in the biblical story rather than controlled by it. In the Southern story, Ham and Japheth became archetypes, respectively, for the black and white

races in America; the relationship between these two brothers in the myth both validated and provided a model for the whites' treatment of blacks in the antebellum South."[27]

Thus, not only was slavery as such seen to have biblical legitimation but, due to the long-held belief among biblical interpreters that Ham was connected to Africa, blacks were singled out as the race that could justifiably be enslaved. The Southern whites, of course, were the ones to do the enslaving.

This fantasy was deeply internalized. One writer portrayed an heir of Japheth instructing a descendant of Ham about this grand white destiny, while Ham's heir humbly submits to God's design for Japheth's descendants:

> Sons of Japhet and children of the white man, you know why we are here. We came not willingly, but we charge not our captivity to you. Yet here we are and we submit to our lot. It may have been for our sins or those of our fathers that we are torn from our native land; but better is it thus than that our race should have been cut off as cumberers of the earth. . . . A great mission you say, awaits you. In our hearts we can believe it true. And something whispers to us that we also, all fallen as we are, have a duty to perform in connexion therewith. We ask not to be admitted to your higher sphere. Would that we were worthy.[28]

The myth not only encodes white superiority but also imagines black acceptance of white domination as the black contribution in God's enduring plan for America.

So imbued were Southerners with this myth that they saw any efforts to disrupt the enslavement of African-Americans as serious breaches in the order that God had ordained for all time. The patriarchal plantation, with its honorable white family and its docile African slaves (prone as they were to "laziness, superstition, and crime" in the white mind) was seen as the logical outgrowth of a biblically centered Providence.[29] Drawing on their "literal" reading of scripture, Southern whites argued that to heed the reformist ideas of Northern abolitionists would be to deny the clear teachings of the Bible. Surely social chaos and theological confusion would ensue if the abolitionists had their way. They threatened to upset the economic applecart by encouraging African-Americans to flee servitude. Over and above that, however, they were flouting God's will. The claim that African-Americans not only were God's children but also democratically equal to whites was anathema to Southern whites. Democratic governance of this sort violated the hierarchy that God had imposed and that Southern white Christians were called to maintain. White Southerners might have wanted their slaves to be religious but certainly not to find in the Bible a justification for their liberation from enslavement.

Peterson shows that the Ham story reverberated throughout the entire fabric of the Southern political, economic, social, and religious order. Citing Clifford Geertz's work on the intimate role of religion in society, he effectively demonstrates that the story functioned as a racial myth that gave the South a "meaningful framework for orienting themselves to one another, to the world around them, and to themselves."[30]

Few in the South raised theological objections to placing the Ham story at the center of the Southern slavery program.[31] Curiously, others rejected the story on "scientific" grounds, arguing that blacks were a demonstrably inferior race with a *separate* genetic and environmental origin to that of whites.[32] This position was adopted, in part, to evade the biblical claim that all people are the descendants of Adam and Eve. Clearly, some feared that a literal reading of the Bible would commit Southerners to press for equality for African-Americans. Common descent might require equal rights and privileges for African-Americans. The theological rejoinder was that one could still adhere to the biblical belief in a common ancestry while also arguing that the Ham story secured a scriptural basis for the unequal treatment of African-Americans. After all, God himself had condemned blacks to servitude.

Whether on "scientific" grounds or through a literal reading of the Bible, most Southern white Christians arrived at the same conclusion: African-Americans were intellectual and social inferiors who could legitimately be enslaved. Peterson's study reveals the pervasive and persuasive character of the Ham myth in upholding the slavery enterprise. He shows the story to be multivalent in nineteenth-century Southern society. It is truly a myth gone wrong. While one must surely remain troubled by what the South did with this tale, we should be doubly disturbed to find that economic domination and social differentiation are encoded in the text itself. Southerners did not so much *abuse* the text as they *made use* of it, invoking the codes of domination that are contained in the story. The challenge today is to know what to do with a Bible that seems to authorize slavery.

How should we deal with a story that has so tainted America's past?

In *The 1993 Trial on the Curse of Ham*, Wayne Perryman offered an unusual and creative response to the persistence of the idea of the curse of Ham in the American psyche. Perryman, described as "an author, lecturer, newspaper publisher, former radio talk show host, minister, and a business employment relations consultant," has committed himself to overturning stereotypes regarding blacks in relation to the Bible.[33] He decided to bring the accursed Ham into a mock courtroom and put 300 years of white prejudice on trial.

The trial was held at the Friendship Baptist Church in Orange County, California, in the summer of 1993. As the trial opens, Perryman calls on several witnesses who offer a variety of interpretations of the Ham incident. These "witnesses" are in fact representative commentaries drawn from the typical fundamentalist fare, each of which puts Ham at the center of some salacious crime. The most outrageous is the so-called *Self-Interpreting Bible* (1896). This commentary states that as a result of the Ham affair, "For about four thousand years past the bulk of the Africans have been abandoned of Heaven to the most gross ignorance, rigid slavery, stupid idolatry, and savage barbarity."[34] This "self-interpretation" tells us more about the interpreter than it ever will about the Bible.

With such biased witnesses before the court, Perryman feels the best defense lies in allowing Mr. Ham to speak for himself. Ham proceeds to exonerate himself by explaining that his son Canaan was the one who was cursed and that he himself had done no wrong. Ham performs his own exegesis on the Noah incident, contending that the writer, Moses, had left all the necessary clues to understand the nature of the misdeed that had been committed. By the use of the term "father's nakedness," Moses intended for us to understand that Ham's son Canaan had had sex with Noah's wife while Noah was drunk. That is why, says Ham, Canaan alone was cursed. Perryman provides us yet another twist on the reading of the text. While Perryman's reading may not do justice to the precise significance of the Hebrew text, he provides food for thought for the literalist who seeks to derive racist certainties from a text that can be understood in a myriad of ways.

During the course of the trial Ham also explains that he was simply born black and was not cursed to be black. In fact, he points out, when the Bible curses people, they turn snow-white (Numbers 12)! Perryman's reading turns the tables on the racism and slavery that others think they can justify from scripture. Perceptively, Perryman's Ham observes, "I believe slavery had more to do with the sins of the people who enslaved them, more than the sins of the slaves themselves."[35] Instead of blaming the victim, one must reflect upon the evils of slave owning and race baiting.

By placing history and scriptural interpretation in the docket, Perryman cleverly removes the Bible from the arsenal of those who would use the sacred text as a weapon of domination and injustice. Much like the medieval rabbis, Perryman shows us the necessity of moving inside the myth both to revitalize our understanding of the tradition and to deconstruct the manipulations made possible by a simplistic treatment of the text.

Cheap literalism will rarely be overcome by rational arguments about the text. Because the argument is operating at such a visceral level, perhaps only a mock trial or some other imaginative counter to such interpretations can make any real difference. Changes of thinking in this regard are usually matters of the heart and not simply of the text or of the intellect. Cheap literalism will probably not be overcome by better literalism or some other kind of rational analysis but through creative carnivalesque performances that jar loose the emotions and open one to the harsh injustices that slavery and oppression impose upon fellow human beings.

This is not to say that a better sort of literalism cannot be helpful. Fortunately, not all in the literalist crowd treat the story in a racist fashion.

D. G. Lindsay, for example, who insists on taking the flood tale "at face value," bucks dangerous trends in his own fundamentalist circles by judging "ridiculous" the attempt to justify the enslavement of African-Americans on the basis of the Bible. An exact literalist like Lindsay knows when the story is being hijacked. He understands that the Book is not being used in a theologically credible fashion. Because the exact literalist must argue that God has created us all from one set of parents, namely, Adam and Eve, the literalist also knows that any attempt to place one race above another violates the spirit and the letter of the tradition as received today.

Lindsay handles the story with kid gloves, not reading into it things that are not there. He joins the abolitionists of the nineteenth century in pointing out that the story is not about Noah's curse of Ham but about the curse of Ham's son Canaan.[36] How often do those who feign literalism, who are what we call "cheap literalists," employ the text for their own selfish ends? Lindsay is on to their game. He talks their language. Thus he can state in no uncertain terms, "There is no place in the Word that suggests that black people are black because they are under a curse of God, and thus, are subject to slavery."[37]

How much misery and pain has been perpetuated by the misuse of the Bible for purposes of racial hatred. It is unfortunate, therefore, that despite his antiracist strictures Lindsay counsels against "mixed marriages" because he thinks the cultural gap and struggles are too great.[38] This does a disservice to his otherwise clear condemnation of racism built on the Bible.[39]

Exact literalism can thus be of value, especially as a way to see through abuses of the scriptural text that are guided by hidden agendas. Yet Lindsay's own cultural blinders regarding interethnic marriage are a sign that we cannot expect the text to do all of the work. We need a way to put the text in dialogue with the issues of our time, rather than continuing to act as if the text were written for our day. The question of slavery is a case in point. Even if the story is about slavery, we need to ask what sort of slavery. In the biblical text, slavery tends to be governed by time limits; slaves are released after seven years of service (Exodus 21:2; Deuteronomy 15:12). If the Southern slave owners had practiced such a literalism, they might have been more cautious about finding a justification for perpetual servitude in Noah's curse.

Moreover, as the abolitionists knew and contemporary liberation theologians continue to remind us, the defining story of the Hebrew Bible is God's liberation of the Hebrew slaves from the tyranny of ancient Egypt. Abolitionist A. Barnes argues that any sensible reader of the Book of Exodus should conclude that God demands "immediate emancipation" for those who are enslaved, whether in ancient Egypt or nineteenth-century America.[40] In the Bible's scheme of things, the Exodus story trumps the Ham story in any century.

Ham's Handiwork and Homosexuality

A more contemporary spin on the Ham story has to do with the question of homosexuality. Randall Bailey seems quite correct, and Haynes concurs, that the very "ambiguity" of the story "leads the reader to resolve that something sexual has transpired."[41] Given the text's failure to specify Ham's transgression, we are compelled to ask what it was that happened between Ham and Noah in the tent that day. Lindsay, who is so careful in his literalism, assumes that Ham's sin was homosexuality. That assumption is supported, Lindsay claims, elsewhere in Genesis where we learn that Ham's son Canaan carried on the family tradition and settled in the land named after him, a land in which the immoral Sodom and Gomorrah continued Ham and Canaan's wicked legacy.[42] The homosexual interpretation is obvious to Lindsay for both the Ham and Sodom stories. How justified is the view that Noah's curse was provoked by a homosexual act and that this curse is still in force against homosexuality today?

The text is rather vague at the very point where the deed occurs. Noah is drunk, and Ham does something inappropriate that warrants the curse of a drunken hero. What did Ham do? Bailey seems right to conjecture that some sort of sexual act has taken place, but the text leaves us in the dark regarding the nature of that act. Whatever Ham did, Shem and Japheth were able quite quickly to remedy the situation. Perhaps we are to see in the story no more than what it says, namely, that Ham exposed (or even simply observed) Noah's private parts and that the other sons covered their father up. This would certainly qualify as a repellant act in the ancient Hebrew value system, but it is hardly the dire homosexual "misdeed" that fundamentalist interpreters see in the text. Who is really being literal here?

Nevertheless, the imputation of a homosexual act is prevalent among fundamentalists and even many biblical scholars. Regina Schwartz, hardly a fundamentalist, is confident that the Ham story is a statement against homosexuality, more specifically "homosexual incest, father-son incest, to be precise."[43] She goes on to give the text a Freudian flavor, suggesting that Ham's homosexual act was designed to displace the father. This evokes Freud's "slaying of the father" motif—a horrific primordial event that for Freud undergirds our collective religiosity.[44] By showing the disaster that results from Ham's deed, the text reinforces "the general biblical hysteria about homosexuality."[45]

This analysis begs many questions. Is incest now to be equated with homosexuality? Homosexuality today is hardly to be tied to parental incest desires. We may also ask if there truly is a general hysteria about homosexuality in the Bible. It is, after all, mentioned very infrequently, if at all (cf. Leviticus 18:22, 20:13; Deuteronomy 23:17). Can we be so precise about a text that is fraught with literary and cultural ambiguities?

Perhaps we should follow Lindsay's lead and bring in the Sodom and Gomorrah story. Unfortunately, similar confusion abounds over the interpretation of this tale later in Genesis (chap. 19). Fundamentalists and other commentators have said confidently that this text, too, concerns homosexuality.[46] Yet does it? The tale is no doubt a brutal one. Abraham's nephew Lot is visited by angelic messengers. He finds his house surrounded by townsmen who demand that he send the visitors out so that the men can "know" them, an obvious reference to rape. Lot offers up his daughters instead, but his offer is rejected. As the angry townsmen begin to storm Lot's house, the angelic messengers cast a spell that blinds them. The angels then warn Lot to flee the town with his family before God destroys the place.

As we read this story, perplexities stand in the way of a straightforward interpretation. Does the passage concern homosexuality or gang rape? Is gang rape between males a homosexual act? What we know about prison experiences might lead us to think otherwise.[47] Could the initial "homosexual" desire of the townsmen be appeased by "heterosexual" rape of Lot's daughters? Lot seemed to think so, which again might suggest that the story is about something other than homosexuality as such. Even if the text can be stretched to read as an ancient statement concerning homosexuality, it is hard to see what it implies with regard to modern committed adult homosexual relationships. While other texts in the Bible may bear on questions of homosexuality, the story of Sodom and Gomorrah in Genesis 19 is about violence and not homosexuality as such. The Ham story is even less clear.[48] That Ham has somehow violated the primacy of his father in the family seems clear (even if Regina Schwartz's Freudian analysis is a bit extreme). That Ham or the men of Sodom were "gay" hardly seems to be the point.

The lesson of the Ham and Sodom stories is that texts that emerge from ancient cultural contexts cannot automatically be applied to the present context without misconstruing the text. We are pressed to find a better way to put the ancient tales in dialogue with the modern world.

A Violent Bible and a Violent God

If it is not about homosexuality, then what sense are we to make of the story of Noah's drunkenness and the curse? Perhaps the violent character of the episode provides a clue. To curse someone was a highly charged act. Even if a sobered-up Noah later came to regret his words, the ancients thought the power of speech was such as to make the curse irrevocable. Yet what would motivate such rage?

Peter Gomes, author of *The Good Book: Reading the Bible with Mind and Heart*, points to rabbinic suggestions "that Ham had engaged in immoral sexual conduct on the Ark." Some rabbis believed that while other humans remained

WHEN MYTHS GO WRONG   141

celibate, Ham joined the dog and the raven as the only beings to have sexual relations aboard the ark, presumably with animals.[49] Others taught that after the flood Ham "had sodomized his drunken father; even that he had castrated Noah so that there could be no more heirs from his father's loins."[50] One rabbinic tradition has Canaan gazing first, and in so doing he becomes an accomplice to Ham's misdeeds.[51] In another, Canaan castrates Noah after binding a thread around his circumcised penis.[52] In this tradition, Ham merely looks on as Canaan does the dirty work but then goes outside to joke with his brothers about the incident, thereby dishonoring his father and neglecting his duties as a son. If any of these horrifying possibilities is implied by the story, the extreme harshness of Noah's response becomes more intelligible. Ham would represent uncontrolled libido at its worst. To make matters worse, so the Talmud tells us, such propensities were passed on by Canaan to his own sons as he groomed them to engage in theft, promiscuity, lying, and rebellion against their masters.[53] Just beneath the surface the text is rife with sexual deviance, violence, unrestrained lust, vengeance, and patriarchal fear.

Gomes strongly suggests that for the American slave era the story encodes the sort of sexual fears and vengeful attitudes that were harbored by Southerners against African-Americans.[54] Like corrupted computer software, the cultural code contained in the Genesis tale reinforced sexual insecurities and desires for revenge in a society that easily found authorization in the text for its repression of African-Americans. Gomes is correct that "it was Bible-reading, churchgoing Christians, chiefly Protestant and largely Baptist, who could and would lynch, castrate, and horribly mutilate errant black men on Saturday night, and pray and praise all day in Church on Sunday, without a hint of schizophrenia or even of guilt. How could they sustain such a culture for so long? The Bible told them so."[55]

Gomes's reading is provocative. While whites in the South may not have consciously used the Ham story to legitimize violence in the raw, Gomes is certainly justified in pointing out the dangers inherent in importing this stormy biblical text into the nineteenth-century Southern context. The net result of promoting this text in that later volatile context is that social violence was legitimized. Regardless of how much this violence was covered over with talk of honor, Christian destiny, or divine authorization, the fact is that the text itself aided and abetted social evil. Gomes is asking us to consider the extent to which the Bible encodes or even encourages vengeance, sexual conflict, and violence. As Regina Schwartz has shown, the pervasive current of violence in the Bible remains a stumbling block to the literalist application of ancient text to modern circumstances. The Bible allowed Lincoln to pronounce "forceful invocations of the Exodus" on behalf of slaves, even as "the South invoked the conquest [story in the Book of Joshua] in order to justify the perpetuation of slavery."[56] Schwartz's unease is warranted: "Clearly, the consequences of overlapping and confusing the exodus and conquest paradigms are deeply troubling."[57]

What are we to do when we find the Bible itself contributing to the ills besetting the world? While some take refuge in the image of the compassionate God who rescues Noah from the flood, others are disturbed that this same God wipes out the entire planet in a fit of anger, calls for the Israelites to annihilate the Canaanites, or, when that campaign of total conquest fails, authorizes the subjugation of those same peoples. The Ham story encapsulates this same set of dilemmas. This is not to say that the question cannot be resolved through deeper reflection, but the trajectory of violence in the Bible ought to be deeply troubling to all sensitive religionists. History—whether the history of the fallen Canaanites or of the African slaves—tells us that we cannot afford to ignore this aspect of the Bible. As Bailey observes, "The problem is, thus, not only with these supremacist ideologies. Our problem is also with the biblical text itself."[58] His call for a "subversive reading" of the Bible may be the best option for handling such passages. The warning is clear: if we remain with an eye-for-an-eye religion based on a violent Bible, we will be bereft of vision for the future. We need new eyes with which to read the Bible before it is too late.

All in the Family: The Incest Question

There is yet another possible angle for approaching the ancient text in its own context. Interpreters often try to make sense of the "nakedness" of Noah. Insight is provided by Leviticus 18:7–8: "Do not uncover your father's nakedness, that is, the nakedness of your mother. She is your mother. You shall not uncover her nakedness. Do not uncover the nakedness of your father's wife. She is the nakedness of your father." Likewise, Leviticus 20:11a concurs: "When a man lies with his father's wife, he uncovers the nakedness of his father."

These passages suggest that a reference to the uncovering of a father's nakedness is really a reference to sexual impropriety with one's own mother or stepmother (see also Deuteronomy 23:1 [English versions = 22:30], 27:20; Ezekiel 22:10). As F. W. Bassett explains in his insightful study "Noah's Nakedness and the Curse of Canaan: A Case of Incest?" the words in question are "used to describe not homosexual but heterosexual intercourse, even when it speaks of a man seeing another man's nakedness. 'To see a man's nakedness' means to have sexual relations with his wife."[59]

R. A. J. Gagnon, author of *The Bible and Homosexual Practice*, who seems to want to find modern homosexual analogues in every nook and cranny of the Bible in search of ammunition to condemn modern practice, actually acknowledges that "father's nakedness" refers to *maternal* incest. Yet he inexplicably insists on reading the Ham passage as "incestuous, homosexual rape."[60]

If Bassett's interpretation that the phrase is an oblique reference to having sex with another man's wife is to be preferred to Gagnon's insistence on reading the drunkenness story as one of homosexual rape, then the story of Ham refers specifically to Ham's violation of his own mother. He would have taken advantage of his father's drunkenness to have sex with his mother, asserting a claim to authority over the house of Noah. In terms of the rules in Leviticus 18 and 20, Ham's deed tops the list of the possible breaches of incest norms. Bassett argues that the later editors of Genesis were ignorant of the idiom and thought that Ham literally looked at a naked Noah. They then added the bit about Japheth and Shem covering up their father to make sense of a difficult text.[61]

The punishment prescribed in the Leviticus incest texts is harsh. Anyone guilty of violating the rules was guilty of defiling the land in the same manner as those whom God had previously driven out of the land. The Bible's way of saying this is vivid: "The land will vomit you out for defiling it, as it vomited out the nation that preceded you. For all who do any of these abhorrent things shall be cut off from their people" (Leviticus 18:28–29). Or, as Leviticus 20:11b says bluntly, "Both shall be put to death. Their bloodguilt is upon them." Against this backdrop, Noah's curse against Ham's son Canaan becomes intelligible, especially if, as Bailey contends, the Ham narrative, like the Leviticus passages, also stems from the Priestly writer's hands.[62] Ham had committed incest with his mother, and his son is numbered among those who are cut off from the people of God. Why the son? Perhaps because Canaan was the product of that incestuous union.[63]

The charge of incestuous conduct can carry nationalistic overtones in scripture, as in the tale of Lot's incestuous liaison with his daughters after the destruction of Sodom and Gomorrah. In this text, the male descendants of the union of the daughters with their father symbolize the peoples of Moab and Ammon (Genesis 19:30–38). Obviously this is meant as a slur on Israel's neighbors. The Noah story represents a sifting on both a personal and a national level. On the personal level, the flood tale separates out the just man from among the wicked of the earth, even in relation to his own heirs. On the national level, the story of the curse of Canaan reflects a broader sifting process. There are wicked people who remain after the flood, but the people of God are promised dominion over the sons of Canaan, children of incest. Later in Genesis those descendants of Canaan are named: "Sidon, his first-born, and Heth; and the Jebusites, the Amorites, the Girgashites, the Hivites, the Arkites, the Sinites, the Arvadites, the Zamarites, and the Hamathites" (Genesis 10:15–18). These are the peoples that the Israelites are later said to have driven out as they established their homeland under Joshua. The Israelites, in other words, are to displace those idolatrous and sexually perverse descendants of Canaan (as well as the sons of Lot's daughters). The scene with Noah foreshadows the conquest, offering a justification for Israelite national superiority over the Canaanites.

The trouble with this reading of the Ham story is that we cannot be certain that the incest categories of Leviticus ought to govern our reading of Genesis. The similarity in language may be coincidental, and we may be guilty of reading more into the story than was intended. After all, the final form of the text, as

even Bassett has to acknowledge, turns on Ham's merely gazing at the nakedness of his father. It seems that, for the final editor of the text at any rate, this
would have been discreditable enough. If this reflects the original composition
of the text and not a later addition, then perhaps the Southern interpretation as
construed by Haynes is right in the end: the central issue at stake in the Ham
story is parental and familial honor. This is the direction in which the later
Qumranites took the story, although with a slightly different twist. Situating the
event during the celebration of a religious festival, the writers of the Dead Sea
Scrolls imagine that "Ham's offense constitutes an act of disrespect not only to
his father, but also to the festival ordinances."[64] Perhaps the tale is more about
honor and less about sex than we might initially think, at least at the final stage
of the tradition, if not its point of origin.

Whether a tale of alcoholic stimulants, dishonor, enslavement, homosexuality, sexual perversity, incest, festival violations, voyeurism, or simple exposure
of the father's flesh, the story of Noah's drunkenness and Ham's response has
exercised the imagination of countless biblical interpreters. The mystery remains
unsolved regardless of how ingenious interpreters are in discovering particular
perversities and specific social evils in the text. The Bible often resists letting us
read into the text theological views that we would like to have authorized by
scripture. In the case of the Ham story, our study tells us more about the Bible's
handlers than it does about the text itself. At the very least, our discussion of
this text points out the folly of trying to take the Bible at "face value."

The lesson here is a negative one but no less important for its negativity.
The mythographer Doty warns of the "danger of getting stuck in fundamental-
isms that leave us trapped in dysfunctional mythostories."[65] In ancient times,
the biblical text may have authorized the Israelite subjugation and enslavement
of the Canaanites. In our own day we must beware of the easy assumption that
we are among the superior crowd authorized to repress others in the name of God
(Leviticus 25:39–46). Gomes throws down the gauntlet before the cheap literalist
when he writes, "Since discerning what God, in the Bible, means for us to hear
and to do is a matter of life and death, we must approach the interpretation of
scripture as we do our own salvation, working it out in fear and trembling."[66]

9

Simone de Beauvoir aboard the Ark

Male Hero Fantasies and the Second Sex

For many readers today, the lack of a significant place for women in the Genesis flood story and the other flood stories from the Middle East is rather disheartening. One wonders what has happened to Noah's wife. All we know of her is that she had three sons and boarded the ark with Noah. In many ways, she typifies the sort of unknown female biblical figure snared by Phyllis Bird's title *Missing Persons, Mistaken Identities: Women and Gender in Ancient Israel.* Noah's wife is the epitome of the missing female figure in the Bible. Humankind could not survive without her, but the attention she and the wives of Noah's sons receive in the Bible is scant indeed. Noah's wife remains unnamed and is simply presented according to her status as wife and mother.[1] She is a cipher in the story. The bare fact of her marital and maternal relationship is underscored, while any deeds remain unrecorded. Is there nothing more to be said? Do males always have to steal the show? Where can we find Simone de Beauvoir's "second sex" in the biblical world and ancient myth?

Ancient flood stories, like so much of ancient literature, reflect gender categories that differ radically from modern sensibilities. The trouble is knowing whether one should try to separate the wisdom of the tale from its male window dressing or simply discard it entirely because of its misogynist deficiencies. Some elect to ignore the male bias of the Bible, treating it as accidental to the Bible's "universal" vision of justice, hope, and survival. The truth of the Bible and of any myth, they would say, can be freed from its time-bound literary and cultural framework. Others balk at accepting the story's "truth," arguing that the androcentric character of the story is precisely what is wrong with it. No universal wisdom can be extracted from the text without seriously distorting its male-dominated legacy. For these critics, the Bible's patriarchal castle is built on sociological quicksand. The sooner we recognize this precarious arrangement, the sooner we will free ourselves from the tyranny of outmoded notions of gender and truth.

Is the biblical world a club to which men alone need apply? Rather than ignore the issue, let us tackle the problem head-on by exploring what mythographers have to say about the "hero's journey" concept and what feminist analysis tells us about women in the biblical world. This two-pronged approach will unlock the Bible's fantasies about its male heroes and restore Israel's second sex, including Noah's wife, to a more central place in the assessment of the enduring meaning of the biblical and ancient flood stories. We need not leave the Bible to its myopic maleness nor discard it as a useless relic of the past.

Dharma Bums on the Road: The Male Hero Fantasy

For some, the absence of women from so many of the major stories and histories in the Bible is a frustrating stumbling block. The Bible, like so much of the literature of the ancient world, is largely, if not exclusively, taken up with male heroes both human and divine. When women do show up, it is to serve as props and stagehands for a play whose main actors are an array of kings, priests, prophets, and warriors—virtually all are male. In mythological circles, the key myths focusing on these male actors are often labeled "heroes' journeys." In such a myth, the main character is typically a lucky-starred but clueless male who is thrust out of his home environment to go on a series of adventures. The adventures, which test and hone the hero's inner resolve and physical prowess, culminate in some great test or trial, which in turn yields a great prize that can be carried back home. Joseph Campbell's book *The Hero with a Thousand Faces* inspired a veritable cottage industry of spin-offs that take us along the hero's journey, often extrapolating implications for how to live one's life today. While others such as Otto Rank and Lord Raglan have developed their own checklists for identifying a hero myth, Campbell's is the best known.[2]

For Campbell the hero's journey is a myth found the world over. Setting dozens of such tales side by side, he argues that the similarities justify labeling the hero's journey theme a "monomyth." This monomyth, according to Campbell, has three fundamental components: departure, initiation, and return. Each of these general phases can exhibit any number of subvariations, but for Campbell the general outlines of the myth can be found throughout all of recorded history in cultures the world over.

The departure phase is instigated, according to Campbell, by some decisive "call to adventure." The hero hears his heart turning to the greater realm of adventure that lies beyond the world he knows. This departure from the familiar can be imposed upon the hero by supernatural forces or self-selected by a change in his immediate circumstances. Regardless of what sparks the journey, the hero must be cut loose from the once-secure moorings of his home turf. The break with the past is marked decisively by what Campbell calls the "crossing of the first threshold." Once the hero is thrust out onto the larger field of adventure, there is no turning back, come what may.

The second phase, the initiation, is a road of many tests and trials and constitutes the bulk of the myth's story line. It can take many forms, sometimes featuring encounters with demons or seductive goddesses, but most often involves a series of trials of strength or mental agility. The period of initiation reaches a climax in one supreme conquest that is filled with grave peril or bitter opposition.

Having overcome all that would thwart him on this road of adventure, after the climactic encounter, the hero is ready for the third phase, namely, the return to life in the mortal realm. According to Campbell, the first steps of the return can take a number of variations. Some heroes refuse to go back, others are rescued, whereas others elect, however reluctantly, to go home. Regardless, the hero finds himself "crossing the return threshold." He cannot remain in the realm of adventure forever. His divine side has emerged, but it must be reunited with the self that he had seemed to leave behind.

Despite his return to the realm of the familiar, the hero is hardly the same man who began the journey. For Campbell, the hero lives out the rest of his days as a "master of two worlds." Once having touched the transcendent or the divine, the hero is forever changed and serves as a model for his fellow men. As a result of his journey to the horizon of human thought and life's possibilities, he knows how to live with greater freedom. The journey precipitates in the hero a realization of all we can achieve, both physically and spiritually.

Examples of the hero's journey abound, but three will have to suffice here. An ancient Buddhist example is that of the founding figure, Siddhartha Gautama (b. 563 B.C.E.). After a youthful encounter with stark examples of disease, old age, and death, Prince Siddhartha rejects his life of ease as pathetically shallow. Much against his father's wishes, he leaves the palace and goes forth resolutely into the world, moving beyond harsh asceticism and overcoming difficult temptations to find enlightenment under the bodhi tree, where he becomes "awake," or the Buddha. That journey yields a boon that can be passed on to his disciples.

George Lucas's *Star Wars* offers an example from pop culture. The film presents us with the restless boy Luke Skywalker, who goes forth into grand adventures in deepest space far beyond his home planet. Lucas confesses, "With *Star Wars* I consciously set about to re-create myths and the classic mythological motifs. I wanted to use those motifs to deal with issues that exist today."[3]

The hero of the space-age myth, the puissant Luke Skywalker, progressively discovers crucial facts about himself, his lineage, and his quasi-supernatural powers. Relying on those newfound abilities, his ties to the mystical Force that underlies all of life, Luke is able to best the evil emperor and the emperor's satanic henchman, Darth Vader. His victory leads to the destruction of the Death Star and the liberation of an enslaved people. Having become the master of two worlds, Luke Skywalker lives on in the hearts of twelve-year-olds everywhere as the space-age hero to emulate, or perhaps we should say the hero with an Iron Age mentality bedecked in futuristic intergalactic garb.

The Bible offers a number of heroes' journeys or at least fragments of such journeys. One can see the bare bones of the pattern in the flood story: Noah is suddenly sent packing by God (departure), rides out the flood in the ark (initiation), and lands in a much-changed world (return). However, the fullest of the biblical hero's journeys is the story of Jacob in the Book of Genesis (chaps. 25–35). The cozy family life of father Isaac and his two sons Jacob and Esau is interrupted by a series of events that ultimately push Jacob onto the road of adventure. With a dangerous destiny foreshadowed by their struggles in their mother's womb, the fraternal twins Esau and Jacob are set at odds by two key events. First, the hungry Esau recklessly sells his birthright to Jacob for a measly bowl of porridge. A short while later, Jacob's mother, Rebekah, disguises her son to deceive the elderly father, Isaac, into thinking that he is Esau. Isaac mistakenly grants his paternal blessing to the younger son, Jacob, much to the consternation of Esau, who finds that a blessing once given cannot be retracted.

Having caused enough trouble at home and fearing the potentially murderous wrath of Esau, Jacob discerns that the better part of valor would be to hightail it away to safer environs in Syria, where his uncle Laban lives. Here the Bible decisively marks the point of transition between the familiar realm of the hero's home and the larger world of adventure. As his journey begins, Jacob has a dream in which he encounters angelic beings who are going up and down a ladder that leads up to heaven. He will meet these same angels when he returns from his adventures.

Jacob has now crossed the threshold into the realm of danger. Here he faces trials that are typical of the major patriarchal figures of Genesis, all of whom have difficulty producing an heir in order to secure the land and prosperity promised by God to the people of Israel. Jacob's initial trial, which foreshadows his success, comes as he enters the territory of his uncle. At a well, Jacob finds the shepherds waiting to water their flocks. The shepherds insist that the rock that covers the well cannot be removed until later in the day when all the flocks have been gathered for watering. The arrival of Laban's daughter Rachel spurs Jacob to roll the rock out of the way in order to water his uncle's flock. He greets his cousin and offers her a kiss. Because the well symbolizes fertility, Jacob's dramatic and decisive action foreshadows his success in ending Rachel's barrenness, although he will have to labor for Laban for fourteen years—seven after which he is tricked into marrying Laban's elder daughter Leah and seven more to secure his marriage to Rachel.[4] Jacob accepts these labors precisely because he loves the younger daughter, Rachel.

The decisive trial for Jacob is the barrenness of Rachel. Leah bears Jacob three sons, and Rachel is consumed with envy. This grief is all the more acute because Rachel is the true love of Jacob. The conflict is further heightened by the countermeasures the sisters take. Rachel gives her handmaid, Bilhah, over to Jacob to bear children on her behalf, and she gains some satisfaction from the success of this stratagem. But Leah, who by now is herself barren, likewise gives her handmaid, Zilpah, over to Jacob in a successful bid to gain added children for her side. The reader senses Rachel's desperation as she bargains to secure an aphrodisiac from Leah. The price of the aphrodisiac is Rachel's willingness to let Leah lie with Jacob yet again, producing still more children. Finally, when neither Rachel nor the reader can take much more of this conflict, the narrator relents and God allows Rachel to bear a son, Joseph, taking away her "disgrace" (Genesis 30:23).

With the birth of Joseph, Jacob is ready to depart from the land of trials and return home, but there are further obstacles that await him before he can leave Laban. There is the question of his wages: Jacob does not wish to incur further obligations to Laban and so devises a plan to trick Laban in return for all the years that he had been virtually enslaved. Jacob asks only for the dark sheep and the speckled and spotted goats from Laban's flock. Laban must have thought this was a bargain, since these were the rarest offspring, requiring either that Jacob remain on for many years to build up a sufficient flock or depart a poor man. Jacob knows his breeding techniques and manages to add to his few partially colored goats and sheep and turn them into a sizable flock. The narrator supplies a bit of folklore, having Jacob mark rods with particular patterns that would cause Laban's flocks to produce more and more dark sheep and speckled and spotted goats. In the end, Laban was the poorer for his choice. Through these trials, Jacob shows himself to be the lord of fertility, both with his wife and with his livestock. His figure now towers over the cowering cheat on the run whom we met at the beginning of the tale.

When Jacob departs, he does so with a vast entourage. In Laban's absence, Rachel has stolen her father's household gods. Laban catches up with the travelers and searches for the idols, but he never finds the deities he seeks because Rachel has hidden them in her camel's saddle. When Laban enters her tent, Rachel sits on the saddle and tells her father she cannot stand up because she is in her time of menstruation. This denouement is a humorous literary allusion to the fact that she is a fertile woman on the road with the master of fertility. Laban is forced to accept defeat as Jacob moves on.

Jacob's return is fraught with danger. The crossing of the threshold is marked once again with angelic encounters. One encounter is simply a vision, but the other is a dramatic wrestling match between Jacob and a mysterious stranger. Jacob has remained alone on the far side of the river after his family has crossed the ford ahead of him on their way toward Canaan. Throughout the entire night he has to hold his own against his powerful, unknown opponent.

Some suggest that this dark figure is Esau come to tangle with his brother one last time. The symmetry between this encounter and the angels Jacob met while leaving Canaan suggests that the ambiguity of the wrestler's identity ought to be respected. Whether it is Esau, a psychological apparition, or some divine figure, Jacob is moved to press his opponent to bless him. The stranger renames Jacob, giving him the name "Israel," which for the narrator signifies that he has "struggled with God and humans, and has overcome" (Genesis 32:29 [English versions = 32:28]). There can be no plainer way for the text to say that through his tests and trials the hero Jacob has become Campbell's "master of two worlds."

The return wraps up with Jacob's reconciliation with Esau. Jacob gifts his brother with wealth, thereby restoring the blessing stolen at the beginning of the story. Together, the reunited brothers bury their father, Isaac.[5] Jacob is no longer the grasping little boy who began this unexpected but formative adventure.

The Male Mystique: A Universal Truth?

Whether it is Lord Buddha, Luke Skywalker, Noah, or the biblical patriarch Jacob, the story of an individual who has suffered separation from home, tackled trials on the road, and experienced a triumphant return (or a profound spiritual realization) is destined to inspire listeners to commit themselves to more meaningful lives. In its ancient, modern, or biblical forms, the monomyth in all its variations governs the thinking of boys and men the world over. There is the crux of the modern dilemma. For my female students the discovery of the hero journey pattern in ancient literature, modern film, or the Bible raises unsettling questions. Typically the debate revolves around the "universality" of the story and its applicability to women.

Even when students recognize flaws in Campbell's pattern of the hero's journey, most will tend to agree that the story is "universal" in the sense that it is found throughout the world's cultures and down through history. Yet strenuous disagreement arises when these same students consider whether or not the monomyth applies equally to men and women.

Some will argue that the literary fact of the main character's maleness is secondary to the message of the myth. For them, what matters is the experiential reality of our lives, which dictates that all people go through definitive stages of growth, including the necessity of moving away from home, facing the challenges of life, and growing into a wisdom that comes from the accumulation of these experiences. The message of the myth, they say, is a universal human message, not one that is exclusive to men.

Many of my female students are inspired by the Buddha story, the *Star Wars* film, the flood legend, or the Jacob story simply because they deal with the trials of life, offering clues to survival and teaching the lessons that can be gained by facing difficult and even terrifying experiences. Women, they contend, can benefit greatly from such stories. Even the flood story, they would say, carries some of these same lessons. Noah is an example to all in his willingness to obey God and stand against the drift of his times. That single-mindedness is rewarded by a divine favor that knows no gender. Noah's survival, they would say, is emblematic of all who trust God in times of crisis. This hero is male, but the enduring meaning of the story does not hinge on his gender.

Others, however, are disturbed that so much of ancient literature and the films that build on those ancient models are caught up in the male mystique. They find it difficult to relate to a hero who is compelled to sever ties with his family, when they themselves would prefer to nurture family ties between parent and daughter. These students have little time for the bravado that drives the hero on from battle scene to battle scene in an attempt to "prove" his manhood. Why, they ask, should anyone think that bludgeoning others to death over and over again has anything to do with human improvement or self-worth or honor? For such women, the *Iliad*, the Bible, the *Epic of Gilgamesh*, the tales of the knights of the Round Table, and *Star Wars* offer examples of the destructive lusts that lurk in the hearts of men in Western culture, not the heroic sentiment they purport to celebrate. For these students, the sexism of the Jacob story is just too much to stomach. Noah, likewise, is just another patriarchal fantasy, where one man's honor is won at the expense of the lives of everyone else on the planet. The psychological and theological cost of the hero's journey, they would say, is no longer worth paying.[6]

Unmasking Medusa: Bringing the Hero's Journey to an End

The feminist critic might be inclined to see the hero's journey as a patriarchal delusion of the worst sort. For these interpreters such myths need to be deconstructed and exposed as the power trips they really are or, even better, smashed and replaced with myths that elevate the feminine to its rightful status.[7] This male myth-smashing does not necessarily mean wholesale rejection of the ancient myths. It can mean rifling through them to retrieve the fragmented and fractured pictures of the feminine that are there. Feminist interpreter Jane Caputi, for example, transforms figures such as the crone, Medusa, and the spinster, arguing that the symbols need not be discarded but instead their inherent power should be tapped to affirm women's worth.

These myth-smashers and transformers point out that while women are often sequestered in subordinate stations in the myths, they nonetheless are figures of formidable power. In fact, they were so powerful both in symbol and in real life that the men felt compelled to use myths to contain and control the feminine presence in society. The frequent restriction of women in myths to such roles as mother, prostitute, temperamental goddess, and mentor of men, while degrading in many ways, serves to accent the power of women in the realms of nature, fertility, sex, and knowledge.

The Epic of Gilgamesh presents wonderful examples of all these roles. Gilgamesh's mother, Ninsun, interprets her son's dreams. She is also an intermediary between the sun god and Gilgamesh during his adventures. To be a mother here is not to be simply a baby-maker but a woman who has deep insight into the inner workings of the human mind and the cosmos. The prostitute Shamhat, who through the power of sex wrests Enkidu away from the animal world and introduces him to civilization, is a woman of great presence. When Enkidu tries to curse Shamhat for bringing him into the civilized realm and thereby paving the road to his death, the gods come to Shamhat's aid. Female guidance is the sine qua non of civilization, and Enkidu had to admit that. The coquettish goddess Ishtar tries to seduce Gilgamesh, another admission of women's seductive powers over men. But here the storyteller presses Gilgamesh to exert restraint in the face of overwhelming desire. Finally, the innkeeper and barmaid Siduri offers Gilgamesh the soundest advice of the epic. As he journeys in search of the survivor of the flood, in order to find consolation after Enkidu's death, Siduri advises him to be content with the simple pleasures of life, the food one can enjoy, and the embrace of one's wife and child.

While it is true that the women of the Gilgamesh epic function as decorative objects in the male-populated landscape, nonetheless feminist interpreters urge us not to ignore the psychological and social significance of the female figures who shape that hero's journey.[8] While they may often be disguised as bit players in the myths, it is obvious that women in ancient times were figures of power. The same can be said for many women in the Hebrew Bible.

Stagehands in an Androcentric Theater?

The Hebrew Bible presents a complex view of women. The so-called patriarchal narratives of Genesis that ostensibly revolve around Abraham, Isaac, and Jacob also contain striking female characters such as Sarah/Sarai, Hagar, Rebekah, Leah, and Rachel. These mothers of Israel get extensive airplay in these stories, so much so that Bloom and Rosenberg, authors of *The Book of J*, have argued that the writer of the J source must have been a woman.[9] Regardless of the gender of the author, the fact is that the tales of the rivalries between the various co-wives are not exactly the feminist's cup of tea. The social structures that ensnare these women are hardly desirable, yet the extended narrative of their travails is unique in the extant literature of the ancient world. The Bible puts a human face on the ancient marital institution of polygyny, a practice otherwise known only in the denatured form of surviving marriage contracts

wherein a wife agrees to secure a co-wife in the event she proves unable to produce an heir. We may deplore the practice itself, but the Bible at least is frank
about its psychological and social costs.

Prostitution is hinted at in a narrative in which Tamar is forced by her circumstances to trick her father-in-law, Judah, into siring her son. This shocking
episode shows Judah lying with a woman he assumes to be a prostitute, when
actually it is his daughter-in-law. Tamar had lost her husband, Er. She was then
jilted by another of Judah's sons, the notorious Onan, who practices coitus in-
terruptus as a way of avoiding his "levirate" marriage obligation to perpetuate
his deceased brother's line by having children with the widow. The text obviously reflects the male preoccupation with the production of heirs. Again, however, the Bible does not shrink from depicting the desperate state of the woman.
Here, as elsewhere in the Bible, woman's plight serves as a measure of the disorder of society.

Others find evidence of prostitution in the Hebrew Bible in references to
the *qedeshah*, which some translate as "cultic prostitute." This figure seems to
be connected to some sort of ritual setting in the law code of the book of
Deuteronomy (23:18–19) and in the harsh judgments of the prophet Hosea
(4:14), but whether the biblical writers are displaying their disapproval of com-
munally sanctioned "sacred prostitution" at temples and shrines is another
question entirely.[10] The Greek historian Herodotus tells a salacious story about
the Babylonians, claiming that before she can be married a women must wait
at the temple of the love goddess for a stranger to come along and pay her for
sex. This tale doubtless represents the fanciful side of Herodotus's "researches"
more than any known social reality of the ancient Near East.[11]

Like the Gilgamesh epic, the Bible does recognize the fact of goddess worship, even though it is condemned. Here and there we find references to women
kneading cakes for the Queen of Heaven (Jeremiah 7:18; 44:15–19), as well as
to women weaving garments for the goddess Asherah (2 Kings 23:7). The latter
is interesting in light of inscriptions discovered at a site known as Kuntillet Ajrud
in southern Israel.[12] Here on various pots and plaster walls have been found
brief notices of votive offerings to "YHWH of Samaria and his Asherah" or to
"YHWH of Teman and his Asherah." The god YHWH is the God of Israel, and
in these cultic inscriptions he is associated with a goddess who is elsewhere
named as the chief goddess of the Canaanite pantheon and wife of the god El,
the most important male deity of that group of gods. Only a thin veil separated
ancient Israelite religion from its Canaanite ancestors, at least as far as the popular imagination was concerned. The Bible's denunciation of these tendencies is
a sign that goddess worship was alive and well in some circles. Perhaps women
turned to goddess worship as a way to cope with their disenfranchisement by
the male priesthood of ancient Israel.

The figure of the wise woman also crops up in the biblical text. Joab, commander of King David's armies, relied on the craftiness of one such woman to

secure the return of Absalom, David's son who had been banished because of his rebellious behavior (2 Samuel 14). The woman comes before David in the guise of a widow whose only surviving son is about to be killed because he had slain his brother in an altercation. David shows mercy and extends his protection to the man. The woman then uses David's own logic to persuade him to show the same sort of mercy to his own son. David realizes that he has been had, that the woman and Joab are in league together, yet he cannot deny the cogency of her argument. The wise woman of Tekoa is thus famous for her insight and persuasiveness.

In addition, there are the heroines, women who stand up for the cause of Israel. The midwives in Exodus risk their own lives to defy Pharaoh's decree that all the male children of Israel be killed at birth. The heroism of the midwives is secondary to the survival of the male line, but the writer has clearly been struck by it. Rahab, the prostitute, conceals the Israelite spies, ensuring Jericho's eventual downfall. The deliverer Deborah and the woman Jael, who kills off an enemy commander, represent women as warriors in Israel. Most noteworthy of all is Esther, the fictional queen of Persia, who is portrayed as a strong actor in the cause of Israel's survival in a world of powerful adversaries. Finally, there is Ruth, the woman of Moab who allies herself with the cause of Israel and becomes an ancestress to King David. Her story is told with great sympathy.

All this is to say that, unlike the stories of the neighboring cultures of ancient Mesopotamia and Egypt, the Bible does offer striking portraits of noteworthy women. It may not be the women's liberation document that many would prefer, but it offers deeper insight into the lives of women than we can find in many places in the ancient world.

Some passages of the Bible put power into the hands of women, but when it is royal power, they are depicted as abusive of that authority. Jezebel, Ahab's wife, becomes synonymous with royal greed as she masterminds the assassination of a fellow countryman, Naboth, in order to add his landholdings to the royal treasuries. The ascent to the throne by Athaliah, the only woman to have become queen of Judah, is viewed as a low point in the nation's history.

More disturbing are the stories of women who are abused, beaten, tortured, or raped. Hagar's mistreatment at the hands of Sarah (Genesis 16, 21), the sacrifice of Jephthah's daughter because of a misguided vow (Judges 11), the horrific gang rape and dismemberment of the Levite's concubine (Judges 19), and the rape of Tamar by Amnon (2 Samuel 13) are deeply distressing tales. Likewise, the story of the women who are forced into cannibalizing their children during a time of war is shocking (2 Kings 6:24–7:2). The Bible by no means condones such behavior. But it is hard to know how to salvage such tales theologically except to read them in memoriam as feminist biblical critic Phyllis Trible has suggested. For Trible, they are evidence about the experience of women in the past. To brush aside that record because the stories are repugnant is to do a disservice to the women they represent. Feminists must recover whatever information they can about women in the past. If that includes a history of abuse inside a patriarchal system that is destructive of women's hopes and aspirations, then that reality must be brought to light. If the patriarchal structure betrays itself by its own literature, then the hindsight of history can help us to rethink such matters in a world that continues to paper over the abuse of women, even after so many centuries.

The Hebrew Bible offers a complex variety of portrayals of women. To the traditional mythic figures such as the mother, wise woman, goddess, and prostitute, we would have to add an array of others as suggested by the title of Susan Ackerman's study *Warrior, Dancer, Seductress, Queen*. For those who would think of the Bible as an "androcentric theater," Ackerman narrates the counterstory, the tales of those women who are military heroes, cult specialists, and queen mothers, figures of mythic power and sexual autonomy.

Noah's Wife: Silent Partner or Carping Critic?

Given all these other portrayals of women in the Bible, the text's silence about Noah's wife is doubly perplexing. She boards the ark with Noah's sons and his sons' wives. That is the end of her story.

Perhaps this is to be expected. Other Middle Eastern flood stories pay scant attention to wives and daughters. In none of these tales do the wives of the flood hero play any significant role. Utnapishtim's wife does appear in the Gilgamesh epic, but only to bake bread. This meager exception proves the rule and underlines cultural stereotypes about women. The flood story is a male preserve in the ancient Middle East. Only when we move outside the region do we find a female flood figure playing a substantive role. In Ovid's tale, Pyrrha raises questions about the value of piety before the gods. Her role is rather profound, but she has no sister spirit in the biblical or related flood legends.

We see here a lost opportunity for the Bible, which suggests elsewhere what is possible. The wife of Noah could have been a deceptive Eve, a supportive Ruth, an authoritarian Jezebel, a misused Hagar, a wily Delilah, a warlike Jael, an abused concubine, a worshiper of the Queen of Heaven, or a woman of wisdom. The writer drops the ball and loses an opportunity to make a theological statement about women through this particular mythical figure.

Imagination is the key here. We have seen the rabbis doing this very sort of work in relation to so many of the biblical characters. Doing theology through literary figures rather than by means of dry propositional logic was the staple of rabbinic thought. Several modern writers have tried this with other women of the Bible, most intriguingly the likewise narrowly construed figure of Job's wife. In the Bible, the only advice the suffering Job gets from his wife is the not so valuable directive "Curse God and die!" (Job 2:9). Yet writers, including Archibald MacLeish and Robert Frost, have seen in her slender literary figure the opportunity to speak to important theological issues.

In MacLeish's play *J.B.*, a Job-like millionaire suddenly finds his banking empire crumbling and his children killed off. Sarah, Job's wife in the play, explores the meaning of God's mercy in a world where families are torn apart. Her ability to affirm life in the face of destruction brings a stirring new message to the jaded tale of Job's rewards at the end of the biblical Book of Job.

Likewise, Frost's vignette *Masque of Reason* presents us with a tough-minded wife for Job, a woman whose feminist tendencies call into question the unsupportable logic of a biblical book that has God scoring theological points off humanity's grim suffering.[13] Job's wife creates a photo opportunity, having God, Job, and Satan pose for posterity. Frost creates an encounter with a feminine voice that undermines the supposed theological depth of the Book of Job. The woman's intrusive presence and use of the camera deconstruct the scenario, exposing the deficiencies of the explanations for evil provided by the book. Frost leaves us wondering what, if anything, was accomplished by torturing that poor, innocent man.

MacLeish and Frost rework the tradition through the eyes of the female figure, offering new insights into old theological dilemmas about human suffering and posing new questions regarding matters of divine justice and the problem of evil.

By comparison with these imaginative efforts, Noah's wife stands as a lost opportunity for creative theological work. Yet there has been one small effort in this regard that should be noted. In her book *Mr. and Mrs. Job*, Ellen van Wolde creates voices for two of the more obscure female characters of the Hebrew Bible. Job's wife and the wife of Noah write an imaginary letter to the readers of her book. In her part of the letter, Noah's wife finally emerges from the shadows. She writes,

> I appear as a character in the flood story in Genesis. I'm not so
> important. My sons are more important than I am. And my husband
> is even more important. He is the famous Noah, the hero of the
> flood. Look it up in your Bible; I'm there, but I'm always named after
> Noah and my sons. I can't complain; my daughters-in-law come off
> even worse than I do. They are only mentioned as a trio. Anonymous
> and just a member of the extended family, that's bad enough.
> Sometimes I think that I was too compliant and that I should have
> raised my voice, so that the author of the story would also have given
> my opinion. But my husband Noah isn't much of a talker either.
> He's a silent man, but a good one. I'm glad to be able to serve him.
> What makes me cross is that the only person who has given me a
> voice, the composer Benjamin Britten in *Noye's Fludde*, has made me

a carping fishwife. I grant that at that time there were lots of fish with all that water, but surely that doesn't make me a fishwife? And he even makes my dear husband hit me.[14]

Van Wolde's little missive, biting as well as humorous, drives home the point that the authors of the flood story and the Book of Job squandered valuable opportunities to explore the plight of women in their societies. The medieval world made matters even worse by concocting the shrewish figure to which van Wolde refers and Britten perpetuates in his version of the Chester miracle play. In the play, Noah's wife is so attached to her gossiping friends that she refuses to board the ark, forcing her sons to whisk her off her feet and drag her aboard. The gossiping friends run off the stage screaming. By contrast, van Wolde understands that the silence of the Bible and the distortions of the Middle Ages must be broken in order to construct a meaningful dialogue between the hallowed traditions of the Bible and the concerns of women in the present. The same could be said for the medieval rabbinic treatment of Noah's wife, who fares little better in the rabbis' hands than with Christian interpreters. The rabbis at least give her a name, Naamah, identifying her with a figure mentioned in Genesis 4:22. Some thought this name signified that she acted in a "pleasing" manner, as her name in Hebrew might seem to imply. Others saw in her name an echo of a Hebrew word for singing, though since her songs are ones of idolatry, she is hardly any nobler than the town gossip conjured up by Christian tradition.[15]

Uncovering the hidden history of women in ancient Israel will be difficult if we wish to go beyond the few tantalizing morsels of the Bible into the lived social world of women at that time and in that culture. Much will remain speculative. Much will continue to be terribly obscure. Later tradition will increase that obscurity. Perhaps this is the legacy of Noah's wife. Her obscurity is a symbol of the obscurity of so many women of ancient Israel and the ancient world. In recognizing this reality, we expose the downside of the enduring meaning of the biblical legends. The world of the flood story was a man's world, and its mythology was a male preserve, but our historical and theological task is not complete until we determine how women factor into the equation and critique that detrimental literary legacy.

IO

Can We Really Dig Up God?

Science, Myth, and the Flood Today

Those who champion the Bible tend to be rather stubborn about the believability of their faith, taking mythic metaphors to be historical events. The lavish popular magazine *Biblical Archaeology Review* and others have profited from the resulting desire to quite literally unearth the ground of faith. Other religions will stress the symbolic character of their stories, but believers in the Bible almost unthinkingly assume that Job, Noah, and Adam and Eve really lived. They do this even if they likewise believe in Darwin's theories of human evolution. This congenital conflation of faith and facts raises a number of sticky questions today. How far are we to press the question of facts when it comes to matters of faith? When the Bible seems to insist on its historical foundations, must the believer be always on the lookout for new corroboration from archaeology and science to shore up belief? The Noah's flood debates put such questions at the heart of the theological discussion. Because archaeology and science deal in data, the believer has little choice but to ask the question posed by John Romer in his chapter "Can We Really Dig Up God?"[1] In this final chapter, I move beneath and beyond the flood story to develop some general perspectives about the nature of religious belief, the workings of science, and the partnership on the horizon between them.

Desperately Seeking Faith's Elusive Facts

When I was much younger and much more naive, two books on the Bible that absolutely fascinated me were *Halley's Bible Handbook* and

Werner Keller's *The Bible as History*. The sheer number of times these books had been reprinted told me that they had to be "important." Halley's book was already in its twenty-fourth edition when I was first looking into these questions as a child, and its sales were well into the millions by that point. Page after fact-laden page, both works eagerly sought to connect the Bible with real historical events and archaeological findings. *The Bible as History*, now boasting over 10 million copies in print, made it appear that the Bible must certainly be historical in all its details. As I leafed through *Halley's Bible Handbook* for hours on end, it seemed that there really was no better way to read the Bible. Was not the Bible simply a collection of historical facts?

These books were compelling to the mind of a teenager in search of certainty at a time when life presents a myriad of unanswered questions. Most would admit that such an approach has its temptations for adults and youth alike. The stakes can seem fairly high to any religiously minded person. If history could deal us that elusive trump card, giving us archaeological artifacts that corroborate the received sacred traditions, believers might be able to breathe a collective sigh of relief. The question of whether or not *all* the rest of the Bible is historical would be forestalled as the "latest discoveries" dispel at least some of the nagging doubts. To recover the historical foundation of the tradition is more than a passing curiosity for the believer. Further headlines in *Discovering Archaeology* are eagerly anticipated.

Yet perplexities seem to dog us at every turn.

When Keller turns to the flood story in *The Bible as History*, he toys with the links to the Mesopotamian flood layers that Woolley discovered. But he backs away from that explanation, observing that the Bible's flood is a global event. He is forced to admit that "the Biblical Flood, at any rate a flood of the unimaginable extent described in the Bible, still remains 'archaeologically not demonstrated.'"[2] Does Keller want us to wait for new findings? Here, the lines between archaeology, the Bible, and the desire to prove its accuracy are too blurry for a keen reader's taste.

Halley, likewise, makes his own compromises. Dispensing with Keller's caution, Halley draws on the evidence of Mesopotamian flood layers to give archaeological credence to the Bible. This forces him to fudge the description of the global flood found in the Bible, which he curiously ascribes to Shem's conversations with his children and grandchildren. Halley is driven by his selection of archaeological evidence to suggest that the peoples of the era had "not spread far outside the Euphrates basin."[3] The Bible is saved by the suggestion that what was global for Shem is not what we would think of as global. Has the story or the archaeology been compromised here? Or both? Somehow the flood tale has been diminished even as the fundamentalist interpreter tries to make the account seem more believable.

The challenge of putting the facts to work in the service of the faith has exercised the imaginations of believers in many periods, but particularly in the early modern scientific era. As Allen points out, prior to the time of Francis Bacon (1561–1626), human reason was viewed by some as "the seed of danger and . . . a dubious gift at best," while others thought of reason as "man's hope," and still others thought of it as "an acceptable source of information provided its findings did not conflict with those of supernatural revelation."[4] As the scientific era began to unfold and reason became the preferred tool of investigation, the balancing act became more difficult. The English poet Francis Quarles (1592–1644) suggested that faith and reason offer different avenues to different sorts of truths, but the believer is still to prefer the former, though with difficulty:

> *Faith* viewes the *Sun*; and *Reason* but the *Shade*:
> T'one courts the Mistresse; t'other wooes the Maide:
> That sees the *Fire*; This, only but the *Flint*;
> *The true-bred Christian alwayes lookes asquint.*[5]

But must shadowy facts always be overwhelmed by the solar flares of faith? Milton obviously thought so, for in his *Paradise Lost* the angel counsels Adam to be content with "knowledge within bounds" but of things beyond "abstain to ask."[6] Yet Milton's contemporaries dared enter the garden of scientific knowledge and eat the forbidden fruit found therein.

Today we insist on eating the fruit of scientific knowledge. As a result, the struggle between fact and faith rages in Western culture. It is true that many early scientists linked fact and faith, believing with Bacon that no one should think "a man can search too far or be too well studied in the book of God's works" or with Robert Boyle (1627–91) that true scientific research will "facilitate . . . submission and adherence to the Christian religion," but the unsettling truth was that science very early on started turning up facts about the world's development and human origins that seemed to contradict the Bible's account.[7]

On the other hand, with such dazzling discoveries as the Dead Sea Scrolls, the "city of David" excavations in Jerusalem, or Black Sea Neolithic core samples, many believers are relying on the archaeologist's spade to support their faith. And why not? If the facts of the case turn out to be as intriguing as the legends, these historical and archaeological discoveries will inspire a greater reverence for the biblical tales. Faith might not require facts, but adherents of this view would say that believers who sift through the dirt of the archaeological dig may possibly recover a few reassuring archaic tidbits.

This wrestling with the facts can be healthy for faith. Saint Paul tells Christians that they live by faith and not by sight (2 Corinthians 5:7). However, most of us quite frankly still prefer to live by sight.

Philosophically speaking, we are children of the ancient Greeks, who early on came to shun myth in favor of rational explanations as to how the universe runs. The pre-Socratic philosopher Thales derived all from water, whereas Anaximander looked to the "infinite" as the fundamental structure of the universe, a structure that Anaximenes further refined as "infinite air."[8] Epicureans, following the teachings of Democritus and Leucippus, thought in terms of atoms, while Stoics, adopting Zeno's system, spoke of an overarching Logos (reason) as the fundamental structure of the universe.[9] Our desire to put faith and its literary traditions on a rational, historical, archaeological, and scientific footing runs deep. Which way is the believer to turn? Must there even be a choice between fact and faith?

Archaeology: Necessary Dimension or Fifth Wheel?

Does archaeology hold the key to unlock the meaning of the biblical text and ancient myth? Is the scientific approach the best? As we have seen, even Bible-thumping believers can be found frequenting the casinos of modernist historical analysis. We watch with bated breath as both secular historians and fundamentalist believers place their bets on the roulette wheel of archaeological investigation. Each imagines that archaeology has become the only real game in town, a high-stakes game of fact and faith. Who will win this antique lottery? Who will get to control the interpretation of the Bible? Should the historical approach, in fact, displace all other methods as obsolete or misleading for believers and nonbelievers alike?

Ryan and Pitman's Black Sea explorations stir great opportunities and pose new challenges for our reading of the Bible. The popularity of their book hints that archaeology has become the eyes and ears of the sacred for most moderns. Even for many believers today, excavation efforts to recover the lands of the Bible or even calibrate the waters of the flood somehow make the distant and curious world of the Bible seem more real. Coffee-table books abound, replete with lush Bible-land pictures, to bring us closer to the travails of Abraham, the wanderings of Moses, the battles of Joshua, the reigns of Judah's kings, the demise of Judah, the footsteps of Jesus, and the fall of Jerusalem at Roman hands. Archaeology would indeed appear to hold out to us the key to the mysteries of faith, clearing up much that was shrouded in darkness for our ancestors. Historical study, according to the modernist, trumps the romantic religious poetry and pious platitudes of the past by providing us a clearer and more sensible way to read the text.

True believers, so the archaeological camp would say, must pin their hopes on the "assured results" of archaeological research, awaiting each month's *Biblical Archaeology Review* with naive enthusiasm (and ready to cancel their subscriptions when archaeology appears to fail the faith test).

This was the promise held out to us in the early part of the twentieth century by pioneering excavators like W. F. Albright, who brought the biblical world to life for many readers. An examination of Albright's contribution can show us the benefits and drawbacks of "biblical archaeology" for the believer's quest.

Albright's *Archaeology of Palestine* begins deep in the prehistoric period and moves in slices right down to the times of the Christian scriptures. References to material artifacts, line drawings, site plans, and ancient writings outside of the Bible litter the text. The expectation is that the Bible, like a rabbit in its cage, will nestle down snugly in this richly articulated landscape. Albright talks confidently, for example, of tying together destruction layers in Palestine around 1200 B.C.E. with the "invasion of the Israelites" found in the Books of Joshua and Judges.[10] If building activity can be connected with King David, the link is made despite the lack of any inscriptions that would justify such a claim.[11] The same goes for Solomon, of whose dominion Albright suggests: "Archaeology, after a long silence, has finally corroborated biblical tradition in no uncertain way."[12] Likewise, the biblical record of the succeeding centuries of Israelite and Judaean monarchic rule finds archaeological connections in the course of Albright's extended discussion of those periods.

The more distant and misty past of the patriarchs in Genesis is similarly illuminated. While passing over the figure of Abraham, Albright is confident "we may date the generation to which Jacob belonged somewhere in the eighteenth or seventeenth century B.C."[13] Linguistic facts, notes of population movements, and Egyptian tomb paintings round out his historical assessment of the Jacob traditions. Albright is not altogether silent about Abraham. In another publication he turns the camel-rich figure of Genesis into an archaeologically correct "donkey caravaneer."[14] The plethora of supposed connections between archaeological artifacts and the patriarchal narratives of Genesis led Albright to conclude: "So many corroborations of details have been discovered in recent years that most competent scholars have given up the old critical theory according to which the stories of the Patriarchs are mostly retrojections from the time of the Dual Monarchy (9th–8th centuries B.C.)."[15]

Albright tackles the flood tale as well in a brief but telling statement that anticipates the direction of Ryan and Pitman's research by several decades:

> I see no reason any longer for refusing to connect the traditions of
> the Great Flood in most regions of Eurasia and America, including
> particularly Mesopotamia and Israel, with the tremendous floods
> accompanying and following the critical melting of the glaciers about
> 9000 B.C.E. It may not be accidental that there are no clear traditions
> of the Deluge in ancient Egypt, which must have escaped the worst
> of these floods.[16]

The Albright school, if such we may call it, spawned a journal, the *Biblical Archaeologist*. Increasingly those who followed Albright's approach gave the downbeat to a historical reading of the text. While there were attempts to flesh out the theology of the text in light of these findings, the emphasis was placed on secular matters of history. It was Albright's view that a proper interpretation of the Bible must "insist on the primacy of archaeology in the broad sense."[17]

Eventually there would be those like archaeologist William Dever who pushed beyond Albright, urging a complete split between Syro-Palestianian excavation and the text analysis of the Bible.[18] Dever and others began to insist that only archaeology takes us into the living world of ancient Israel. The biblical text, which can be so misleading in many aspects, must be corrected by the story the artifacts tell. There was a time when it seemed that Dever and others might push the text completely off the radar screen. Lately, in his book, *What Did the Biblical Writers Know and When Did They Know It?* Dever has backed off somewhat, calling for more dialogue between archaeologists and text scholars. The legacy of his crusade, however, can be measured by the ignominious fate of the *Biblical Archaeologist* which has been deposed by the safer-sounding *Near Eastern Archaeology*. Ironically, Albright's materialist reading of the Bible, his "inductive organismic philosophy" of Israelite history, so cogent in its general formulation, has birthed a journalistic child that no longer recognizes its parent!

Dever's latest book only adds fuel to the fire. Despite protesting that his brand of archaeology shores up the Hebrew Bible against the onslaught of the "minimalists" (who appear to wish to throw out the Bible entirely), the fact is that Dever's "Hebrew Bible" has taken a hard fall on the battlefield of archaeological analysis. While he seeks links between the biblical text and an endless array of artifacts from the time of the monarchy in Israel, many parts of the Hebrew Bible are "missing in action." Gone is Genesis's patriarchal age; gone are the Exodus and conquest stories; gone is the editorial frame of the Deuteronomistic History; gone are the "late" and "non-Israelite" wisdom texts; gone are Ruth, Esther, Job, and Daniel ("historical novellae with contrived 'real-life' settings"); gone are the "Oriental love-songs" of Song of Songs; gone are the Priestly books of Leviticus and Numbers (which are "preoccupied with notions of ritual purity"); gone are the latecomers among the minor prophets.[19] Indeed, apart from the books of 1 and 2 Samuel, 1 and 2 Kings, and a few of the prophetic texts, it looks like the bulk of the Bible has gone AWOL.

Far from bringing the Bible and archaeology together, Dever has demonstrated how much the Bible needs to be read on another basis. If archaeology is the only key, then the lockbox Dever has put his Bible into must be quite small. Sadly, this is what can happen to the Hebrew Bible when archaeologists dissect the text. While they claim to put the Bible on a richer historical basis, in fact the text is sent through the secular archaeologist's shredder to emerge in fragments that no longer fit together as a meaningful literary tradition. This approach fails to recognize the validity of other methods of reading the text, especially as a record that bears historical *significance* even if it does not accurately recount historical events. More importantly for our purposes, this shredding fails to acknowledge the Bible's theological impact and mythical insight.

The demise of biblical archaeology is not entirely the fault of secularists who would rather not deal with the biblical text or who shun theological questions.

It also has its roots in the failure of the Albright program. Albright's vivid re-construction of the various biblical periods has suffered over time precisely because it tried to make too much of the archaeological record. It is no longer possible to locate the stories of Abraham, Isaac, and Jacob in the deep past as Albright so confidently asserted.[20] The Israelite conquest of Canaan has turned out to be less than clearly supported by the archaeological record. Whereas some continue to speak of an Israelite invasion, others insist the process was one of peaceful nomadic settlement or even a peasants' revolt.[21] While we seem to be on surer ground with the Israelite and Judaean monarchies, as Dever *has* shown, the data merely fill out the background and do not tell us what to do with the Bible's own view that the end of the kingship was of profound *theological* sig-nificance for the people of Israel.

Doubtless, the Bible gains from the work of the archaeologist, as its world is more definitively revealed. The deep cultural moorings of the biblical tradi-tions are exposed. Nevertheless, the shifting archaeological tides from Albright to Dever and beyond should caution believers not to tie their faith to particular historical reconstructions. Even so, there is still value to be found in an ongo-ing dialogue between secular archaeologists, text scholars, and theologians, provided faith and fact are allowed to reach new accommodations as our view of the ancient Middle East and our estimate of biblical religion inevitably un-dergo further revisions. The secularists should not have the last word in this dialogue, if only because it narrows the frame of the discussion.

Dumbing Down the Mystery?

Like the secular archaeologists, believers also have their own way of narrowing the discussion. They, too, can become fixated on the facts of history and the results of archaeology, as if this is the core of their own story.

In this religionists cannot entirely be faulted. Believers invariably read the metaphors of the Bible as history because the Bible itself insists on a God who acts in history. The Bible opens with a God who creates the universe, fashions humans, and floods the world. The Bible depicts a God who strikes down wicked Pharaohs in their stubbornness. The Bible gives us a God who directs armies against rebellious Israel and Judah. The Bible acclaims a God who restores God's people from the far-flung lands of their captivity. The Bible presents us with a God who builds whole nations and tears them down again. The writers of the Bible were good ancients. They joined their Mesopotamian counterparts in believing that the gods not only direct the sun, wind, and rain but also govern a warrior's deeds on the battlefield, treaties forged between nations, and the affairs of the human heart. Far more than mere meteorological metaphors, the gods of ancient Mesopotamia and the God of the Bible contend with humanity on the plain of history.[22]

There is a tendency, then, for believers not to read the Bible as myth but to look for historical corroboration in the hopes that the stories will turn out to be "real." Most important for this discussion of the flood story, Bible readers have looked to the archaeologist's spade to find support for their beliefs, lending weight to the idea that the root metaphors of the Bible are best read as history.

Is this approach really productive for faith? Should we wait for the archaeologist's spade to turn up a global flood? Must the believer balance precariously on the knife edge, waiting for word from the dig before accepting the religious truth of the story?

Such a desperate search for facts carries a heavy price. Believers can be continually caught in a struggle between fact and faith. Faith would seem to call for belief in things that are not possible, such as miracles, or to accept as historical things that cannot possibly be historical, such as massive catastrophic floods that sweep away the entire world.

The temptation in this situation is to hope for more and more facts to secure one's faith. The pressure to hunt down the final fact that solidifies all of one's faith can become unbearable. Ironically, behind each new fact lie further doubts. The doubts press on to still further facts, which in turn bring forth further doubts. In the boxing match between fact and faith, it appears that faith is ever in danger of being knocked out of the ring.

Allen extends a stark warning to those who would secure their faith by more and more historical facts: "It seems to me that the efforts of the theologians to prove that this legend [the Noah story] was completely credible in every detail ended with almost a complete disavowal of the story itself."[23] He thinks of these efforts as "one of the glorious failures" of Western thought insofar as the attempt to prove the legend true spurred new thinking about geology, botany, human history, and natural science.

As captivating as this search for more facts may be, there are still more perils to negotiate. The gravest danger is that too many facts will render the mystery of faith mundane. If the fiery Lord turns out to be nothing more than a volcano, the mystery is explained and cheapened at one and the same moment. If the parting of the Red Sea is the result of a timely tidal wave, the majesty of the moment is reduced to fodder for the Weather Channel. If the Noah story owes its existence to an ancient local flood, is the power of the story thereby exhausted?

Focusing on the minutiae of the story will erode its value as either history or myth. One John Hall, cited by Allen, offered this satirical reductio ad absurdum of the Adam and Eve story to prove the point:

Whether ye reinforce old times, and con
What kind of stuff Adam's first suit was on;
Whether Eve's toes had corns; or whether he
Did cut his beard spadewise or like a T.[24]

Those who take myth seriously, on the other hand, will find in the tale of the pious Noah, his ark, and the preservation of the world's animals from divine judgment a story that resists scientific demonstration. If the story is to continue to have faith value, perhaps that value must rest on its mythic power and not its status as a fragment of hydrological history.

This is not to say that we should return to prescientific ways of thinking about seismic activity or storm currents. It is just to say that myths, when understood as such, point beyond themselves to the wonders that govern all of life. If we reduce myths to historical events and natural processes that are acceptable to the modern scientific mind, we run the risk of missing the reasons those myths have spoken to successive generations for literally millennia. To read the seven-day creation story of Genesis 1 as a poem, for example, might unlock more of its power than if we insist on its possible parallels with big bang cosmology. Perhaps the same is true of the flood story. Let us at least ask if the myth has anything to teach us before we shear away its truths to uncover its supposed "real" geological background.

The Unambiguous Text Is Not Worth Reading

The mature faith is content to live with ambiguity and multiplicity. Science and archaeology provide insight but not the sole way to read the text. Human experience is not so simply dissected, and neither is the Bible. We can learn from interpreters in the Middle Ages who played not only with the literal sense of scripture but also with its allegorical, anagogical (mystical), and tropological (moral) senses. To impress these possibilities on the student, the schools employed this ditty:

> Littera gesta docet, quid credas allegoria,
> Moralis quid agas, quo tendas anagogia.

Which translated means:

> The letter teaches events, allegory what you should believe,
> Morality teaches what you should do, anagogy what mark you should
> be aiming for.[25]

Certainly much in these medieval readings of the text was misguided. The corrective of the Reformation has also affected Roman Catholics, who now prefer a historical-critical reading based on the Hebrew-language texts of the Jewish scriptures and the Greek text of the Christian Testament.[26] Yet the centuries have taught both communions, Protestant and Catholic, that severe literalism can breed a fanaticism about the text that undermines the very values the text seeks to promote. Reading the Bible as a many-layered text, informed by the many different methods adopted by interpreters throughout the ages, can be a healthy corrective to wooden literalism about legends like the flood story.

Jewish tradition offered a similar corrective. Rabbis of the late Middle Ages came to read the biblical text on a variety of levels. Like their Christian contemporaries, they codified their insights in a memorable fashion. To remind students that scripture can be read on many levels, the rabbis used the four consonants in the Hebrew word *pardes* (enclosure, park, pleasure garden) to create a kabbalistic acronym for the fourfold layering of the Torah. As Schwartz explains, "*Peshat* is the literal level. *Remez* is the first hint of another level of meaning: in literary terms it is the use of metaphor. *Drash* stands for midrash, when the interpretation takes the form of a legend, or, in literary terms, of allegory. . . . *Sod* is the level of mystery."[27] Only one who penetrated to the fourth level could really be said to have understood the text. At this level the text has taken up residence inside the interpreter, illuminating the inner recesses of the heart and mind.

What is the lesson here?

Perhaps we should acknowledge that not all questions can be answered definitively. This is the nature of the human quest, whether in the realm of science or religion. The answers we have are merely provisional. The search for any final truths is an all-consuming, lifelong task. Faith should not shun the historian's discoveries, but neither will faith expect the historian to solve all questions. Faith can certainly benefit from seeing in the archaeologist's persistent probing a kindred spirit in the search for elusive truths. Historical truth is a moving target, not a rock upon which to build faith. Faith, likewise, has its own work to do and cannot wait for the arrival of the latest issue of *Near Eastern Archaeology* before trying to sort things out. Or, as physicist-philosopher Sir Arthur Eddington more eloquently observes:

> Verily, it is easier for a camel to pass through the eye of a needle than for a scientific man to pass through a door. And whether the door be a barn door or a church door it might be wiser that he should consent to be an ordinary man and walk in rather than wait till all the difficulties involved in a really scientific ingress are resolved.[28]

So I return to the question with which I began this chapter, namely, Can we really dig up God? Is nothing lost when we turn sacred myths into videotapes of the past? Karen Armstrong, in *A History of God*, identifies our challenge today as knowing when to take our scriptures literally and when to read them mystically. We must accept that archaeology helps us only with the literal side but does not exhaust the layers of meaning that faith can uncover in these ancient tales.

The power of the spade, in other words, does not exhaust the power of the story.

Taking the Quantum Leap of Faith

Joseph Campbell once said that there is no conflict between science and religion; the conflict is between the science of 2000 B.C. and the science of A.D. 2000. For Campbell, it was religion's task to penetrate the new scientific knowledge and reveal the mysteries that always lie beyond what science observes. The one needs the other. In more recent years, religion and science have been like two kingdoms at war.[29] Whereas religiously minded literalists have fiercely maintained that the sun stood still in obedience to God's law as Joshua fought at Jericho (Joshua 10:12–14), scientists find an ever-evolving universe obeying laws of its own making. Religion and science have been at odds on the two sides of a wall as beleaguered as that of Jericho. For a time it looked like religion was hopelessly trapped, while science's battalions were besieging the city and about to conquer their foe. Yet of late the walls have begun to tumble, with no clear victor emerging from the struggle. Both opponents remain standing in amazement, wondering who will make the next move. Will there be renewed strife or a newfound alliance?

Many scientists are becoming more candidly cautionary regarding the explanatory powers of their art. Although the decoding of the human genome "will revolutionize our understanding of our biology," says molecular biologist Johnjoe McFadden, "it will not tell us what it means to be human. For the time being, in searching for the answer to that riddle, I would still put my faith in Dostoyevsky."[30] In his college days, McFadden writes, the back cover of his student copy of *The Brothers Karamazov* made the claim that "all life is in 'The Brothers Karamazov.'" McFadden recalls that "to a young man with intellectual pretensions, the possibility of discovering the important truths about the human condition in two (admittedly hefty) volumes, and all for less than $10, seemed like a good investment." Apparently the investment is still paying dividends despite his advances in other realms of knowledge.

No doubt Dostoyevsky makes good reading. No doubt, too, science in the narrow sense ought not to have the last word on the meaning of life. Still, must one choose between them? What might happen if instead of setting aside cold scientific facts for inspiring fiction we insisted that scientists and humanists talk to one another to see where the commonalities lie? In fact, many today would argue that the equation has changed for both religion and science. Perhaps we do not have to choose between Dostoyevsky and dissecting the genome. What if the Jericho wall that has separated religionists and scientists for so long is falling down, never to be rebuilt?

On the one hand, science has increasingly opened to mystery. Recent quantum mechanics finds a universe far stranger than the mechanists of the nineteenth century could ever have imagined. As Werner Heisenberg once quipped, "Those who are not shocked when they first come across quantum theory cannot possibly have understood it."[31] When the revolution in twentieth-century science began to unfold, geneticist J. B. S. Haldane observed, "Now my suspicion is that the universe is not only queerer than we suppose but queerer than we can suppose."[32] Books attempting to plumb science's depths have poured forth in recent years. Most would agree with Roger Jones, the author of *Physics for the Rest of Us*, who as a theoretical physicist confesses, "Perhaps we all speak too soon and too glibly about space and time. They represent deep mysteries— metaphors for the very nature of being and existence. All the laws of science do not even begin to explain the mystery. They do, however, give us some insight and an important viewpoint, and they are certainly valuable."[33]

Other changes have arisen from religion's side, at least among the non-fundamentalists who are open to science's discoveries. A major player in this revitalization is the Church of Rome. The Vatican has rehabilitated Galileo and called for a religious appreciation of the wonders of human evolution. In a 1996 address to the Pontifical Academy of Sciences entitled "Truth Cannot Contradict Truth," Pope John Paul II calls for an open dialogue with the scientific community "to inform the Holy See in complete freedom about developments in scientific research, and thereby to assist him in his reflections." The pope acknowledges that the "apparent contradictions" between religion and science must be put squarely on the table. The hope is that mutual investigation and discussion will lead to a unified field theory of human knowledge, one in which the truths of science and the truths of religion are put at the service of the betterment of humankind before the Creator. While some might argue solely for the "materialist" or "reductionist" reading of the evolutionary record, the pope holds out the hope that good minds working in concert will discern the "spiritualist interpretation" of these findings. Religious truth insists on the "dignity of the person" by resisting the view that spirit and consciousness are merely accidental by-products of directionless physical processes. The pope's remarkable statement rescues the church from the old stereotype which holds that religion of necessity must denounce the findings of science when they appear to contradict the Bible or church dogma. The church is not still shadowboxing with Galileo.[34] The pope's forward-looking statement encourages good science and a thoughtful faith. Such a combination will not only promote the expansion of the horizons of knowledge but also encourage researchers to remain fully conscious of the humanistic values that must guide and inform that exploration.

This openness has not always been evident on the side of science. The nineteenth-century apostle of scientific rationalism T. H. Huxley, for example, led science's troops against a host of enemies, including the overly practical men of business, the misguided purveyors of religion, and the hopelessly nostalgic classicists who were stuck somewhere in the Renaissance as far as Huxley could determine. Huxley described the latter as seeking to thwart science "in their capacity of Levites in charge of the ark of culture and monopolists of liberal education."[35] Science was civilization's only hope of rescue from the clutches of those who held the human mind and societal progress in chains. Huxley ranges his scientific forces against those who would place literature at the heart of the academic enterprise: "I find myself wholly unable to admit either nations or individuals will really advance, if their common outfit draws nothing from the stores of physical science."[36] The certain knowledge provided by science counters the narrow-minded mythology of religion, its "mediaeval way of thinking."[37] Religion's day has come to an end for Huxley. The "scientific method" has become the "sole method of reaching truth."[38]

By contrast, Gary Zukav's exuberant treatise *The Dancing Wu Li Masters* seeks to build a dreamy Golden Gate Bridge of religio-quantum mechanics between the citadel of faith and the wild headlands of science, across the stormy waters that have increasingly divided the two disciplines. Although now dated in some aspects, Zukav's book remains relevant to current discussions about the relationship between science and religion. In the wild headlands, pioneering physicists have found a land far stranger than their nineteenth-century counterparts had ever imagined, raising deep philosophic and religious questions. Students of religion have begun to take notice.

Zukav points out the limitations of the older scientific rationalism by drawing our attention to the prolific inventor and researcher Lord Kelvin (1824–1907), for whom the Kelvin temperature scale is named and who in 1900 thought that "there were only two 'clouds' on the horizon of physics, the problem of black-body radiation and the Michelson-Morley experiment." For Kelvin, as Zukav notes, "There was no doubt . . . that they soon would be gone."[39] Science would solve all questions and presumably render philosophic musing and religious questioning moot.

In Lord Kelvin's estimation, science was standing at the end of the era of human exploration. In one sense he was right. The Newtonian era was over. What Kelvin did not see was that the spot where science was erecting its last housing project was at the edge of an abyss of startling new discoveries. Relativity thinking and quantum analysis jarred the scientific certainties of the nineteenth century, sending Kelvin's conceptual cottage hurtling down the uncharted cliffs into a mysterious realm of new possibilities and ideas. The two seemingly final problems of physics were actually chinks in the armor of the old Newtonian system. The confrontation with these and other oddities demanded the creation of new formulas, new theories, and a new era of exploration.

The Michelson-Morley experiments in the 1880s, for example, revealed the strange properties of the absolute velocity of light in a vacuum that, in part, paved the way for the general acceptance of Einstein's thinking about the time-warping and mass-enhancing events that occur as one approaches the speed of light. The study of black-body radiation led Max Planck to discern that energy was absorbed and emitted at the atomic level in "energy packets," or quanta.[40] Out of the two final problems of Newtonian physics, in other words, an entirely new view of the universe was born!

In this changing theoretical context, what do people of faith and ancient philo-sophic traditions have to offer science? For Zukav, "The new physics sounds very much like old eastern mysticism."[41] There are qualities about the new physics that Zukav finds anticipated in Hindu, Taoist, and Buddhist reflections about such imponderables as the illusory quality of our sense perceptions, the transience of the material realm, the impermanence of the ego, and the interconnectedness of all beings. Zukav champions ancient religious sensibilities that are primed for the new science's insights about the nature of reality. Quantum physics tells us that the universe is a place that generates an "endless profusion of possibilities" better studied through probability statistics than through rigid Newtonian grids. Our own participation in that realm of possibility actualizes what comes to be in our world. Zukav finds these insights alive especially in Buddhist psychology and philosophy.[42] In the interplay between Western physics and Eastern philosophy, we are opened to a realm better suited to the mystical musing of the ancients than to the mere mechanistic machinations of nineteenth-century rationalists such as T. H. Huxley and Lord Kelvin.

Thus, while some may wish for a strict division of labor, assigning "subjec-tive belief" to religion and "objective verification" to science, it appears that on the frontier between ancient philosophies and modern physics the lines between fact and faith have become very blurry. Modern physicists are increasingly aware of how our own subjective situations factor into research and analysis. For these researchers, science is no longer simply an investigation into objective physical matter by means of disembodied mathematical categories; it is also an explora-tion of our deepest selves as participant observers of this wondrous universe. Likewise, religion can no longer content itself with isolated or abstract specula-tion about the highest questions. Religion cannot afford to shun the realities of the material world in favor of blind belief.[43] In the renewed encounter between ancient and modern, our two sparring partners, science and religion, have much to offer one another. Their combined encounter with the universe's "patterns of organic energy" (Zukav's *wu li*) can reveal to each participant some of nature's closely guarded secrets and even a reflection of our deepest selves:

> Imagine that a group of young artists have founded a new and revolutionary school of art. Their paintings are so unique that they have come to share them with the curator of an old museum. The curator regards the new paintings, nods his head, and disappears into the vaults of the museum. He returns carrying some very old paintings, which he places beside the new ones. The new art is so similar to the old art that even the young artists are taken aback. The new revolutionaries, in their own time and in their own way, have rediscovered a very old school of painting.[44]

We should not overstate what the ancients have to offer, as if modern sci-ence has discovered nothing that could not already have been found in old reli-

gious texts; nonetheless, the curious findings of quantum science call for a reasoned response from the religious mind even as the scientific mind bids us to
grapple with the language of the mystics of the past.[45] We have arrived at a new
point in the dialogue between religion and science.

Zukav is hardly alone in wanting to find ways to put us in the hands of both
religion and science. Insofar as each mode of thought enables us to penetrate
deeper realities, neither can be neglected. J. B. S. Haldane thinks of each as a
necessary element in our response to life and the universe:

> Perhaps a summary of the ideal relationship of religion and science
> would be somewhat as follows:—Religion is a way of life and an
> attitude to the universe. It brings men into closer touch with the
> inner nature of reality. Statements of fact made in its name are
> untrue in detail, but often contain some truth at their core. Science is
> also a way of life and an attitude to the universe. It is concerned with
> everything but the nature of reality. Statements of fact made in its
> name are generally right in detail, but can only reveal the form, and
> not the real nature, of existence. The wise man regulates his conduct
> by the theories both of religion and science. But he regards these
> theories not as statements of ultimate fact but as art forms.[46]

This complementarity of science and religion, of physics and poetry, is captured a bit more elegantly by Max Planck: "Science enhances the moral values
of life because it furthers a love of truth and reverence—love of truth displaying
itself in the constant endeavor to arrive at a more exact knowledge of the world
of mind and matter around us, and reverence, because every advance in knowledge brings us face to face with the mystery of our own being."[47] In Planck we
arrive at a kind of scientific mysticism not unlike that of the Eastern religious
masters.

Zukav, Haldane, Planck, and others recognize that the wall that has gradually built up between science and religion in the western world over the past
several centuries and especially during the late nineteenth and early twentieth
centuries, like Joshua's walls at Jericho, is starting to fall at the trumpet blasts
of the new physics and a renewed appreciation of Eastern mysticism. Students
of religion have begun to take note of these developments and are encouraging
the conversation to move forward. On this frontier, older insights will be reap-
propriated and new perspectives will expand a very ancient horizon.

Is There Wisdom in the Western World?

There is much to commend in Zukav's work, but while he has been quite open
to Western physics, he has been less than fair to the Western religious tradition. There has in the West been long and lively discussion of the interconnec-

tions between the Christian faith and the findings of reason. Fritjof Capra, author of *The Tao of Physics*, a work that shares Zukav's blend of Eastern philosophy and new physics, admits in his Afterword to the third edition that Western mystical traditions ought to take their place beside Eastern mysticism when we are speaking about the links between ancient religion and modern physics.[48]

To make amends, Capra initiated a stimulating dialogue with Benedictine monks David Steindl-Rast and Thomas Matus, a conversation recorded in their book, *Belonging to the Universe*. This wide-ranging and penetrating discussion demonstrated that the Western religious tradition has much to offer to the dialogue between science and religion.

Matus, in particular, points out that the face of that interaction has changed over time among Christian thinkers.[49] In the first centuries the focus was on the mystical experience of God. The church fathers read the Bible on many different levels to come to grips with this experience. While Matus does not mention the early church councils, I would add that these gatherings paved the way for the more intellectual approach to faith that culminates in the achievements of Thomas Aquinas and the Scholastics. We find in the early Christian centuries and in the late Middle Ages a desire in many quarters to situate faith on a solid foundation of reason. The intellectual heirs of Thomas Aquinas and other Scholastics took a wrong turn, according to Matus, during the Reformation period. The hyperscholasticism that emerged among Catholics was focused on fighting the Protestants on dogmatic grounds, much to the detriment of the mystical side of the faith.

Matus goes on to suggest that the twentieth century saw a renewal of the experiential question and that Vatican II had opened the doors for a search for a "new paradigm." Matus and Steindl-Rast believe this paves the way for quantum physicists, monks, mystics, environmentalists, liberation theologians, and feminists to rethink the foundations of faith and the scope of science.[50] The Western religious tradition, in other words, also has a rich and diverse contribution to make to the ongoing discussion.

Within the Western religious tradition before Thomas Aquinas, Saint Augustine is a hallmark of the collaboration between science and faith. In his *Confessions*, Augustine situates the story of his own personal faith journey within the larger context of the philosophic pursuit of truth concerning the workings of the universe. He devotes large portions of his book to the workings of the mind, especially memory, which he terms the "stomach of the mind."[51] Were it not for memory, the mind would have no way to place sense perceptions in a wider frame. For Augustine, memory and the mind create certain illusions, in particular our experience of time. We ordinarily think of time in terms of past, present, and future. Augustine recognized that this is a mental construct built up out of our current sense perceptions and from our memories, and does not reflect the way the world actually is. Only God, who sees all times, experiences the world as it is. Human circumstances and limitations force us to fall back on our narrow mental capacities, which permit us only to perceive the world in short spurts of time. All times are present to God.

Time seems to be as much of an illusion for Augustine as it is for Buddhist philosophy. Our experience of the world is as much a mental construct for Augustine as for the formidable Hindu thinkers of the Upanishads, a Buddhist phenomenologist, or the philosophically reflective modern particle physicist.

If we can add Augustine to Zukav's list of ancient wu li masters, then we have to admit that the dialogue between rational investigation and religion is an ancient yet vigorous tree whose philosophic roots stretch both east and west.

Mystery and the Languages of Science and Theology

The Western tradition, whether theological, philosophic, or scientific, tells us that mystery is inseparable from our quest for truth but also that mystery alone is not enough. Both science and theology are conceptual systems that rely on language to investigate data, analyze, draw inferences, create hypotheses, and postulate conclusions. The nature of their respective targets of investigation may ultimately be unknowable, but their modes of expression are dependent on language, even if that language consists of abstractions such as mathematical equations and formulas in the case of science or abstruse philosophic reasoning and use of spiritual symbols in theology. Language matters. What form can the dialogue take between religion and science, with their diverging languages, such that the deeper realities are respected?

The structure of our study of Noah's flood story may point the way. "Literalism" about the Bible may indeed lead to great literary insights, but this path represents a dead end for dialogue between religion and modern science. Battles inevitably result. "Loose literalism," on the other hand, grants an entrée to science, quite often with favorable results, though sometimes leading to imbalances that favor secular science and history and leave religion out of the loop or in a secondary position. The "myths as nonsense" secularist stands at the opposite end of the spectrum from the biblical literalist, championing a secular naturalism and historical materialism that ignore the human need for faith and our spiritual depths. The more positive "mythic approach" affords an opportunity to draw together various strands so that the text, science, history, the human dimension, and theological awe find points of contact. Beyond "mystery," the mythic approach uses a language built around symbols, structures, and philosophic constructs and is elastic enough to foster further dialogue between religion and science. I hope that this book might contribute in some small way toward more fruitful engagement between these disciplines.[52]

The flood story has played every character in this ongoing drama of religion and science. It has been a source of conflict and back-turning independence. It has been the occasion for dialogue and the probing of life's mysteries. It has also served as a symbol of the possibilities of integration between science, myth, and belief. Undoubtedly the flood story will recede into the background, becoming a bit player at least insofar as the earth's geological history and human evolution are concerned. However, before Noah's flood takes its grand exit from the historical stage, it is worth noting the lessons gained from our study and the implications raised for the dialogue between religion and science. The world's oldest story has been at the center of a long-standing discussion, right at the heart of the Western world's theological and scientific progress. Imagining Noah's flood has been a time-honored pastime both for those who have affirmed the story in religious terms and for those who wish to expunge that story from the annals of science. Now, however, we must pen new tales to carry us into a very different theological and scientific future.

Telling New Tales of Religion and Science

Religious thinkers, at times resistant to scientific progress, are now offering olive branches to scientists. Likewise, the sciences are beginning to fashion a language that would warm the heart of any ancient mystic. Oscar Wilde once quipped, "Religions die when they are proved to be true. Science is the record of dead religions."[53] Now, however, a new horizon of thought is upon us, shaking up all our preconceptions of the relation of religion to matters of fact and the contributions of science to the affairs of the heart. It is a time to tell new tales about religion and science.

This fundamental shift has been captured imaginatively by the Buddhist monk Thich Nhat Hanh, who in a poignant short story about an ailing child brings together three worlds, those of the scientist, the artist, and the pious believer. Following a life-threatening operation for a brain tumor that had been misdiagnosed, a boy's condition worsens. His mother remains by his side at the hospital. Out of her heartfelt devotion she offers traditional prayers to the Buddha. The boy's more sophisticated uncle, an artist who practices meditation, takes a more exalted path, seeking through sitting meditation to come to grips with the boy's imperiled state. But the focus is on the scientifically minded father, who is thrust into a deep mental and emotional crisis by the possibility of his son's death. The particulars of the situation have forced the scientist-father to remain at home alone; only the mother is allowed to stay with the boy at the hospital. Restless, awaiting some news, he is unable to either eat or work because of his fear for his son.

Neither a humble believer like his wife nor a rigorous practitioner of sitting meditation like the boy's artist-uncle, the father is thrown back onto the intellectual resources at his disposal, namely, his knowledge of subatomic physics. He comes to a profound realization: "He knew that all phenomena are interdependent, that we are all part of the entire universe, and it is because we exist that other phenomena and the universe exist."[54] Moving from mere technical observation to the deeper and more humanistic penetration of reality, the father joins the Zen artist and the pious wife in an appreciation of the mystery of life and its sufferings, finding some measure of comfort. While the scientist, artist, and pious person may not be *saying* the same thing, at some profound level they are *seeing* the same thing.

When Science Spins Its Myths

Today many scientists are realizing that science's own story is akin to myth in significant ways. Ryan and Pitman offer a digested version of their own theories in a stylized outline entitled "On a Golden Pond." The contemporary reader can see in it a striking resemblance to "A Postmodern Fable," a tale penned by the French cultural theorist Jean-François Lyotard.[55]

Lyotard's basic idea is that the great myths of the Western world are dead, having dismantled themselves. Gone are the "grand narratives" that have sustained political movements and entire nations since the dawn of the Enlightenment. The biggest mythic tales of the West, the story of Liberty's triumph through the power of Democracy and Marxism's tale of the defeat of the capitalistic economic forces of evil by the workers' revolution, have faltered, betraying their ideological character.

If the great political narratives about the inevitable onward march of history toward either a Marxist utopia or a Land of Liberty no longer persuade, what remains? For Lyotard in his postmodern myth, we come to rely on science's materialistic story of the big bang with its minidrama of accidental human evolution, a dance of particles without a divine choreographer.

How does this tale end?

Lyotard carries the story on billions of years into the future to a time when the sun burns out and the earth meets its cold demise. It is truly Shakespeare's "tale full of sound and fury, signifying nothing." Escape from the solar system must be our sole aim and source of hope given the grim prospect of earth's annihilation.

Lyotard's postmodern story is, as he is clever enough to realize, a myth of the Western world. Not myth in the sense that it is scientifically false or without factual support, but in the sense that this is the narrative that governs our thinking and shapes our values more deeply than most of us consciously realize or are willing to admit.

Perhaps Ryan and Pitman also recognize that science's myth of human origins, or even their own tale of Neolithic catastrophe and dispersion, is compelling because it draws on the ancient tales to construct a new "myth" rather than using science to sidestep our ancestor's literary legacy. Loose literalists, in other words, seek today to balance our common mythic inheritance with a critical use of science. Whether the stories science tells are sufficient to overcome philosophic anxiety about our minuscule place in this vast universe is another issue entirely. Only serious dialogue between religion and science can answer that question.

Dialogue between Equals

If humans are nothing else, we have proven ourselves over the millennia to be mythmakers. The Bible's legend of Noah, the scientific tale of the Neolithic flood, and the story of the big bang are kindred intellectual spirits. If we do not acknowledge the mythic qualities of our postmodern contribution, we will delude ourselves into thinking we have traveled farther beyond the mind-set of our Neolithic forebears than we actually have. Einstein was quite right when he said, "The unleashing of the power of the atom bomb has changed everything except our mode of thinking and thus we head toward unparalleled catastrophes."[56] A chastened science can fashion tales that will call us back from the brink of nuclear madness. Francis Crick treated science as the antidote to belief in myth, but Arno Penzias, a Jewish believer who shared a Nobel Prize with Robert Wilson for astronomical work related to the big bang, regards Crick's attitude as "complete scientific arrogance." For Penzias, ancient religious teachings and myths have opened doors that science can also enter.[57] Such a dialogue at this precarious juncture in human history is a moral imperative if we want to secure a viable future for planet Earth.

In this changing intellectual climate and period of global awakening, we must encourage archaeology and biblical faith to see if they might have new things to say to each other. As archaeology literally uncovers the ground of faith, faith can rekindle a sense of wonder for that newly unearthed terrain. While theology may no longer be the queen of the sciences as it was in the Middle Ages, recent developments in scientific thought no longer permit science to play the part of an arrogant Henry VIII chopping off the heads of unwanted theological brides. According to physicist Sir Arthur Eddington, the "iron bound" period of the "dominion of . . . physics" is finished: "That overweening phase, when it was almost necessary to ask the permission of physics to call one's soul one's own, is past."[58] Both realms of thought are exploring profound realities, even as each speaks its own unique language. Slowly but steadily each is learning to appreciate the very real truths the other has to offer.

Many definitions are possible for science and religion. Setting my own side by side reveals something of the difference and similarity in theory and practice:

Science	Religion
The investigation and analysis of the essential patterns and structures of the material world.	The individual and communal ritualization of sacred symbols and spiritual stories that are of transcendent significance.
This analysis is done in terms of systematic observations that rely on a range of rationally based investigatory methods (such as classification, experimentation, field research, mathematical models, and falsifiable theoretical constructs).	This ritualization is done in terms of meditative and worship practices that can (but need not) involve an intellectual interpretative component (such as exegesis, allegorization, philosophic speculation, apologetics, or other systematic theological constructs).

How can these two systems speak to one another? Is this like asking whether there is an intersection between art and science, two very different realms of human experience that complement one another but need not be in regular dialogue? Or is it more like asking about ethics and medical research, which need to be in constant contact with one another? In the case of ethics and medi- cal research, when these disciplines fail to regularly interact, we are left in a dangerous place as a society. What is the mode of interaction that is required of science and religion?

Stephen Jay Gould points the way toward a more constructive conversation. His lively and insightful volume *Rocks of Ages: Science and Religion in the Full- ness of Life* depicts two domains in dialogue. How can religion and science be put on an equal footing, to stand together as partners rather than against one another as combatants? Gould does not make the mistake of fusing the realms together, as if religion and science were merely flip sides of the same method- ological coin. Rather, he insists that each partner to the conversation be given free rein in its own domain, wherein science superintends the facts of the ma- terial world even as religion regulates the affairs of the heart. Or in Gould's epigrammatic formulation, "Science gets the age of rocks, and religion the rock of ages."[59] Establishing differing game plans in this vigorous though respectful intellectual sparring match, Gould suggests that "each domain frames its own rules and admissible questions and sets its own criteria for judgment and reso- lution."[60] Gould dubs this relationship, "non-overlapping magisteria" (NOMA). While this might seem like a recipe for an end to meaningful conversation, Gould finds that if each partner can honor the mode of inquiry and findings of the other, a fruitful dialogue can actually emerge: "Instead of supposing that a single ap- proach can satisfy our full set of concerns ('one size fits all'), we should prepare to visit a picture gallery, where we can commune with several different canvases, each circumscribed by a sturdy frame."[61]

If we create room for both solid science and rich religious reflection, Gould suggests, their candid conversation and intelligent integration (not fusion!) will produce both the factual understanding we need and the ethical underpinnings we must have to live a life of wisdom.[62] But each must see the other as a genuine dialogue partner, not simply a foil. Gould is especially concerned about unconstructive interference of one side in the domain of the other. Each side must acknowledge its limits, so that religionists stop mounting creation science forays into science's domain and scientists stop launching moral crusades on the basis of supposed scientific "truth." As Gould explains, "NOMA . . . cuts both ways. If religion can no longer dictate the nature of the factual conclusions residing properly within the magisterium of science, then scientists cannot claim higher insight into moral truth from any superior knowledge of the world's empirical constitution."[63] When it comes to matters of "morals and aesthetics," in other words, "science cannot answer these questions alone and science cannot dictate social policy."[64] Only a savvy science and a robust religion—"Religion just can't be equated with Genesis literalism"—will serve society at this critical time in human history.[65]

The need for that dialogue comes into focus with a rather ironic and disturbing modern twist on the flood story. Even as God's power to send a worldwide flood to destroy the earth has been called into question by the historian's rewriting of the biblical past, science has enabled us to arrogate that world-destroying power to ourselves. Many physicists are pressing us to confront the moral dilemmas that arise when we elect to put the new physics in the service of war and destruction. The terrible dangers are faced squarely by quantum physicist Louis de Broglie, famed discoverer of the wave nature of electrons, who writes, "The era of atomic energy can be an era of admirable progress, an era of a better and easier life. But it can also be an era of inexpiable strife, surpassing in extent and horror all the wars of the past where, with the aid of terrifying means of destruction, humanity runs the risk of completely destroying itself."[66] Science gives us the knowledge of unlimited energy, the godlike power to shake the earth. But will we have the moral courage to follow the flood God's example and make a covenant not to destroy the earth with a storm of nuclear devastation? Can we devise a modern equivalent to God's commitment not to kill again?: "When I make clouds appear over the land, the war bow will be seen in the clouds. In that moment, I will call to mind my agreement between myself and all of you, with every living being, and with every animal: the flood water will never again destroy all creatures" (Genesis 9:14–15). Ironically, while moderns find distasteful this image of a vengeful God who punishes the planet, we remain blind to the fact that this image is but a reflection of our collective selves in our worst moments. The Bible urges us beyond vengeance toward compassion and renewal. How can we make the move? De Broglie pins his hopes on a recovery of the mystical way: "Often the feeling of the imminence of a danger gives birth in the heart of men to sentiments or mysticisms which can serve to avoid it."[67] We can only hope that he is right. Now, more than ever, we need a renewed dialogue between science and religion not just out of an antiquarian interest to recover the meaning of ancient myths but to ensure there is a future in which we can continue to tell those tales.

We arrive, then, at a new place in the age-old battle between faith and fact. When integration is pursued cautiously and insightfully, faith can be nourished by facts, and facts can underscore faith. To be sure, faith should not be reduced to the facts, made mundane rather than mysterious. Likewise, while piety does not necessarily arise out of proof, the facts can breed the amazement that is the ground of a healthy faith. Certainly, faith will be cautious about the facts, since faith must not become dependent on a particular scientific theory or historical reconstruction. Indeed, faith will refuse to be taken hostage by specific theories and reconstructions precisely because every time this has happened, faith has been the loser and has had to race to catch up to the scientists and historians who discarded the old theories and historical reconstructions and moved on. Yet faith will not turn its back on the facts, being willing to be challenged and deepened by the encounter between facts and faith. Faith will not become wedded to Ryan and Pitman's ideas, but it will still be inspired by their achievement and until a better theory emerges will at least be informed by their compelling argument. In the end, however, faith must remain free to set its own terms for entering the dialogue, if only to remain a vital partner in what is sure to be a long-term discussion whose final word has yet to be uttered. Likewise, faith will respect the fact that science must also set its own terms for participation. No longer will we allow scripture to dictate what science must "find." For there to be genuine discussion, the give-and-take between science and religion must likewise be genuine. This is the best ground for future progress in both realms as faith and fact weave anew the garments of truth.

Whatever the outcome, our effort to know the truth of the matter changes irrevocably the way we receive those tales and how we understand ourselves. While we may seem to have moved far away from the story of the flood in this chapter, our study of that story has provoked a new assessment of the relationship between fact and faith. As we turn from the ancient story to the new stories that are being written about science and belief, we see that we can excavate beneath the sea and sands to seek to discern the meaning of the myth for its own time, or we can reverse the process and use the myth to excavate ourselves both personally and collectively. The flood story offers us examples of some of the possibilities that arise. Historical archaeology can help us to ground the myth in historical realities that guide us to its point of origin and ancient significance, while through inner archaeology we use the myth, as Joseph Campbell would say, to explore the inner reaches of outer space.[68]

Let us continue, then, to dig for the flood, but let us also continue to let the flood story dig away at our deepest selves. We not only will discover the wisdom the ancients wish to pass on to us but also will look at ourselves and our civilization steadfastly in the mirror to judge what we can contribute to this ancient and ongoing conversation between fact and faith.

Conclusion

Telling Many Different Stories

I began this book by asking, What is the truth of Noah's flood story, and how is that truth to be found?

The pages in between have taken us on an oceanic odyssey spanning the ages. We have traversed great waves of tradition and encountered rough ideological waters. The four camps and their various nuances have pointed to very different ways to read the text and have drawn very different lessons concerning its essential meaning. Each reading tends to pitch itself as the best way to read the text. While I have been pulled toward the mythic reading, I readily admit that each offers insight. If we are careful not to limit ourselves to one reading or one school of thought, we will find that there are many truths contained in the flood story and that there are many different ways of unlocking those truths.

What, by way of summation, do the camps have to offer?

The strict literalists, our first camp, press us to pay attention to the text as such. They do not want us diverted by the glitz and glamour of geological explanations or by historical theories that frequently vie for center stage. Thus, we have tried to look at the text itself in all its detail. We have seen that Genesis is a world unto itself, a rich land-scape that, like a scenic overlook on a picturesque highway, invites us back again and again to discover an ever-changing array of engrossing sights. Strict literalism, despite its limitations, underscores the fact that the text always has its own tale to tell, a tale that we should not overlook in our zeal to find the "meaning behind the text."

Loose literalism, the second camp, takes us into that world behind the text. While this is a more speculative enterprise, perhaps the reader will have at least appreciated the spirit that has energized so many efforts to try to make rational, historical, scientific, and geological sense out of the flood story. Loose literalism offers a fascinating jumble of perspectives, even if we are not entirely convinced by the various "theories of the earth," fundamentalist flood geologies, ancient Near Eastern connections, climbs up Mount Ararat, or Ryan and Pitman's more sophisticated reading. These efforts may not actually take us into the world that produced the text or explain the "true history" behind the text, but they do tell us a lot about ourselves as we seek, however vainly, to put religion on some sort of rational basis.

Those who see the story as myth but who also prefer to treat myth in a cautious manner, our third camp, are right to observe that religion often obscures the truth when it insists on having veto power over the perspectives of science. This scientifically minded assessment recognizes that there are strains of religiosity that are threatened at the prospect of having to revise long-held beliefs. There are believers who are perplexed by new discoveries that stand outside the purview of cherished doctrines. If nothing else, the secularists remind us that truth is wider than any single system of religious teachings can encompass and that the search for truth can take many forms beyond spiritual speculation. While I have tried to press the secular reading of myth beyond its own narrow construal, nonetheless references to more secular views have kept us from engaging in mythic and religious flights of fancy ungrounded in sound scientific thinking and good historical investigation. More dialogue is needed. Clearheaded science will prod us along. Religiosity without these elements must surely fall short of a complete vision of the truth.

As for the fourth camp, those who promote a deeply humanistic appreciation of myth as sacred literature offer us an additional perspective and may even hold out the possibility of a healthy compromise among all four approaches. By treating these stories as sacred myths that speak deeply to enduring questions, we tie together loose ends. Many readers, regardless of which camp they belong to, should be sympathetic with this approach: it takes the stories seriously as stories (which ought to please the strict literalist at some level), it remains curious about the world behind the text (which should win over the loose literalist), and it acknowledges the dangers of unchecked mythic speculation (such that even T. H. Huxley will find something to affirm here), particularly in matters of race and gender. Yet to be fair, even this view has its limitations insofar as it prefers to study the stories rather than live them out. Much as I am enamored with the "power of myth" language, I realize that this is a modernist's way of mediating between the ancient world where myth once lived and the religious studies department office bookshelf, where those same myths run the risk of either gathering dust or being dissected under a microscope. The fourth camp, in other words, needs the others to keep its own understanding vibrant and alive.

There are four sets of lessons that can be gleaned from the approaches taken by our interpreters. In some ways these lessons run parallel to the four camps

we have distinguished in this book, but they also tend to bleed across the boundary lines, reminding us that the separate camps have more in common than
each might admit.

Those who focus on the biblical text itself, no matter from what perspective, ask us to do *literary* archaeology. While the fundamentalist, the liberal, and
the ancient rabbis do not agree on what they derive from the tale, their digging
into the literature unearths a stunning mosaic of meanings lodged beneath the
crusty surface of the text. The three groupings find quite different truths. Fundamentalists uncover unifying themes and underlying patterns. Liberals discern
conflicting voices. And the rabbis disclose divergent points of departure for their
fertile theological imaginations. However, they are united in their primary orientation: the truth of the matter is to be found by dissecting the text. While literary archaeology may have its drawbacks, there seems to be an endless array
of literary artifacts that await our discovery whenever we decide to seriously
ponder the inner workings of the text.

Those who read the text more loosely ask us to look beyond the text to find
the truth behind the story. And so we have turned to *spade* and *seagoing* archaeology to see what the story is that lies back of the written word. The work of
Ryan, Pitman, and Ballard is the latest in a long series of attempts to put the
story of the flood on some more rational basis. Ever since the advent of modern
science, we have found ourselves increasingly looking to the tools of human
reason to excavate for us the true meaning of the tale. In this latest phase, dirt
archaeology and marine exploration have become for us the eyes and ears of
the sacred. The possibilities are dramatic and tantalizing, even if in the end we
remain unconvinced in all the details. Like the literary archaeologist, the spade
and marine archaeologists present a wide range of views. Despite the diversity,
however, these theorists are united in insisting that the truth of the matter is
not imprisoned under biblical lock and key but is best found where the text in-
terfaces with the record of the past. This view takes the text seriously as an arti-
fact of ancient society, reflecting the values, beliefs, and experiences of that world.
While such an approach must be speculative, we are reminded not to neglect
the tools that permit a sifting of the world behind the text.

Those who read the story as myth strike out on a different trail. Secular
writers and archaeologists who treat myths as nonsense are warning us against
doing *bad* archaeology and *bad* theology.

In terms of bad archaeology, they worry about our using the Bible as if it
were some sort of Michelin guide to the undersoils of the Middle East. They
fear that we will confuse fables in a book with the facts on the ground. They are
concerned that we will interpret what we find through the distorted lenses created when myths and biblical stories are read as if they recount actual historical
events. Their worries are well-founded. How often have we seen interpreters go
awry when they try to turn the Bible into a science textbook? The data scream
out for a more cautious and scientific assessment, but believers have often in-

sisted that material facts be forced to conform to their particular reading of the Bible. Putting the Bible first has often led to bad excavation results precisely because all the artifacts arc made to support a predetermined understanding of the biblical record. It is true that those who rely solely on philosophic reason or experimental science may too easily dismiss vital perspectives that come from serious literary excavation of myths, the Bible, and even from archaeology, but we have also seen that an excessive reliance on the biblical text can lead to abuses of both the ancient stories and science itself. If the "science-only" types do not have all the answers, at least their worries are sound ones. We will only get to the truth of the matter to the extent that we construct a solid conversation between informed scientific observation and religious commitments grounded in good theoretical sense.

If we are going to speak about bad archaeology, we must also note the dangers of bad theology. Those who practice bad theology, as we know from elsewhere in the Hebrew Bible, are scolded by God. In the Book of Job, Job's theological buddies were chided by God for offering religious views that may have been traditionally accurate but were woefully inadequate in the challenging circumstances faced by the suffering Job (Job 42:7–9). For the writer of the Book of Job, old views of God had to give way to new insights based on new experiences. The same holds true for Genesis. Twisting the flood story to authorize racist attitudes, the persecution of sexual minorities, or the disenfranchisement of women is to make inappropriate use of the Bible. Such readings deserve the caveat offered by feminist interpreter Elizabeth Schüssler Fiorenza: *"Caution! Could be dangerous to your health and survival."*[1] Bad biblical theology, like bad biblical archaeology, short-circuits the openness required by the renewed dialogue between religion and science that is now under way. From the religious side, we need a sophisticated view of the Bible that is adequate to the new challenges posed by science and secular analysis. We need a Bible that is a genuine partner to the dialogue, not simply a relic of the past that stifles new wisdom about matters of race, society, and gender. The secularist may not supply the final answers to questions of faith, but the skeptical approach offers valuable insight by insisting that theology and biblical interpretation stand up to rigorous scrutiny.

In the course of this discussion, we have also seen that the flood stories can be read as anthropological artifacts that attest to our collective pursuit of enduring truths. From this vantage point, the meaning of the tales here becomes clear only through *psychic* archaeology. To probe the mythic meaning of the ancient flood legends is to probe our deepest selves. Through such tales we come to see the integral character of the core values and virtues that have woven together entire civilizations throughout the centuries. To look into these tales is to look into the mirror of the human past, where we discern the traits and dispositions that make us who we are, provided we are willing to face the fact that our "modern" minds are still fueled by fumes from the distant Bronze and Iron Ages.

The psychic excavator finds disturbing truths in these flood stories: in myth, we are confronted with the darker potentialities of our deepest selves.

Literary archaeology, spade and seagoing archaeology, bad archaeology (and bad theology), or psychic archaeology? Which approach shall we take? There are many routes, signposts, detours, and roadblocks on a journey toward discovering the truth of the flood story. This book has taken us down all these paths. We have had to ask many different questions of the texts and the artifacts, and we have found that they have many different stories to tell. Each excavator, whether of the text, the ground, the sciences, or the mind, opens a multitude of possible readings of the stories and the past. Some become fixated on one particular reading or one restricted understanding of the truth. But if we can step back and listen to the seemingly chaotic undertones of the ongoing debates, we will also begin to hear a chorus of symbols and truths that should arouse a sense of wonder over stories that have stood at the heart of the human enterprise for centuries, stories that are even now receiving a new hearing from religionists and scientists.

To conclude our exploration of this enduring tale, it seems fitting to end with a story about stories.

Salman Rushdie offers us another sort of aquatic tale in his children's book, *Haroun and the Sea of Stories*. In this thinly veiled political farce, the elder Rashid Khalifa, derided by his critics as the Shah of Blah, loses his gift of storytelling. He is saved by his son, Haroun, and his son's ragtag companions, who learn how to outwit the evil Khattam-Shud (Mr. "Completely Finished"), who was poisoning the Ocean of the Streams of Story with potent "anti-stories." This ocean "contained different sorts of stories, and as all the stories that had ever been told and many that were still in the process of being invented could be found here, the Ocean of the Streams of Story was in fact the biggest library in the universe."[2] This ocean was in danger of toxic destruction at the hands of one who wanted to control what people wished for, demanding uniformity of thought and conformity of opinion.

Rushdie warns us not to prematurely cut off our search by privileging one tale and stamping out all others. His call to water-lovers and storytellers is potent: plunge deep into the Ocean of the Streams of Story. The final chapter has yet to be written in our scientific and mythic saga. Who knows what questions we must now ask? Who knows what new yarn we must yet spin? Doubtless there are many stories of archaeology and myth that remain to be told.

Dive in!

Appendix

The J and P Versions of the Flood Story

For the reader's reference, I have broken down the two versions
of the biblical flood story into their component parts. The first
selection is the Yahwist story (J), wherein the volatile YHWH
judges the world. The second selection presents the more staid
and verbose God of the Priestly writers (P). I indicate the verse
numbers so that the reader can see how the two stories have been
woven together by the Genesis editor. Scholars will quibble about
the precise divisions between the J and P material, especially
where the final editor may have embellished J here and there
with P-like wording (Genesis 6:7; 7:3a) as Gunkel observed in his
commentary on Genesis; I rely here on the identifications presented
in Friedman's *Who Wrote the Bible?* The translation is my own.
Despite any embellishments by the final redactor, the two versions
of the flood story are virtually self-contained, except insofar as the
extant J version lacks a description of the actual construction of
the ark. This segment may have been omitted by the editor in favor
of the more extensive P version of the ark's construction or may
not have been present in the original J version. The J material
reads well enough without the scene. The two versions differ in
significant ways, especially in terms of chronological details and
their portrayals of the deity, suggesting that neither version was
originally a conscious expansion of the other but formed separate
streams of tradition that were merged well into the period of exile
in Babylon, where the various Israelite versions of the flood tale

may have arisen in the first place. Putting all of the J segments in order highlights the temperamental YHWH known from the Garden of Eden expulsion story, the Cain and Abel episode, and the subsequent story of the Tower of Babel. Likewise, treating the P segments as a unit helps to clarify the literary connections to Genesis 1. The puzzle, of course, is why the two versions were merged rather than having one simply displace the other.

The J Version of the Flood Story

Genesis 6:1–8

When people began to increase in number throughout the land and daughters were born to them, the divine sons took note of how delightful the mortal daughters were and selected as wives whomever they wished. As a result YHWH exclaimed, "My spirit will not contend with these people for ever, for they are merely flesh. Henceforth their lifetimes shall be no more than 120 years." The giants were in the world in those days and also afterward when the divine sons had intercourse with the mortal daughters who bore offspring to them, those mighty heroes who have been hailed since ancient times. Then YHWH saw that people were doing evil everywhere in the world; every intention was toward wickedness every day. And YHWH regretted that he had brought people into the world. Because he was troubled within, YHWH said, "I will wipe from the surface of the land the people I have created, the entire lot: people, cattle, crawlers, and the birds of the sky because I regret that I ever made them." But YHWH liked Noah.

Genesis 7:1–5

So YHWH said to Noah, "Go, you and all your family into the ark, for I have seen that you are a just person before me in this generation. Take for yourself some of the ritually pure cattle, seven pairs, the man and its woman, and from the impure take two, the man and its woman. The same with the birds of the sky, seven pairs, the male and the female, so that seed will survive throughout the world. Because in seven days I am going to send rain over the world, for forty days and forty nights, wiping away from the surface of the land every creature that I made." So Noah did everything that YHWH ordered him to do.

Genesis 7:7

Noah entered the ark along with his sons, his wife, and his sons' wives to escape the flood.

Genesis 7:10

Then, seven days later the flood befell the world.

Genesis 7:12

The storm raged over the world for forty days and forty nights.

Genesis 7:16b–20

YHWH had shut [the door] behind him. The flood covered the world for forty days. The water swelled, lifting up the ark so that it rose above the world. The water was energized, swelling even more over the world as the ark rode on the surface of the water. The water showed great force throughout the world, covering all of the highest mountains beneath the broad sky. Covering the mountains by fifteen cubits, the waters revealed their strength.

Genesis 7:22–23

Everything that once lived on the dry ground died, all that had life's breath in its nostrils. He wiped away every creature that lived on the surface of the land, whether human, cattle, crawler, or bird of the sky. They were wiped from the world; only Noah and those with him in the ark remained.

Genesis 8:2b–3a

He stopped the storm in the sky. The water turned away from the world, backing further and further away.

Genesis 8:6

When forty days had passed, Noah opened the window of the ark that he had made.

Genesis 8:8–12

He sent forth the dove to see whether the water had receded from the surface of the land. But the dove did not find a resting place for the bottoms of its feet, so it returned to him in the ark because the water still covered the surface of the world. With his hand, he reached out and drew the dove back into the ark. He waited for another seven days and again sent out the dove from the ark. When the dove returned in the evening there was a freshly plucked olive branch in its beak! Then Noah knew that the water had receded from the world's surface. Still, he waited yet another seven days and sent out the dove, but this time it did not return.

Genesis 8:13b

Noah drew back the ark's lid and saw that the surface of the land was dry.

Genesis 8:20–22

Then Noah built an altar to YHWH, and he offered up sacrifices from some of the ritually pure cattle and some of the pure birds. YHWH smelled the pleasing aroma and thought to himself, "I will never again curse the land because of its inhabitants even though their minds are set on evil from their youth. I will never again strike every living being as I have done. So long as the world endures there will be sowing and harvest, cold and heat, summer and winter, day and night. They will not come to an end."

The P Version of the Flood Story

Genesis 6:9–22

This is the line of descent from Noah: Noah was just and blameless among his contemporaries. In fact, he walked with God. Noah fathered three sons, Shem, Ham, and Japheth. The land was corrupt before God; the land was filled with violence. God saw the world, that it was corrupt because all living beings had come to live corruptly throughout the land. So God said to Noah, "The end of every living being in my sight has arrived. The land is full of violence because of them. I am about to destroy them and the land. Make an ark using *gopher*-trees. You must put rooms in the ark. You will need to cover it inside and out with tar. Here is how you will make it: 300 cubits long, 50 cubits wide, and 30 cubits high. You must make a roof [skylight?] for the ark, finishing it one cubit above. You must put a door for the ark in its side. You will need to make a bottom level, a second, and a third. I am about to bring the flood throughout the land to destroy every living being in it—those that breathe beneath the sky. Everything in the world will perish, but I will make my agreement with you. You will enter the ark—you, your sons, your wife, and your sons' wives along with you. Of all that lives, all flesh, you may bring two of each into the ark so that they may survive along with you. They will be male and female, from every type of bird, from every type of cattle, from every type of thing that crawls on the ground; two of each will come to you in order to survive. And as for yourself, take some of every kind of food that is eaten; gather it up for yourself, so that it can serve as food for yourself and for them." Taking into account all that God ordered him to do, Noah did just that.

Genesis 7:6

Noah was 600 years old when the flood hit the land.

Genesis 7:8–9

From the ritually pure cattle and from those cattle that were not pure, from the birds, and from the creatures that crawl on the ground, two pairs came to Noah in the ark, male and female, in just the way that God had instructed Noah.

Genesis 7:11

In the 600th year of Noah's life, in the second month, on the seventeenth day of the month, all the hidden reservoirs of the great abyss burst open, and the windows of the sky opened up.

Genesis 7:13–16a

On that same day, Noah, Shem, Ham, and Japheth—the sons of Noah—together with Noah's wife and the three wives of his sons all entered the ark, along with every type of beast, all types of cattle, every kind of crawling thing that crawls along the ground, every type of bird, any bird with any kind of wing. Representatives of every sort of living creature that breathes came in pairs to Noah into the ark. Those that came were male and female from every type of animal, just as God had instructed Noah.

Genesis 7:21

Every creature perished, those that crawled in the land or lived among the birds, cattle, beasts, or other creatures that swarmed the world. Indeed, every person died.

Genesis 7:24–8:2a

The water exerted its force throughout the world for 150 days. Then God took note of Noah, of every beast, and of all the cattle that were with him in the ark. God drew a wind across the land, and the water receded. The hidden reservoirs of the deep were shut along with the windows of the sky.

Genesis 8:3b–5

The water diminished at the end of the 150 days. The ark came to a rest on the mountains of Urartu in the seventh month, on the seventeenth day of the month.

The water kept thinning out until the tenth month. On the first day of the tenth month the tops of the mountains were visible.

Genesis 8:7

He sent forth the raven, and it flitted about until the water on the land dried up.

Genesis 8:13a

In the 601st year, on the first day of the first month, the water on the land dried up.

Genesis 8:14–19

In the second month, on the twenty-seventh day of the month, the land was completely dry. So God said to Noah, "Depart from the ark, you, your wife, your sons, and your sons' wives with you. Bring out every animal—the birds, the cattle, and the crawlers that crawl on the land—so that they can swarm throughout the land, and be fruitful, and increase throughout the land." Then Noah went out along with his sons, his wife, and his sons' wives. Every beast, every crawler, every bird, everything that crawls on the land came out of the ark by families.

Genesis 9:1–17

God blessed Noah and his sons, saying to them, "Be fruitful! Increase! Fill the land! All who live in the land and every bird in the sky will be overcome with fear and dread because of you. Furthermore, everything that crawls on the ground and all the fish in the sea are given over into your power. Every crawler that lives will become your food. Just as I have given you the green plants, I also give everything to you. Just do not eat meat with its life, its blood, still inside. I will make an exaction for your lives, for your blood. I will make an exaction from every beast, from each person, each person in connection with his brother, making an exaction for the life of that person. As for the one who sheds blood, on account of that person his blood will also be shed because [God] made people in God's image. But as for you, be fruitful and multiply! Swarm throughout the world! Increase in it!" Then God said to Noah and his sons, "I am about to confirm my agreement with you, with your heirs after you, and with every living being that is with you—birds, cattle, every wild animal, all who came out of the ark, indeed every creature of the world. I will confirm my agreement with you. Never again will all beings be cut down through such a flood. Never again will there be a flood to destroy the world." God said, "This is the sign of the agreement that I am about to make with you and with every living being that is with you for all generations ever after. I have put my war bow in the clouds to serve as the sign of the agreement between myself and the world. When I make clouds appear over the land, the war bow will also be seen in the clouds. In that moment I will call to mind my agreement between myself and all of you, with every living being, and with every animal: the flood water will never again destroy all creatures. When the war bow is in the clouds, I will see it and recall the permanent agreement between God, all living beings, and all creatures in the world." Then God said to Noah, "This is the sign of the agreement that I have confirmed between myself and all the creatures that are in the world."

Notes

CHAPTER I

1. W. Ryan and W. Pitman, *Noah's Flood: The New Scientific Discoveries about the Event That Changed History* (New York: Simon and Schuster, 1998), pp. 95–96.

2. Ibid., pp. 97–99.

3. Ibid., p. 101.

4. Ibid., pp. 101–2.

5. Ibid., pp. 119–42.

6. Ibid., pp. 143–51.

7. Ibid., p. 160.

8. Ibid., p. 160.

9. Ibid., p. 184.

10. Ibid., p. 187.

11. Ibid., chaps. 16–18.

12. Ibid., p. 213.

13. Ibid., chap. 19.

14. Ibid., p. 238.

15. See also R. Ballard, "Mysteries of the Deep Black Sea," *National Geographic* 199, no. 5 (2001): 52–69. Ballard's Black Sea adventure is also detailed in R. Ballard and M. McConnell, *Adventures in Ocean Exploration: From the Discovery of the Titantic to the Search For Noah's Flood* (Washington, D.C.: National Geographic 2001), pp. 260–79.

16. www.ngnews.com/news/1999/11/111899/ ballard_flood.asp.

17. www.ngnews.com/news/2000/09/09132000/blackseadisc_3014.asp).

18. www.ngnews.com/news/1999/11/111899/ballardflood_7432.asp.

19. See B. Z. Wacholder, *Nicolaus of Damascus* (Berkeley: University of California Press, 1962), p. 55; Josephus, *Antiquities* I.95 (Loeb edition);

L. R. Bailey, *Noah: The Person in History and Tradition* (Columbia: University of South Carolina Press, 1989), pp. 63–64.

20. Bailey, *Noah*, chap. 4.

21. J. W. Montgomery, *The Quest for Noah's Ark*, 2d ed. (Minneapolis, Minn.: Bethany Fellowship, 1974), pp. 70–74.

22. Ibid., pp. 80–81.

23. Polo, *The Travels*, trans. R. Lathan (New York: Penguin, 1958), p. 48.

24. F. Parrot, *Journey to Ararat*, trans. W. D. Cooley (London: Longman, Brown, Green, and Longmans, 1845); Montgomery, *The Quest for Noah's Ark*, pp. 141–47.

25. Montgomery, *The Quest for Noah's Ark*, p. 167.

26. Ibid., p. 211.

27. Ibid., p. 193.

28. F. Navarra, *The Forbidden Mountain*, trans. Michael Legat (London: Macdonald, 1956), p. 12.

29. Ibid., p. 13.

30. Ibid., p. 95.

31. Ibid., p. 90.

32. Ibid., pp. 165–66.

33. Bailey, *Noah*, pp. 92–105.

34. Also see F. Navarra, *Noah's Ark: I Touched It* (Plainfield, N.J.: Logos International, 1974).

35. For additional climbs see Montgomery, *The Quest for Noah's Ark*, pp. 247–88. For a compendium of fearless but failed efforts at scaling Mount Ararat in search of the Ark, see also B. J. Corbin, ed., *The Explorers of Ararat and the Search for Noah's Ark* (Long Beach, Calif.: Great Commission Illustrated Books, 1999).

36. Noted by Montgomery, *The Quest for Noah's Ark*, p. 111, referencing F. G. Coan, *Yesterdays in Persia and Kurdistan* (Claremont, Calif.: Saunders Studio, 1939), pp. 164–65.

37. Coan, *Yesterdays*, p. 165.

38. R. L. Numbers, *The Creationists: The Evolution of Scientific Creationism* (Berkeley: University of California Press, 1992), p. 138.

39. D. C. Allen, *The Legend of Noah: Renaissance Rationalism in Art, Science, and Letters* (Urbana: University of Illinois Press, 1963), p. 3.

40. www.answersingenesis.org/docs2/4377news9–14–2000.asp

41. D. G. Lindsay, *The Genesis Flood: Continents in Collision* (Dallas: Christ for the Nations, 1992), p. 12.

42. Ibid., p. 14.

43. www.talkorigins.org/faqs/flood-myths.html.

CHAPTER 2

1. Lindsay, *The Genesis Flood*, p. 14.

2. B. Batto, *Slaying the Dragon: Mythmaking in the Biblical Tradition* (Louisville, Ky.: Westminster/John Knox, 1992), pp. 115–18.

3. H. Lindsell, *The Battle for the Bible* (Grand Rapids, Mich.: Zondervan, 1976), pp. 174–76.

4. Ryan and Pitman, *Noah's Flood*, p. 239.

5. Ibid., p. 225.

6. T. Paine, *The Age of Reason* (New York: Freethought Press, n.d.), p. 89.

7. F. Crick, *Life Itself: Its Origins and Nature* (New York: Simon and Schuster, 1981), p. 158, quoted in D. Brian, *Genius Talk: Conversations with Nobel Scientists and Other Luminaries* (New York: Plenum, 1995), pp. 170–71.

8. J. Campbell and B. Moyers, *The Power of Myth*, (New York: Doubleday, 1988), p. 3.

9. R. Jones, *Physics for the Rest of Us: Ten Basic Ideas of Twentieth-Century Physics That Everyone Should Know and How They Have Shaped Our Culture and Consciousness* (Chicago: Contemporary Books, 1992), p. 93.

10. O. Rank, "Die Symbolschichtung im Wecktraum und ihrer Wiederkehr im mythischen Denken," *Jahrbuch für psychoanalytische und psychopathologische Forschungen* 4 (1912): pp. 51–115.

11. P. Vandermeersch, "Where Will the Water Stick? Considerations of a Psychoanalyst about the Stories of the Flood," in *Interpretations of the Flood*, ed. F. G. Martinez and C. P. Luttikhuizen (Leiden: Brill, 1998), pp. 167–93.

CHAPTER 3

1. G. Wenham, "The Coherence of the flood Narrative," *Vetus Testamentum* 28 (1978): 336–48.

2. J. A. Emerton, "An Examination of Some Attempts to Defend the Unity of the Flood Narrative in Genesis: Part II," *Vetus Testmentum* 37, no. 4 (1988); 6–15.

3. ourworld.compuserve.com/homepages/CW_Arnhem/Genesis.html.

4. Talmud, b. Kodoshim Menachoth 30a, b. Mas. Baba Bathra 15a.

5. Soncino Talmud, b. Kodoshim Menachoth 30a, b. Mas. Baba Bathra 15a.

6. J. Astruc, *Conjectures sur Genèse: Introduction et Notes de Pierre Gilbert* (Paris: Éditions Noêsis, 1999).

7. One might compare Astruc's formulation to the popular book by R. E. Friedman, *Who Wrote the Bible?* (New York: Summit Books, 1987).

8. See A. F. Campbell and M. A. O'Brien, *Sources of the Pentateuch: Texts, Introductions, Annotations* (Minneapolis, Minn.: Fortress, 1993).

9. Astruc's A, or Elohim, sections are as follows: 6:9–22; 7:6–10, 19, 22, 24; 8:1–19; 9:1–10, 12, 16–17, 28–29. Astruc's B, or YHWH, sections are 6:1–8; 7:1–5, 11–18, 21, 24; 8:20–22; 9:11, 13–15, 18–27, 28–29.

10. D. Dimant, "Noah in Early Jewish Literature," in *Biblical Figures outside the Bible*, ed. M. E. Stone and T. A. Bergren (Harrisburg, Pa.: Trinity Press International, 1998), p. 140.

11. For a full study of the preceding, see ibid.

12. For representative translations of the Targumic material, see B. Grossfeld, *The Targum Onqelos to Genesis, Translated with a Critical Introduction, Apparatus, and Notes* (Wilmington, Del.: Michael Glazier, 1988); and M. McNamara, *Targum Neofiti 1: Genesis, Translated with Apparatus and Notes* (Collegeville, Minn.: Michael Glazier, 1992).

13. Josephus, *Antiquities* I, 3, 5–6 (89–95).

14. See R. Cornuke and D. Holbrook, *In Search of the Lost Mountains of Noah: The Discovery of the REAL Mts. of Ararat* (Nashville, Tenn.: Broadman and Holman, 2001).

15. H. Schwartz, *Reimagining the Bible: The Storytelling of the Rabbis* (New York: Oxford University Press, 1998), p. 6.

16. Ibid., p. 16.

17. For the Qumran links, see Dimant, "Noah in Early Jewish Literature," pp. 127–29.

18. H. N. Bialik and Y. H. Ravnitzky, *The Book of Legends*, trans. W. G. Braude with an introduction by D. Stern (New York: Schocken, 1992), 26:113 and note. This volume offers a convenient compendium of talmudic materials regarding the flood story. Not all of the talmudic texts, however, are collected here and those that remain will be indicated with the relevant reference to the Talmud as I proceed in this discussion.

19. Ibid., 9:23.

20. Ibid., 10:28.

21. Ibid., 25:108.

22. Ibid., 27:118.

23. Ibid., 27:119.

24. Ibid., 27:120.

25. Talmud, b. Sanhedrin 108b.

26. Bialik and Ravnitzky, *Book of Legends*, 25:111.

27. Ibid., 31:1.

28. Ibid., 27:120.

29. Ibid., 25:112.

30. Ibid., 26:114.

31. Ibid., 27:121; Talmud, b. San 108b.

32. Talmud, b. Sanhedrin 108b.

33. Bialik and Ravnitzky, *The Book of Legends*, 28:130, 131, and Talmud, b. San 108b, for the preceding several paragraphs.

34. Bialik and Ravnitzky, *The Book of Legends*, 27:122.

35. Talmud, b. Zevachim 113b.

36. Ibid.

37. Talmud, b. Sanhedrin 108b.

38. Bialik and Ravnitzky, *The Book of Legends*, 28:127.

39. Ibid., 29:134.

40. Ibid., 453:484–485.

41. Schwartz, *Reimagining the Bible*, p. 29.

42. Reprinted in M. Drosnin, *The Bible Code* (New York: Simon and Schuster, 1997), pp. 236 ff.

43. Ibid., p. 20.

44. Ibid., pp. 117–20, 19, 33, 108–10, 40, 34, 48, 85–93, 121–47, 164–67.

45. R. Hendel and S. Sternberg, "The Bible Code: Cracked and Crumbling," *Bible Review* 13, no. 4 (1997): 22–25. For McKay's calculations consult http://cs.anu.edu.au/~bdm/dilugim/moby.html.

CHAPTER 4

1. Numbers, *The Creationists*, p. 209.

2. A. C. Dixon, L. Meyer, and R. A. Torrey, eds., *The Fundamentals: A Testimony to the Truth* (Chicago: Testimony Publishing Co., 1909–15), 8:27–35.

3. Ibid., p. 31.

4. Ibid., pp. 36–48.

5. Ibid., p. 37.

6. Ibid., 7:5–20.

7. For full-scale studies, see D. N. Livingstone, *Darwin's Forgotten Defenders: The Encounter between Evangelical Theology and Evolutionary Thought* (Grand Rapids, Mich.: Eerdmans, 1987); and J. H. Roberts, *Darwinism and the Divine in America: Protestant Intellectuals and Organic Evolution, 1859–1900* (Notre Dame, Ind.: University of Notre Dame Press, 1988).

8. Dixon, Meyer, and Torrey, *The Fundamentals*, 4:97, 103.

9. Ibid., 6:93.

10. Ibid., 4:100; 6:93.

11. Ibid., 6: 97.

12. Numbers, *The Creationists*, p. 59.

13. A. I. Brown, *Evolution and the Bible* (Vancouver: Arcale Printers, n.d.), p. 5.

14. Ibid., pp. 11–14.

15. Ibid., p. 7.

16. Ibid., p. 9.

17. Ibid., pp. 26, 30.

18. A. I. Brown, *Men, Monkeys and Missing Links* (Findlay, Ohio: Fundamental Truth Publishers, n.d.), p. 9.

19. Ibid., p. 39.

20. Quoted in Numbers, *The Creationists*, p. 60.

21. Ibid., p. 62.

22. Ibid., p. 63.

23. H. Rimmer, *Monkeyshines: Fakes, Fables, Facts concerning Evolution* (Duluth, Minn.: Research Science Bureau, 1926), pp. 3–4.

24. Ibid., p. 4.

25. Ibid., p. 13.

26. Ibid., p. 4.

27. Ibid., p. 5.

28. Ibid., p. 33.

29. Ibid., p. 39.

30. Ibid., p. 43.

31. Ibid., p. 48.

32. Numbers, *The Creationists*, p. 66.

33. Rimmer, *Monkeyshines*, p. 30.

34. Ibid., pp. 5–7.

35. G. McCready Price, *Q.E.D. or the New Light on the Doctrine of Creation* (New York: Fleming H. Revell, 1917), p. 118.

36. G. McCready Price, *Illogical Geology: The Weakest Point in the Evolution Theory* (Los Angeles: Modern Heretic Company, 1906), p. 9.

37. Price, *Q.E.D.*, p. 11.

38. Ibid., p. 128.

39. Numbers, *The Creationists*, p. 99.

40. Ibid., p. 311.

41. Ibid., chap. 7.

42. Ibid., pp. 198–99.

43. By far the best treatment is E. J. Larson, *Summer for the Gods: The Scopes Trial and America's Continuing Debate over Science and Religion* (Cambridge, Mass.: Harvard University Press, 1997).

44. L. W. Levy, ed., *The World's Most Famous Court Trial*: State of Tennessee v. John Thomas Scopes, (New York: Da Capo, 1971), p. 138.

45. Ibid., p. 113.

46. Ibid., p. 302.

47. Ibid., pp. 285–87.

48. Ibid., p. 285.

49. Ibid., pp. 289–94.

50. Ibid., p. 296.

51. Ibid., pp. 287–89.

52. Ibid., p. 297.

53. Ibid., p. 301.

54. Ibid., p. 298.

55. Ibid., p. 303.

56. Ibid., pp. 302–3.

57. Ibid., p. 304.

58. Ibid., p. 299.

59. See, e.g., L. Gilkey, *Creationism on Trial: Evolution and God at Little Rock* (Minneapolis, Minn.: Winston, 1985); L. A. Witham; *Where Darwin meets the Bible: Creationists and Evolutionists in America* (New York: Oxford University Press, 2002).

60. Notably absent from "intelligent-design" discourse is any talk of the flood story. Here we have a tacit acknowledgment that modern science is writing the better story. We have come a long way since Thomas Burnet, for whom God had designed into the created order the mechanisms that eventually produced the flood. Intelligent-design theorists omit discussing a part of the Bible that would be inconvenient to their thesis, making Genesis 1 look more relevant to modern scientific discourse. Certainly, this sleight of hand would make magician David Copperfield envious: the ark has disappeared! Yet Christian intelligent-design enthusiasts need to stop and gauge the significance of omitting large chunks of biblical prehistory from their cosmic calculations. Is this any way to read the Bible? Is this any way to do science? Such biblicists will eventually have to admit that the Bible does not contain the only scientific truths we moderns need. Omitting *all* the early chapters of Genesis may be the better approach. This will only happen when Genesis 1 is no longer force-fit into intelligent-design theorizing as if the chapter were about science rather than myth. For convenient overviews of the current intelligent-design craze, see B. McMurtrie, "Darwinism under Attack," *Chronicle of Higher Education* 48, no. 17 (December 21, 2001): A8–A10; and R. Monastersky, "Seeking the Deity in the Details," *Chronicle of Higher Education* 48, no. 17 (December 21, 2001): A10–A11, and the literature cited there. The on-line debate sparked on this issue by the *Chronicle of Higher Education* provides a barometer of the ferocity of this question. See http://chronicle.com/colloquy/2001/design/design.htm.

61. See, e.g., M. Ruse, *The Evolution Wars: A Guide to the Debates* (New Brunswick, N.J.: Rutgers University Press, 2000), chap. 10.

62. J. C. Whitcomb and H. Morris, *The Genesis Flood: The Biblical Record and Its Scientific Implications* (Philadelphia: Presbyterian and Reformed, 1961), pp. 239–58. See Numbers, *The Creationists*, p. 316.

63. J. C. Whitcomb, *The World That Perished* (Grand Rapids, Mich.: Baker Book House, 1988), p. 36.

64. Ibid., pp. 139, 144–45.

65. Ibid., p. 21.

66. Ibid., pp. 24–26.

67. Ibid., pp. 26–34.

68. Ibid., pp. 35–37.

69. Ibid., pp. 37–41.

70. Ibid., pp. 41–43; Psalm 104:6–9.

71. Whitcomb, *The World That Perished*, pp. 42–43, 102, 107; S. J. Gould, *Time's Arrow, Time's Cycle: Myth and Metaphor in the Discovery of Geological Time* (Cambridge, Mass.: Harvard University Press, 1987), pp. 2 3.

72. Whitcomb, *The World That Perished*, p. 121.

73. Ibid., pp. 68–69, 103.

74. Ibid., pp. 118, 120.

75. Ibid., p. 118, Whitcomb's emphasis.

76. Ibid., pp. 58–60, 95–97, 107–12.

77. Gould in A. Dundes, *The Flood Myth* (Berkeley: University of California Press, 1988), pp. 435–36.

78. J. R. Van de Fliert, "Fundamentalism and the Fundamentals of Geology," *Journal of the American Scientific Affiliation* 21, no. 3 (1969): 69–81.

79. Ibid., pp. 74–78.

80. Ibid., p. 80, van de Fliert's emphasis.

81. Ibid., p. 80.

82. Gilkey, *Creationism on Trial*, p. 40.

83. Ibid., p. 61.

84. Ibid., p. 171.

85. Ibid., pp. 191, 206–7.

86. Ibid., pp. 186–87.

87. Ibid., p. 191.

88. Austin in R. Youngblood, ed., *The Genesis Debate: Persistent Questions about Creation and the Flood* (Nashville, Tenn.: Thomas Nelson, 1986), p. 219.

89. M. J. Oard, *An Ice Age Caused by the Genesis Flood* (El Cajon, Calif: Institute for Creation Research, 1990), p. 23.

90. Ibid., p. 26.

91. Austin in Youngblood, *The Genesis Debate*, p. 224.

92. Oard, *An Ice Age Caused by the Genesis Flood*, pp. 80–91, 128–33.

93. Lindsay, *The Genesis Flood*, pp. 95–96.

94. Whitcomb, *The World That Perished*, pp. 76–82, similarly skirts this question.

95. K. R. Miller, *Finding Darwin's God: A Scientist's Search for Common Ground between God and Evolution* (New York: Cliff Street Books, 1999), p. 77.

96. M. Hall, *The Earth Is Not Moving* (Cordelia, Ga.: Fair Education Foundation, 1991),

204 NOTES TO PAGES 63–69

97. D. Nelkin, *The Creation Controversy: Science or Scripture in the Schools* (San Jose, Calif.: toExcel Press, 2000). The radical divergence between P. E. Johnson (*Darwin on Trial*, 2d ed. [Downers Grove, Ill.: Inter Varsity Press, 1993]), who uses prosecutorial language to define evolution out of existence in favor of creationism, and N. Eldredge (*The Triumph of Evolution and the Failure of Creationism* [New York: Freeman, 2000]), who capably demonstrates the fact of evolution from a judicious review of the evidence, could not be more telling.

98. The PBS *Evolution* series presents a program entitled "What about God?" that shows there are conservative Christians who are taking seriously evolutionary ideas and who are working to integrate their faith with the best that modern science has to offer.

99. L. Woolley, *Ur of the Chaldees: A Revised and Updated Edition of Sir Leonard Woolley's Excavations at Ur by P. R. S. Moorey* (Ithaca, N.Y.: Cornell University Press, 1982), pp. 25–35.

100. M. E. L. Mallowan, "Noah's Flood Reconsidered," *Iraq* 26 (1964):62–82.

101. Ibid., p. 63; cf. p. 66.

102. Ibid., p. 64.

103. Ibid., p. 67.

104. Ibid., p. 75.

105. Ibid., p. 78.

106. Ibid., pp. 78–79.

107. Ibid., p. 80.

108. J. B. Pritchard, ed., *Ancient Near Eastern Texts Relating to the Old Testament, Third Edition with Supplement* (Princeton, N.J.: Princeton University Press, 1969), p. 265.

109. A. Parrot, *The Flood and Noah's Ark* (New York: Philosophical Library, 1955), pp. 45–53.

110. Ryan and Pitman, *Noah's Flood*, p. 248.

111. On the fundamentalist culture war and a refreshing attempt at constructing a dialogue between religion and science, see Eldredge, *The Triumph of Evolution*, chap. 7.

CHAPTER 5

1. For detailed discussions of specific phases of the history of interpretation of the flood story in Jewish and Christian tradition, see F. Garcia Martinez and G. P. Luttikhuizen, eds., *Interpretations of the Flood* (Leiden: Brill, 1998).

2. Genesis Rabbah 31:11; N. Cohn, *Noah's Flood: The Genesis Story in Western Thought* (New Haven, Conn.: Yale University Press, 1996), pp. 33–34.

3. Genesis Rabbah 31:10–11.

4. For a survey see R. W. Unger, *The Art of Medieval Technology: Images of Noah the Shipbuilder* (New Brunswick, N.J.: Rutgers University Press, 1991).

5. Allen, *The Legend of Noah*, p. 71.

6. Ibid., p. 79.

7. Ibid., p. 76.

8. As quoted in ibid., p. 76.

9. Talmud, b. Sanhedrin 108b; Genesis Rabbah 36:7. Ham's sexual exploits form the basis for Stephen Minot's novelistic farce *Surviving the Flood* (New York: Atheneum, 1981).

10. Cohn, *Noah's Flood*, pp. 41–42.

11. Allen, *The Legend of Noah*, p. 130.

12. Ibid., p. 120.

13. J. Woodward, *An Essay towards a Natural History of the Earth and Terrestrial Bodies, especially Minerals: As also of the Sea, Rivers, and Springs. With an account of the Universal Deluge: And of the Effects that it had upon the Earth* (London: Ric Wilkin, 1695; reprint, New York: Arno, 1978), pp. 166–69.

14. Quoted in E. Mayr, *The Growth of Biological Thought: Diversity, Evolution, and Inheritance* (Cambridge, Mass.: Belknap/Harvard University Press, 1982), pp. 872–73.

15. Noted by Allen, *The Legend of Noah*, p. 80.

16. Cohn, *Noah's Flood*, p. 43.

17. Ibid., p. 44; W. Ralegh, *The History of the World: A New Edition, Revised and Corrected, Volume 1* (Edinburgh: Archibald Constable, 1820), .

18. Quoted by Campbell in C. A. Patrides, ed., *Sir Walter Ralegh, The History of the World* (Philadelphia: Temple University Press, 1971), p. xii.

19. Ralegh, *The History of the World*, pp. 220–21.

20. Ibid., p. 222.

21. Ibid., p. 223.

22. Ibid., pp. 234–35.

23. Cohn, *Noah's Flood*, pp. 40–41.

24. Allen, *The Legend of Noah*, p. 78.

25. Ralegh, *The History of the World*, p. 237.

26. Ibid., pp. 240–43.

27. Ibid., p. 247.

28. Noted in Patrides, *Sir Walter Ralegh, The History of the World*, p. 11.

29. Quoted in ibid., p. 39.

30. Lloyd quoted in ibid., p. 3.

31. Ralegh, *The History of the World*, p. 210.

32. Pictured in Cohn, *Noah's Flood*, p. 40.

33. Allen, *The Legend of Noah*, p. 184.

34. Ibid., p. 187.

35. Reprinted as Thomas Burnet, *The Sacred Theory of the Earth, with an Introduction by Basil Willey* (Carbondale: Southern Illinois University Press, 1965).

36. Gould, *Time's Arrow, Time's Cycle*, chap. 2, rightly rescues Burnet from the misconception that his views were the product of irrational theological speculation.

37. Cohn, *Noah's Flood*, pp. 48–61; Allen in Dundes, *The Flood Myth*, pp. 362–67.

38. Allen, *The Legend of Noah*, p. 100, characterizing Warren's views.

39. Allen in Dundes, *The Flood Myth*, pp. 375–78. For a brief discussion of Whiston's calculations in their historical context, see M. Gorst, *Measuring Eternity: The Search for the Beginning of Time* (New York: Broadway Books, 2001), chap. 5.

40. Allen, *The Legend of Noah*, p. 109.

41. Reprinted as W. Whiston, *A New Theory of the Earth* (New York: Arno, 1978); cf. Cohn, *Noah's Flood*, pp. 62–72.

42. Allen, *The Legend of Noah*, p. 112.

43. Rappaport in Dundes, *The Flood Myth*, pp. 388–90.

44. Ibid., p. 391.

45. Ibid., p. 399.

46. Ibid.

47. Ibid., p. 400.

48. See A. Hallam, *Great Geological Controversies*, 2d ed. (Oxford: Oxford University Press, 1989), chap. 1.

49. G. Cuvier, *Essay on the Theory of the Earth*, 3d ed. (Edinburgh: W. Blackwood, 1817), pp. 39–40.

50. Ibid., p. 159.

51. Ibid., p. 164.

52. Ibid., p. 171.

53. As defined and delineated by Gould, *Time's Arrow, Time's Cycle*, chap. 4.

54. C. Lyell, *Principles of Geology; or, The Modern Changes of the Earth and its Inhabitants* (New York: Appleton, 1860), p. 25.

55. See Gould, *Time's Arrow, Time's Cycle*, chaps. 2, 4.

56. N. A. Rupke, *The Great Chain of History: William Buckland and the English School of Geology (1814–1849)* (Oxford: Clarendon Press, 1983), chap. 7.

57. A. Sedgwick, "Address to the Geological Society," *Proceedings of the Geological Society of London* 1 (1831): 313.

58. W. Buckland, *Vindiciae Geologicae, or the Connexion of Geology with Religion Explained* (Oxford: Oxford University Press, 1820), p. 24.

59. Ibid., dedication page.

60. Ibid., p. 24.

61. Ibid.

62. Ibid., pp. 23–24, 35–37.

63. Ibid., p. 12.

64. W. Buckland, *Geology and Mineralogy Considered with Reference to Natural Theology*, 2d ed., 2 vols. (London: William Pickering, 1837), p. 16.

65. Rupke, *The Great Chain of History*, chaps. 7–8.

66. See the wonderful study of C. McGowan, *The Dragon Seekers: How an Extraordinary Circle of Fossilists Discovered the Dinosaurs and Paved the Way for Darwin* (Cambridge: Perseus, 2001),

67. Buckland, *Geology and Mineralogy*, pp. 12–13. Even Buckland's *Reliquiae Diluviae* caused consternation among some biblical literalists. See Rupke, *The Great Chain of History*, chap. 3.

68. Buckland, *Geology and Mineralogy*, pp. vii–viii, 14.

69. On Buckland's intellectual development in the context of the clerical interests at Oxford, see Rupke, *The Great Chain of History*.

70. Buckland, *Vindiciae Geologicae*, p. 14.

71. Buckland, *Geology and Mineralogy*, p. 24.

72. Ibid., pp. 21–22.

73. Ibid., pp. 25–26.

74. Moore in Dundes, *The Flood Myth*, p. 414.

75. Sedgwick, "Address to the Geological Society," p. 314; a passage cited approvingly in J. Pye Smith, *Scripture and Geology, on the Relation between the Holy Scriptures and Some Parts of Geological Science* (New York: D. Appleton, 1840), p. 122.

76. Allen, *The Legend of Noah*, p. 93.

77. Quoted in ibid., p. 93.

78. N. Steno, *The Prodromus of Nicolaus Steno's Dissertation: Concerning a Solid Body Enclosed by Process of Nature within a Solid*, intro. and trans. J. G. Winter (London: Macmillan, 1916; reprint, New York: Hafner, 1968), pp. 257–58.

79. Ibid., p. 205.

80. Ibid., pp. 211–25, 249–61.

81. Ibid., p. 262.

82. Ibid., p. 258.

83. Ibid., pp. 258, 266.

84. Ibid., p. 267.

85. Quoted in Allen, *The Legend of Noah*, p. 94.

86. Woodward, *Essay towards a Natural History of the Earth*, preface.

87. Ibid., p. 88.

88. Ibid., p. 239.

89. Ibid., pp. 83–102, 148–49.

90. Ibid., pp. 87–90.

91. Ibid., pp. 1–3.

92. Ibid., pp. 13–28, 38, 162–65.

93. Ibid., p. 39.

94. Ibid., pp. 46, 72, 82.

95. Ibid., pp. 116–31, 157–61, 270–71.

96. Ibid., p. 135.

97. Ibid., pp. 29–30, 71–82, 108–111.

98. Ibid., pp. 261–63.

99. Ibid., preface.

100. Ibid., pp. 67–68, 165.

101. Ibid., p. 67.

102. Ibid., pp. 55–59.

103. Ibid., p. 81.

104. Cohn, *Noah's Flood*, pp. 89–90.

105. R. Kirwan, *Geological Essays* (London: D. Brenner, 1799; reprint, New York: Arno, 1978), p. 56; On the background, see F. L. Filby, "Noah's Flood: Noah and the Neptunists," *Faith and Thought* 100 (1972): 143–58.

106. Kirwan, *Geological Essays*, p. 54.

107. Ibid., pp. 73–74.

108. Ibid., p. 54.

109. Ibid., pp. 54–55.

110. Ibid., pp. 56–60.

111. Ibid., pp. 71–72.

112. Ibid., pp. 65–66.

113. Ibid., pp. 84–85.

114. Ibid., p. 86.

115. Mayr, *The Growth of Biological Thought*, pp. 371–86.

116. The heading for this section of the chapter is a play on the title of an important study of this trend in flood interpretation in nineteenth-century America by R. L. Stiling, "The Diminishing Deluge: Noah's Flood in Nineteenth-Century American Thought" (Ph.D. diss., University of Wisconsin–Madison, 1991).

117. Numbers, *The Creationists*, pp. x–xi.

118. Smith, *Scripture and Geology*, p. 139.

119. Ibid., p. 245.

120. Ibid., pp. 243–59.

121. Ibid., pp. 258.

122. Ibid., pp. 165–68.

123. Ibid., p. 70.

124. Ibid., p. 39.

125. Ibid., p. 21.

126. Ibid., p. 33.

127. Ibid., pp. 142, 143.

128. See Ibid., p. 181.

129. Quoted by Moore in Dundes, *The Flood Myth*, p. 424; the characterization as an oracle is Numbers, *The Creationists*, p. 11.

130. For a complete study of the development of Hitchcock's thought from a believer in the global flood to his eventual conversion to a limited, non-traceable flood, see Stiling, "The Diminishing Deluge," chaps. 2–3.

131. The thirtieth edition retains Smith's notice; E. Hitchcock, *Elementary Geology* (New York: Ivison and Phinney, 1856).

132. Hitchcock, *Elementary Geology*, p. xvii.

133. Ibid., p. xviii.

134. Ibid., pp. 351–53.

135. E. Hitchcock, *The Religion of Geology and Its Connected Sciences*, (Glasgow: William Collins, 1851), p. 42.

136. Ibid., p. 30.

137. Hitchcock, *Elementary Geology*, p. 362.

138. As amply demonstrated by Livingstone, *Darwin's Forgotten Defenders*, chap. 3.

139. D. Crofton, *Genesis and Geology: or, An Investigation into the Reconciliation of the Modern Doctrines of Geology with the Declarations of Scripture* (Boston: Phillips, Sampson and Company, 1853), p. iii.

140. Ibid.

141. Ibid., p. 11.

142. Ibid., p. 25.

143. Ibid., p. 62.

144. Ibid., pp. 70, 77, 82.

145. Ibid., p. 19.

146. For earlier attacks on Buckland, see Rupke, *The Great Chain of History*, chap. 3.

147. Smith, *Scripture and Geology*, p. 180; Smith tackles some of the early exceptions on pp. 175–94.

148. E. Lord, *The Epoch of Creation: The Scripture Doctrine Contrasted with the Geological Theory* (New York: Scribner, 1851), chap. 3.

149. Ibid., p. 97.

150. Ibid., chaps. 5, 9.

151. Ibid., p. 185.

152. Ibid., pp. 201–3.

153. Ibid., p. 142.

154. Ibid., p. 144.

155. Ibid., pp. 160–61.

156. Ibid., p. 254; see also pp. 168–73.

157. Ibid., pp. 181–94.

158. Ruse, *The Evolution Wars*, offers an insightful and entertaining overview.

159. Livingstone, *Darwin's Forgotten Defenders*, chaps. 2–3; Roberts, *Darwinism and the Divine in America*, chap. 3.

160. Livingstone, *Darwin's Forgotten Defenders*, chap. 3.

161. Cohn, *Noah's Flood*, pp. 95–96. Actually Ussher set the beginning of creation as 6 P.M. on Saturday, October 22, 4004 B.C.E., but the 23rd has long held sway in scholarly lore. For a convenient discussion of Ussher's life and work, see M. Gorst, *Measuring Eternity: The Search for the Beginning of Time* (New York: Broadway Books, 2001), chap. 2.

162. Campbell, *The Power of Myth*.

CHAPTER 6

1. For the Gladstone discussion, see T. H. Huxley, *Science and Hebrew Tradition: Essays* (New York: D. Appleton, n.d.), chaps. 4–5.

2. Ibid., p. 234.

3. Ibid., p. 215.

4. Ibid., pp. 201–2.

5. Ibid., p. 205.

6. Ibid., p. 203.

7. Ibid., p. 252.

8. Ibid., pp. 256–59.

9. Ibid., pp. 256–59.

10. Ibid., p. 229.

11. Ibid., p. 226.

12. Ibid., p. 211.

13. Ibid., pp. 267, 279.

14. Ibid., pp. 267–82.

15. Ibid., p. 225.

16. Ibid., p. 237.

17. M. Fishbane, *Text and Texture: Close Readings of Selected Biblical Texts* (New York: Schocken, 1979), chap. 1.

18. For a discussion of the Babylonian New Year's festival, see J. A. Black, "The New Year Ceremonies in Ancient Babylon: 'Taking Bel by the Hand' and a Cultic Picnic," *Religion* 11 (1981): 39–59; and K. Van der Toorn, "The Babylonian New Year

Festival: New Insights from the Cuneiform Texts and Their Bearing on Old Testament Study," in *Congress Volume: Leuven 1989*, ed. J. A. Emerton (Leiden: Brill, 1991), pp. 331–44.

19. P. Lal, *The Mahabharata of Vyasa*, vol. 21 (Calcutta: Writer's Workshop, 1970), p. 11.

20. For a translation, see Pritchard, *Ancient Near Eastern Texts*, pp. 42–44.

21. For a translation, see S. Dalley, *Myths from Mesopotamia: Creation, the Flood, Gilgamesh, and Others* (Oxford: Oxford University Press, 1989), pp. 9–35.

22. For translations of the following texts, see A. George, *The Epic of Gilgamesh: The Babylonian Epic Poem and Other Texts in Akkadian and Sumerian* (London: Penguin, 1999).

23. For representative recent translations, see ibid. and Dalley, *Myths from Mesopotamia*, pp. 50–125.

24. E. A. Budge, *The Rise and Progress of Assyriology* (London: Martin Hopkinson, 1925), p. 153.

25. Smith, "The Chaldean Account of the Deluge," in Dundes, *The Flood Myth*, p. 47.

26. Ibid., p. 48; for additional sources, see R. Campbell Thompson, *A Century of Exploration at Nineveh* (London, 1929), pp. 48–54; and G. Smith, *Assyrian Discoveries* (New York: Scribner, Armstron, and Co., 1875). pp. 9–14.

27. J. Tigay, *The Evolution of the Gilgamesh Epic* (Philadelphia: University of Pennsylvania Press, 1982), p. 224.

28. Ibid., p. 224.

29. Ibid., p. 231.

30. Ibid., p. 231.

31. Ibid., p. 226.

32. Ibid., p. 226.

33. Ibid., p. 288.

34. Ibid., p. 231.

35. Parrot, *The Flood and Noah's Ark*, pp. 37–38.

36. As pointed out by Allen, *The Legend of Noah*, p. 74.

37. G. P. Verbrugghe and J. M. Wickersham, *Berossos and Manetho, Introduced and Translated: Nature Traditions in Ancient Mesopotamia ar Egypt* (Ann Arbor: University of Michigan Press, 1996), p. 50.

38. Ibid., p. 50; cf. also Parrot, *The Flood and Noah's Ark*, pp. 38–40.

39. Lucian, *De Dea Syria*, 12–13.

40. Apollodorus 1.7.1–3.

41. See, e.g., Voltaire, "Genesis," *Philosophical Dictionary*, trans. P. Gay (New York: Harcourt, Brace, and World, 1962), pp. 284–97, esp. p. 295; Frazer, "The Great Flood," in Dundes, *The Flood Myth*, pp. 113–23.

42. Frazer, "The Great Flood," p. 117.

43. For a convenient distillation, see C. Lévi-Strauss, *Myth and Meaning: Cracking the Code of Culture* (New York: Schocken, 1978).

44. M. Casalis, "The Dry and the Wet: A Semiological Analysis of Creation and Flood Myths," *Semiotica* 17, no. 1 (1976): 35–67.

45. Ibid., p. 64.

46. See, e.g., the selections in R. A. Segal, ed., *Jung on Mythology* (Princeton, N.J.: Princeton University Press, 1990),

47. Ryan and Pitman, *Noah's Flood*, p. 251.

48. Allen, *The Legend of Noah*, pp. 169–70.

49. Ibid., p. 173.

CHAPTER 7

1. W. G. Lambert and A. R. Millard, *Atra-hasis: The Babylonian Story of the Flood* (Oxford: Clarendon Press, 1969), p. 47.

2. Ibid., p. 57.

3. Ibid., p. 59.

4. Ibid., p. 103.

5. Ibid., pp. 87, 89.

6. Malinowski, "The Role of Myth in Life," in Dundes, *Sacred Narrative*, p. 198.

7. Ibid., p. 199.

8. Ryan and Pitman, *Noah's Flood*, pp. 246–47.

9. For background consult Z. Meshel, "Kuntillet Ajrud," in *The Anchor Bible Dictionary*, ed. D. N. Freedman (New York: Doubleday, 1992), 4:103–9.

10. For a representative translation, see Dalley, *Myths from Mesopotamia*, pp. 233–74.

11. Psalms 29, 47, 93, 95, 96, 97, 98, and 99. For a discussion see J. D. Pleins, *The Psalms: Songs of Tragedy, Hope and Justice* (Maryknoll, N.Y.: Orbis, 1993), chap. 9.

12. For texts and translations, see J. C. L. Gibson, *Canaanite Myths and Legends* (Edinburgh: T. and T. Clark, 1977).

13. Friedman, *Who Wrote the Bible?* chap. 2.

14. For the link between J and the Deuteronomistic History or at least the first parts devoted to David and Solomon, see R. E. Friedman, *The Hidden Book in the Bible* (San Francisco: HarperSanFrancisco, 1998).

CHAPTER 8

1. H. H. Cohen, *The Drunkenness of Noah* (University: University of Alabama Press, 1974), chap. 8.

2. Ibid., p. vii.

3. Ibid., p. x.

4. Ibid., chap. 1.

5. Ibid., pp. 7–8.

6. Ibid., p. 8.

7. Ibid., p. 12.

8. Ibid., p. 12.

9. Ibid., pp. 21–22.

10. Ibid., chap. 2.

11. Ibid., p. 29.

12. Dalley, *Myths from Mesopotamia*, pp. 107–9.

13. Ovid, *Metamorphoses*, book I.

14. H. F. Stander, "The Church Fathers on (the Cursing of) Ham," *Acta Patristica et Byzantina* 5 (1994): 113.

15. Stringfellow, *Scriptural and Statistical Views in Favor of Slavery* (Richmond, Va.: J. W. Randolph, 1856), p. 9.

16. Ibid., p. 8.

17. Astonishingly, R. L. Dabney (*A Defense of Virginia: And through Her, of the South, in Recent and Pending Contests against the Sectional Party* [E. J. Hale and Son, 1867; reprint, New York Negro Universities Press, 1969], pp. 101–4) continued to invoke the Ham story to support slavery even after the civil war! He readily acknowledged that some would find his arguments "wholly unseasonable" given the postwar realities, but those facts on the ground did not temper his enthusiasm for the "peculiar institution."

18. For a complete study, see S. R. Haynes, *Noah's Curse: The Biblical Justification of American Slavery* (New York: Oxford University Press, 2002), See also H. Eilberg-Schwartz, *God's Phallus: and Other Problems for Men and Monotheism* (Boston: Beacon 1994), pp. 86–91.

19. Quoted in Haynes, *Noah's Curse*, p. 72.

20. Cited in ibid., p. 73.

21. S. R. Haynes, "Original Dishonor: Noah's Curse and the Southern Defense of Slavery," *Journal of Southern Religion* 3 (2000); on-line, available: http://jsr.as.wvu.edu/honor.htm.

22. Haynes, *Noah's Curse*, p. 80.

23. T. V. Peterson, *Ham and Japheth: The Mythic World of Whites in the Antebellum South* (Metuchen, N.J.: American Theological Library Association, 1978), pp. 48–49.

24. Ibid., chap. 2.

25. Stringfellow, *Scriptural and Statistical Views*, pp. 8–9.

26. Peterson, *Ham and Japheth*, chap. 5.

27. Ibid., p. 7.

28. Ibid., p. 94.

29. Ibid., p. 82. A fairly degrading though not untypical assessment of African-Americans is offered by S. Robinson, who invokes the Ham story throughout as an integral factor in his explanation of the black condition and culture. See Robinson, "Negro Slavery at the South," *De Bow's Review* 7, no. 3 (September 1849): esp. pp. 211–14, 217–19.

30. Peterson, *Ham and Japheth*, p. 1.

31. Ibid., p. 102.

32. See, e.g., A. Ely, "On the Common Origin of the Human Races," *De Bow's Review* 17, no. 1 (July 1854): 25–39. Also, Peterson, *Ham and Japheth*, chaps. 2, 4, 5.

33. W. Perryman, *The 1993 Trial on the Curse of Ham: With Liberty and Justice for All* (Bakersfield, Calif.: Pneuma Publishing, 1994), p. 5.

34. Quoted in ibid., p. 13.

35. Perryman, *The 1993 Trial*, p. 33.

36. Lindsay, *The Genesis Flood*, p. 24.

37. Ibid., p. 229.

38. Ibid., p. 201.

39. Ibid., p. 243.

40. A. Barnes, *An Inquiry into the Scriptural Views of Slavery* (Philadelphia: Parry and McMillan, 1855; reprint, Detroit: Negro History Press, n.d.), p. 104.

41. R. C. Bailey, "They're Nothing but Incestuous Bastards: The Polemical Use of Sex and Sexuality in Hebrew Canon Narratives," in *Readings from this Place*, vol. 1, *Social Location and Biblical Interpretation in the United States*, ed. F. F. Segovia and M. A. Tolbert (Minneapolis, Minn.: Fortress, 1994), p. 134.

42. Lindsay, *The Genesis Flood*, p. 227.

43. Schwartz, *The Curse of Cain*, p. 107.

44. Ibid., pp. 108–13.

45. Ibid., p. 111.

46. For a discussion, see R. A. J. Gagnon, *The Bible and Homosexual Practice: Texts and Hermeneutics* (Nashville, Tenn.: Abingdon, 2001), pp. 77–91.

47. See the Human Rights Watch report *No Escape: Male Rape in U.S. Prisons*, http://hrw.org/reports/2001/prison/report4.html#_1_26.

48. For an alternate analysis, see Eilberg-Schwartz, *God's Phallus*, pp. 91–97.

49. Talmud, b. Sanhedrin 108b; Genesis Rabbah 36:7.

50. P. Gomes, *The Good Book: Reading the Bible with Mind and Heart* (New York: Morrow, 1996), p. 49. For the rabbinic material, see Rashi, *Bereshis*, Genesis 9:22; Talmud b. Sanhedrin 70a; Tanhuma Buber 2:21; and (use with caution!) R. Graves and R. Patai, *Hebrew Myths: The Book of Genesis* (New York: McGraw-Hill, 1963), p. 121.

51. Genesis Rabbah 36:7.

52. G. Friedlander, trans., *Pirke de Rabbi Eliezer* (London, 1916; reprint, New York: Hermon Press, 1970), p. 170.

53. Talmud b. Pesahim 113b.

54. Which is different than saying that the talmudic traditions were known or understood by nineteenth-century Southern interpreters. See D. H. Aaron, "Early Rabbinic Exegesis on Noah's Son Ham and the So-Called 'Hamitic Myth,'" *Journal of the American Academy of Religion* 63 (1995): 721–59.

55. Gomes, *The Good Book*, p. 50.

56. Schwartz, *The Curse of Cain*, p. 58.

57. Ibid., p. 58.

58. Bailey, "They're Nothing but Incestuous Bastards," p. 138.

59. F. W. Bassett, "Noah's Nakedness and the Curse of Canaan: A Case if Incest?" *Vetus Testamentum* 21 (1971): p. 235.

60. Gagnon, *The Bible and Homosexual Practice*, p. 64.

61. Bassett, "Noah's Nakedness," p. 237.

62. Bailey, "They're Nothing but Incestuous Bastards," pp. 134–35.

63. Bassett, "Noah's Nakedness," p. 235.

64. Dimant, "Noah in Early Jewish Literature," p. 139.

65. Doty, *Mythography: The Study of Myths and Rituals*, 2d ed. (Tuscaloosa: University of Alabama Press, 2000), p. 46.

66. Gomes, *The Good Book*, p. 52.

CHAPTER 9

1. P. Bird, *Missing Persons, Mistaken Identities: Women and Gender in Ancient Israel* (Philadelphia: Fortress, 1997), p. 58.

2. For a general discussion of the various approaches, see R. A. Segal, *In Quest of the Hero* (Princeton, N.J.: Princeton University Press, 1990).

3. "Of Myth and Men: A Conversation between Bill Moyers and George Lucas on the Meaning of the Force and the True Theology of *Star Wars*," *Time*, April 26, 1999, p. 90.

4. R. Alter, *The Art of Biblical Narrative* (New York: Basic Books, 1981), chap. 3.

5. On the idea of the balancing character of the narrative, see Fishbane, *Text and Texture*, chap. 3.

6. For a discussion of an array of alternatives, see W. G. Doty, "From the Traditional Monomythic Hero to the Contemporary Polymythic Hero/ine," *Forum* 8 (1992): 337–69.

7. J. Caputi, "On Psychic Activism: Feminist Mythmaking," in *The Feminist Companion to Mythology*, ed. C. Larrington (London: Pandora, 1992), pp. 425–40.

8. For a Jungian approach to the Gilgamesh epic, see R. Schärf Kluger, *The Archetypal Significance of Gilgamesh: A Modern Ancient Hero* (Einseideln, Switzerland: Daimon, 1991).

9. H. Bloom and D. Rosenberg, *The Book of J* (New York: Vintage, 1991).

10. R. Oden, *The Bible without Theology* (Urbana: Univesity of Illinois Press, 1987), chap. 5.

11. Herodotus I, 199.

12. See D. N. Freedman, ed., *The Anchor Bible Dictionary* (New York: Doubleday, 1992), 4:103–9.

13. E. C. Latham, ed., *The Poetry of Robert Frost: The Collected Poems, Complete and Unabridged* (New York: Holt, Rinehart and Winston, 1979), pp. 473–90.

14. E. Van Wolde, *Mr. and Mrs. Job* (London: SCM, 1997), pp. 18–19.

15. Midrash Rabbah 23:3. For a brief discussion, see E. Goldstein, ed., *The Women's Torah Commentary: New Insights from Women Rabbis on the 54 Weekly Torah Portions* (Woodstock, Vt.: Jewish Lights, 2000), pp. 53–56.

CHAPTER 10

1. J. Romer, *Testament: The Bible and History* (New York: Henry Holt, 1988), chap. 2.

2. W. Keller, *The Bible as History*, 2d rev. ed. (New York: Morrow, 1981), p. 49.

3. H. H. Halley, *Halley's Bible Handbook: An Abbreviated Bible Commentary*, 24th ed. (Grand Rapids, Mich.: Zondervan, 1965), p. 74.

4. Allen, *The Legend of Noah*, p. 15.

5. Ibid., p. 34.

6. Ibid., p. 38; *Paradise Lost*, VII, 118–30.

7. Ibid., pp. 16, 28.

8. For representative texts, see J. Barnes, *Early Greek Philosophy* (London: Penguin, 1987).

9. Their views are conveniently summarized in J. M. Robinson, *An Introduction to Early Greek Philosophy* (New York: Houghton Mifflin, 1968). Their debates are captured by Cicero, *On the Nature of the Gods.*

10. Albright, *The Archaeology of Palestine*, p. 109.

11. Ibid., p. 122.

12. Ibid., p. 124.

13. Ibid., p. 204.

14. See, e.g., W. F. Albright, *Yahweh and the Gods of Canaan: A Historical Analysis of Two Contrasting Faiths* (Winona Lake, Ind.: Eisenbrauns, 1968), pp. 64–73.

15. W. F. Albright, *From the Stone Age to Christianity: Monotheism and Historical Process*, 2d ed. (New York: Doubleday, 1957), p. 241.

16. Ibid., p. 9.

17. Ibid., p. 2.

18. W. G. Dever, "'Will the Real Israel Stand Up?': Part I: Archaeology and Israelite Historiography," *Bulletin of the American Schools for Oriental Research* 297 (1995): 61–80; Dever, "'Will the Real Israel Stand Up?': Part II: Archaeology and the Relgions of Ancient Israel," *Bulletin of the American Schools for Oriental Research* 298 (1995): 37–58.

19. W. G. Dever, *What Did the Biblical Writers Know*, pp. 98–101.

20. T. L. Thompson, *The Historicity of the Patriarchal Narratives: The Quest for the Historical Abraham* (New York: Walter de Gruyter, 1974); J. Van Seters, *Abraham in History and Tradition* (New Haven, Conn.: Yale University Press, 1975).

21. The models are conveniently characterized in N. Gottwald, *The Tribes of Yahweh: A Sociology of the Religion of Liberated Israel 1250–1050 B.C.E.*, (Maryknoll, N.Y.: Orbis, 1979), chaps. 20–22.

22. The supposed contrast that Wright sought to defend between the Bible's "God who acts in history" and the Mesopotamian "nature" gods has been roundly challenged. See B. Albrektson, *History and the Gods: An Essay on the Idea of Historical Events as Divine Manifestations in the Ancient Near East and Israel* (Lund. Gleerup, 1967); B. S. Childs, *Biblical Theology in Crisis* (Philadelphia: Westminster, 1970); H. W. F. Saggs, *The Encounter with the Divine in Mesopotamia and Israel* (London: Athlone, 1978); G. E. Wright, *God Who Acts: Biblical theology as Recital* (London: SCM, 1952); Wright, *The Old Testament Against Its Environment* (London: SCM, 1950).

23. Allen, *The Legend of Noah*, p. 66.

24. Ibid., p. 69 citing Hall, *Poems, The Caroline Poets*, ed. Saintsbury (Oxford, 1906), II, 187.

25. H. de Lubac, *Medieval Exegesis*, vol. 1, *The Four Senses of Scripture* (Grand Rapids, Mich.: Eerdmans, 1998), p. 1.

26. For a general discussion, see J. A. Fitzmyer, *Scripture, the Soul of Theology* (New York: Paulist, 1994).

27. Schwartz, *Reimagining the Bible*, p. 37.

28. Quoted in K. Wilber, ed., *Quantum Questions: Mystical Writings of the World's Great Physicists* (Boston: Shambhala, 1984), p. 208.

29. To be fair, religionists have often been far more open to the sciences than many scientists care to admit. The picture of constant warfare provided by Draper

and White overstates the case, although one has to admit that pockets of religious resistance have been there since the advent of the Copernican revolution. See J. W. Draper, *History of the Conflict between Religion and Science* (New York: D. Appleton, 1875); and A. D. White, *A History of the Warfare of Science with Theology in Christendom: In Two Volumes* (New York: D. Appleton, 1925 [1896]). Note the corrections of J. H. Brooke, *Science and Religion: Some Historical Perspectives* (Cambridge: Cambridge University Press, 1991).

30. J. McFadden, "Bravo! We're Decoded, but a Mystery Still," *Washington Post*, February 18, 2001, pp. B1, B5.

31. Quoted in Wilber, *Quantum Questions*, pp. 33–34.

32. Quoted in Brian, *Genius Talk*, p. 135.

33. Jones, *Physics for the Rest of Us*, p. 84.

34. For a succinct and sensible treatment of the Galileo affair and its lasting impact on the dialogue between religion and science, see R. J. Blackwell, *Science, Religion and Authority: Lessons from the Galileo Affair* (Milwaukee, Wis.: Marquette University Press, 1998).

35. T. H. Huxley, "Science and Culture," in *Essays: English and American*, ed. Charles W. Eliot (New York: Collier, 1938), p. 210.

36. Ibid., p. 214.

37. Ibid., p. 218.

38. Ibid., p. 219.

39. G. Zukav, *The Dancing Wu Li Masters: An Overview of the New Physics* (New York: Morrow, 1979), p. 328.

40. Ibid., p. 75.

41. Ibid., p. 97.

42. Ibid., p. 102.

43. Ibid., pp. 110–11.

44. Ibid., p. 235.

45. Ibid., p. 272.

46. J. B. S. Haldane, *Possible Worlds and Other Papers: A Scientist Looks at Science* (New York: Harper and Brothers, 1928), 252.

47. Quoted in Wilber, *Quantum Questions*, pp. 151–52.

48. F. Capra, *The Tao of Physics* (Boston: Shambhala, 1991), p. 340.

49. F. Capra and D. Steindl-Rast, with Thomas Natus, *Belonging to the Universe: Explorations on the Frontiers of Science and Spirituality* (San Francisco: HarperSanFrancisco, 1991), pp. 50–55.

50. Ibid., pp. 110–12, and chap. 5.

51. Saint Augustine, *Confessions: Translated with an Introduction and Notes by Henry Chadwick* (Oxford: Oxford University Press, 1991), p. 191.

52. To a certain extent, the manner in which the issues tackled in this book have unfolded parallels, after a fashion, the views of the relationship between religion and science elaborated in Ian Barbour's writing, most recently encapsulated in his book *When Science Meets Religion: Enemies, Strangers, or Partners?* (San Francisco: HarperSanFrancisco, 2000), For Barbour, there are essentially four possible relationships to be had between religion and science. Two are rather unconstructive: "conflict" and "independence." Two are constructive: "dialogue" and "integration."

In Barbour's understanding, "conflict" is the mode that dominates when each side retreats into its narrowest posture, namely, biblical literalism and scientific materialism. This posture combines to some extent my literalist view and the myths-as-nonsense tendency. Barbour's second category of "independence" sees science and religion as two separate domains, each speaking a unique language and operating in a kind of hermetically sealed intellectual isolation. In a way, my own "loose literalism" captures something of this mode, especially when each partner is dancing gingerly around the other, being careful not to step on each other's toes. More vigorous is Barbour's third possibility, namely, "dialogue," where each side speaks from its own stance but does so in a complementary and comparative fashion. In part, my loose literalism and mythic approach parallel this element, especially when loose literalism is at its best and gives ample room to the religious questions. Finally, Barbour suggests that "integration" is, in fact, possible. Here the advances of science, the challenges of contemporary society, and the theological quest find common cause today. At its strongest, my "mythic approach" finds integration in this sense a rather congenial prospect.

53. O. Wilde, *Epigrams: Phrases and Philosophies for the Use of the Young* (Boston: Aldine, 1910), p. 141.

54. T. Nhat Hanh, *The Stone Boy and Other Stories* (Berkeley, Calif.: Parallax, 1996), p. 212.

55. J.-F. Lyotard, *Postmodern Fables* (Minneapolis: University of Minnesota Press, 1997), chap. 6.

56. *New York Times Magazine*, August 2, 1964, quoted in A. Claprice, *The Expanded Quotable Einstein* (Princeton, N.J.: Princeton University Press, 2000), p. 184.

57. Quoted in Brian, *Genius Talk*, p. 170.

58. Quoted in Wilber, *Quantum Questions*, p. 201.

59. S. J. Gould, *Rocks of Ages: Science and Religion in the Fullness of Life* (New York: Ballantine, 1999), p. 6.

60. Ibid., pp. 52–53.

61. Ibid., p. 53.

62. Ibid., pp. 58–59, 175.

63. Ibid., p. 10.

64. Ibid., p. 169.

65. Ibid., p. 209.

66. Quoted in Wilber, *Quantum Questions*, p. 123.

67. Ibid., p. 125.

68. J. Campbell, *The Inner Reaches of Outer Space: Metaphor as Myth and as Religion* (New York: Harper and Row, 1986).

CONCLUSION

1. E. Schüssler Fiorenza, "The Will to Choose or to Reject: Continuing Our Critical Work," in *Feminist Interpretations of the Bible*, ed. L. M. Russell (Philadelphia: Westminster, 1985), pp. 125–36, esp. p. 130.

2. S. Rushdie, *Haroun and the Sea of Stories* (London: Granta, 1990), p. 72.

Bibliography

Aaron, D. H. "Early Rabbinic Exegesis on Noah's Son Ham and the So-
  Called 'Hamitic Myth.'" *Journal of the American Academy of Religion* 63
  (1995): 721–59.
Ackerman, S. *Warrior, Dancer, Seductress, Queen: Women in Judges and
  Biblical Israel.* New York: Doubleday, 1998.
Albrektson, B. *History and the Gods: An Essay on the Idea of Historical
  Events as Divine Manifestations in the Ancient Near East.* Lund:
  Gleerup, 1967.
Albright, W. F. *The Archaeology of Palestine.* Baltimore, Md.: Penguin, 1956.
———. *From the Stone Age to Christianity: Monotheism and the Historical
  Process*, 2d ed. New York: Doubleday, 1957.
———. *Yahweh and the Gods of Canaan: A Historical Analysis of Two
  Contrasting Faiths.* Winona Lake, Ind.: Eisenbrauns, 1968.
Allen, D. C. *The Legend of Noah: Renaissance Rationalism in Art, Science, and
  Letters.* Urbana: University of Illinois Press, 1963.
Alter, R. *The Art of Biblical Narrative.* New York: Basic Books, 1981.
Armstrong, K. *A History of God.* New York: Knopf, 1993.
Astruc, J. *Conjectures sur Genèse: Introduction et notes de Pierre Gibert.* Paris:
  Éditions Noêsis, 1999.
Augustine, Saint. *Confessions: Translated with an Introduction and Notes by
  Henry Chadwick.* Oxford: Oxford University Press, 1991.
Bailey, L. R. *Noah: The Person in History and Tradition.* Columbia: Univer-
  sity of South Carolina Press, 1989.
Bailey, R. C. "They're Nothing but Incestuous Bastards: The Polemical Use
  of Sex and Sexuality in Hebrew Canon Narratives." In *Readings from
  This Place, Vol. 1: Social Location and Biblical Interpretation in the United
  States*, ed. F. F. Segovia and M. A. Tolbert, 121–38. Minneapolis,
  Minn.: Fortress, 1994.

Ballard, R. and M. McConnell *Adventures in Ocean Exploration: From the Discovery of the* Titanic *to the Search for Noah's Flood with Malcolm McConnell.* Washington, D.C.: National Geographic, 2001.

Barbour, I. *When Science Meets Religion: Enemies, Strangers, or Partners?* San Francisco: HarperSanFrancisco, 2000.

Barnes, A. *An Inquiry into the Scriptural Views of Slavery.* Philadelphia: Parry and McMillan, 1855. Reprint, Detroit: Negro History Press, n.d.

Barnes, J. *Early Greek Philosophy.* London: Penguin, 1987.

Bassett, F. W. "Noah's Nakedness and the Curse of Canaan: A Case of Incest?" *Vetus Testamentum* 21 (1971): 232–37.

Batto, B. *Slaying the Dragon: Mythmaking in the Biblical Tradition.* Louisville, Ky.: Westminster/John Knox, 1992.

Bialik, H. N., and Y. H. Ravnitzky. *The Book of Legends.* Translated by W. G. Braude with an introduction by D. Stern. New York: Schocken, 1992.

Bird, P. *Missing Persons, Mistaken Identities: Women and Gender in Ancient Israel.* Philadelphia: Fortress, 1997.

Black, J. A. "The New Year Ceremonies in Ancient Babylon: 'Taking Bel by the Hand' and a Cultic Picnic." *Religion* 11 (1981): 39–59.

Blackwell, R. J. *Science, Religion and Authority: Lessons from the Galileo Affair.* Milwaukee, Wis.: Marquette University Press, 1998.

Bloom, H., and D. Rosenberg, *The Book of J.* New York: Vintage, 1991.

Brian, D. *Genius Talk: Conversations with Nobel Scientists and Other Luminaries.* New York: Plenum, 1995.

Britten, B. *Noye's Fludde: The Chester Miracle Play.* New York: Boosey and Hawkes, 1958.

Brooke, J. H. *Science and Religion: Some Historical Perspectives.* Cambridge: Cambridge University Press, 1991.

Brown, A. I. *Evolution and the Bible.* Vancouver: Arcade Printers, n.d.

———. *Men, Monkeys and Missing Links.* Findlay, Ohio: Fundamental Truth Publishers, n.d.

Buckland, W. *Vindiciae Geologicae; or the Connexion of Geology with Religion Explained.* Oxford: Oxford University Press, 1820.

———. *Reliquiae Diluvianae or, Observations in the Organic Remains Contained in Caves, Fissures, and Diluvial Gravel and on Other Geological Phenomena Attesting to the Action of a Universal Deluge.* London: John Murray, 1823. Reprint, New York: Arno, 1978.

———. *Geology and Minerology Considered with Reference to Natural Theology.* 2d ed., 2 vols. London: William Pickering, 1837.

Budge, E. A. *The Rise and Progress of Assyriology.* London: Martin Hopkinson, 1925.

Burnet, T. *The Sacred Theory of the Earth, with an Introduction by Basil Willey.* Carbondale: Southern Illinois University Press, 1965.

Campbell, A. F., and M. A. O'Brien. *Sources of the Pentateuch: Texts, Introductions, Annotations.* Minneapolis, Minn.: Fortress, 1993.

Campbell, J. *The Hero with a Thousand Faces,* 2d ed. Princeton, N.J.: Princeton University Press, 1968.

———. *The Inner Reaches of Outer Space: Metaphor as Myth and as Religion.* New York: Harper and Row, 1986.

Campbell, J. and B. Moyers, *The Power of Myth*. New York: Doubleday, 1988.

Campbell Thompson, R. *A Century of Exploration at Nineveh*. London, 1929.

Capra, F. *The Tao of Physics*. Boston: Shambhala, 1991.

Capra, F., and D. Steindl-Rast with Thomas Matus. *Belonging to the Universe: Explorations on the Frontiers of Science and Spirituality*. San Francisco: HarperSanFrancisco, 1991.

Caputi, J. "On Psychic Activism: Feminist Mythmaking." In *The Feminist Companion to Mythology*, ed. C. Larrington, 425–40. London: Pandora, 1992.

Casalis, M. "The Dry and the Wet: A Semiological Analysis of Creation and Flood Myths." *Semiotica* 17, no. 1 (1976): 35–67.

Childs, B. S. *Biblical Theology in Crisis*. Philadelphia: Westminster, 1970.

Cicero. *On the Nature of the Gods*, trans. H. C. P. McGregor. New York: Penguin, 1972.

———. *The Nature of the Gods and On Divination*. Trans. C. D. Yonge. Amherst, N.Y.: Prometheus, 1997.

Claprice, A. *The Expanded Quotable Einstein*. Princeton, N.J.: Princeton University Press, 2000.

Coan, F. G. *Yesterdays in Persia and Kurdistan*. Claremont: Saunders Studio, 1939.

Cohen, H. H. *The Drunkenness of Noah*. University: University of Alabama Press, 1974.

Cohn, N. *Noah's Flood: The Genesis Story in Western Thought*. New Haven, Conn.: Yale University Press, 1996.

Corbin, B. J., ed. *The Explorers of Ararat and the Search for Noah's Ark*. Long Beach, Calif.: Great Commission Illustrated Books, 1999.

Cornuke, R., and D. Halbrook. *In Search of the Lost Mountains of Noah: The Discovery of the REAL Mts. of Ararat*. Nashville, Tenn.: Broadman and Holman, 2001.

Crick, F. *Life Itself: Its Origins and Nature*. New York: Simon and Schuster, 1981.

Crofton, D. *Genesis and Geology; or, An Investigation into the Reconciliation of the Modern Doctrines of Geology with the Declarations of Scripture*. Boston: Phillips, Sampson and Company, 1853.

Cuvier, G. *Essay on the Theory of the Earth*. 3d ed. Edinburgh: W. Blackwood, 1817.

Dabney, R. L. *A Defense of Virginia: And through Her, of the South, in Recent and Pending Contests against the Sectional Party*. E. J. Hale and Son, 1867. Reprint, New York: Negro Universities Press, 1969.

Dalley, S. *Myths from Mesopotamia: Creation, the Flood, Gilgamesh, and Others*. Oxford: Oxford University Press, 1989.

Dawkins, R. "Science, Delusion and the Appetite for Wonder," Richard Dimbleby Lecture, BBC 1 Television, November 12, 1996. On-line. Available: http://www.positiveatheism.org/writ/dawkins2.htm.

Dever, W. G. "'Will the Real Israel Stand Up?': Part I: Archaeology and Israelite Historiography." *Bulletin of the American Schools for Oriental Research* 297 (1995): 61–80.

———. "'Will the Real Israel Stand Up?': Part II: Archaeology and the Religions of Ancient Israel." *Bulletin of the American Schools for Oriental Research* 298 (1995): 37–58.

———. *What Did the Biblical Writers Know and When Did They Know It? What Archaeology Can Tell Us about the Reality of Ancient Israel*. Grand Rapids, Mich.: William B. Eerdmans, 2001.

Dimant, D. "Noah in Early Jewish Literature." In *Biblical Figures outside the Bible*, ed. M. E. Stone and T. A. Bergren, 123–50. Harrisburg, Pa.: Trinity Press International, 1998.

Dixon, A. C., L. Meyer, and R. A. Torrey, eds. *The Fundamentals: A Testimony to the Truth.* 12 vols. Chicago: Testimony Publishing Co., 1909–15.

Doty, W. G. "From the Traditional Monomythic Hero to the Contemporary Polymythic Hero/ine." *Forum* 8 (1992): 337–69.

———. *Mythography: The Study of Myths and Rituals.* 2d ed. Tuscaloosa: University of Alabama Press, 2000.

Draper, J. W. *History of the Conflict between Religion and Science.* New York: D. Appleton, 1875.

Drosnin, M. *The Bible Code.* New York: Simon and Schuster, 1997.

Dundes, A., ed. *Sacred Narrative.* Berkeley: University of California Press, 1984.

———. *The Flood Myth.* Berkeley: University of California Press, 1988.

Eilberg-Schwartz, H. *God's Phallus: And Other Problems for Men and Monotheism.* Boston: Beacon, 1994.

Eldredge, N. *The Triumph of Evolution and the Failure of Creationism.* New York: Freeman, 2000.

Ely, A. "On the Common Origin of the Human Races." *De Bow's Review* 17, no. 1 (July 1854): 25–39.

Emerton, J. A. "An Examination of Some Attempts to Defend the Unity of the Flood Narrative in Genesis: Part I." *Vetus Testamentum* 37, no. 4 (1987): 401–20.

———. "An Examination of Some Attempts to Defend the Unity of the Flood Narrative in Genesis: Part II." *Vetus Testamentum* 37, no. 4 (1988): 1–21.

Filby, F. L. "Noah's Flood: Noah and the Neptunists." *Faith and Thought* 100 (1972): 143–58.

Fishbane, M. *Text and Texture: Close Readings of Selected Biblical Texts.* New York: Schocken, 1979.

Fitzmyer, J. A. *Scripture, the Soul of Theology.* New York: Paulist, 1994.

Freedman, D. N., ed. *The Anchor Bible Dictionary.* New York: Doubleday, 1992.

Friedlander, G., trans. *Pirke de Rabbi Eliezer.* London, 1916. Reprint, New York: Hermon Press, 1970.

Friedman, R. E. *Who Wrote the Bible?* New York: Summit Books, 1987.

———. *The Hidden Book in the Bible.* San Francisco: HarperSanFrancisco, 1998.

Gagnon, R. A. J. *The Bible and Homosexual Practice: Texts and Hermeneutics.* Nashville, Tenn.: Abingdon, 2001.

Garcia Martinez, F., and G. P. Luttikhuizen, eds. *Interpretations of the Flood.* Leiden: Brill, 1998.

George, A. *The Epic of Gilgamesh: The Babylonian Epic Poem and Other Texts in Akkadian and Sumerian.* London: Penguin, 1999.

Gibson, J. C. L. *Canaanite Myths and Legends.* Edinburgh: T. and T. Clark, 1977.

Gilkey, L. *Creationism on Trial: Evolution and God at Little Rock.* Minneapolis, Minn.: Winston, 1985.

Goldstein, E., ed. *The Women's Torah Commentary: New Insights from Women Rabbis on the 54 Weekly Torah Portions.* Woodstock, Vt.: Jewish Lights, 2000.

Gomes, P. *The Good Book: Reading the Bible with Mind and Heart.* New York: Morrow, 1996.

Gorst, M. *Measuring Eternity: The Search for the Beginning of Time*. New York: Broadway Books, 2001.

Gottwald, N. *The Tribes of Yahweh: A Sociology of the Religion of Liberated Israel 1250–1050 B.C.E.* Maryknoll, N.Y.: Orbis, 1979.

Gould, S. J. *Time's Arrow, Time's Cycle: Myth and Metaphor in the Discovery of Geological Time*. Cambridge, Mass.: Harvard University Press, 1987.

———. *Rocks of Ages: Science and Religion in the Fullness of Life*. New York: Ballantine, 1999.

Graves, R., and R. Patai. *Hebrew Myths: The Book of Genesis*. New York: McGraw-Hill, 1963.

Grossfeld, B. *The Targum Onqelos to Genesis, Translated with a Critical Introduction, Apparatus, and Notes*. Wilmington, Del.: Michael Glazier, 1988.

Gunkel, H. *Genesis*. Macon, Ga.: Mercer University Press, 1997.

Haldane, J. B. S. *Possible Worlds and Other Papers: A Scientist Looks at Science*. New York: Harper and Brothers, 1928.

Hale, M. *The Primitive Origination of Mankind: Considered and Examined according to the Light of Nature*. London: William Godbid, 1677.

Hall, M. *The Earth Is Not Moving*. Cornelia, Ga.: Fair Education Foundation, 1991.

Hallam, A. *Great Geological Controversies*. 2d ed. Oxford: Oxford University Press, 1989.

Halley, H. H. *Halley's Bible Handbook: An Abbreviated Bible Commentary*. 24th ed. Grand Rapids, Mich.: Zondervan, 1965.

Haynes, S. R. "Original Dishonor: Noah's Curse and the Southern Defense of Slavery." *Journal of Southern Religion* 3 (2000). On-line. Available: http://jsr.as.wvu.edu/honor.htm.

———. *Noah's Curse: The Biblical Justification of American Slavery*. New York: Oxford University Press, 2002.

Hendel, R., and S. Sternberg. "The Bible Code: Cracked and Crumbling." *Bible Review* 13, no. 4 (1997): 22–25.

Hitchcock, E. *The Religion of Geology and Its Connected Sciences*. Glasgow: William Collins, 1851.

———. *Elementary Geology*. New York: Ivison and Phinney, 1856.

Huffmon, H. "The Origin of Prophecy." In *Magnalia Dei: The Mighty Acts of God: Essays on the Bible and Archaeology in Memory of G. Ernest Wright*, ed. F. M. Cross, W. E. Lemke, and P. D. Miller, 171–86. Garden City, N.Y.: Doubleday, 1976.

Hunter, G. W. *A Civic Biology: Presented in Problems*. New York: American Book Company, 1914.

Huxley, T. H. "Science and Culture." In *Essays: English and American*, ed. Charles W. Eliot, 209–23. New York: Collier, 1938.

———. *Science and Hebrew Tradition: Essays*. New York: D. Appleton, n.d.

Johnson, P. E. *Darwin on Trial*. 2d ed. Downers Grove, Ill.: InterVarsity Press, 1993.

Jones, R. *Physics for the Rest of Us: Ten Basic Ideas of Twentieth-Century Physics That Everyone Should Know and How They Have Shaped Our Culture and Consciousness*. Chicago: Contemporary Books, 1992.

Keller, W. *The Bible as History*. 2d rev. ed. New York: Morrow, 1981.

Kirwan, R. *Geological Essays*. London: D. Bremner, 1799. Reprint, New York: Arno, 1978.

Kluger, R. Schärf. *The Archetypal Significance of Gilgamesh: A Modern Ancient Hero*. Einseideln, Switzerland: Daimon, 1991.

Lal, P. *The Mahabharata of Vyasa*. Vol. 21. Calcutta: Writer's Workshop, 1970.

Lambert, W. G., and A. R. Millard. *Atra-hasis: The Babylonian Story of the Flood*. Oxford: Clarendon Press, 1969.

Larson, E. J. *Summer for the Gods: The Scopes Trial and America's Continuing Debate over Science and Religion*. Cambridge, Mass.: Harvard University Press, 1997.

Latham, E. C., ed. *The Poetry of Robert Frost: The Collected Poems, Complete and Unabridged*. New York: Holt, Rinehart and Winston, 1979.

Lévi-Strauss, C. *Myth and Meaning: Cracking the Code of Culture*. New York: Schocken, 1978.

Levy, L. W., ed. *The World's Most Famous Court Trial: State of Tennessee v. John Thomas Scopes*. New York: Da Capo, 1971.

Lindsay, D. G. *The Genesis Flood: Continents in Collision*. Dallas: Christ for the Nations, 1992.

Lindsell, H. *The Battle for the Bible*. Grand Rapids, Mich.: Zondervan, 1976.

Livingstone, D. N. *Darwin's Forgotten Defenders: The Encounter between Evangelical Theology and Evolutionary Thought*. Grand Rapids, Mich.: Eerdmans, 1987.

Lord, E. *The Epoch of Creation: The Scripture Doctrine Contrasted with the Geological Theory*. New York: Scribner, 1851.

Lubac, H. de. *Medieval Exegesis*. Vol. 1, *The Four Senses of Scripture*. Grand Rapids, Mich.: William B. Eerdmans, 1998.

Lyell, C. *Principles of Geology; or, the Modern Changes of the Earth and its Inhabitants*. New York: Appleton, 1860.

Lyotard, J.-F. *Postmodern Fables*. Minneapolis: University of Minnesota Press, 1997.

MacLeish, A. *J.B.* Boston: Houghton Mifflin, 1961.

Malinowski, B. "The Role of Myth in Life." In *Sacred Narrative: Readings in the Theory of Myth*, ed. A. Dundes, 193–206. Berkeley: University of California Press, 1984.

Mallowan, M. E. L. "Noah's Flood Reconsidered." *Iraq* 26 (1964): 62–82.

Mayr, E. *The Growth of Biological Thought: Diversity, Evolution, and Inheritance*. Cambridge, Mass.: Belknap/Harvard University Press, 1982.

McFadden, J. *Quantum Evolution*. London: HarperCollins, 2000.

————. "Bravo! We're Decoded, but a Mystery Still." *Washington Post*, February 18, 2001, B1, B5.

McGowan, C. *The Dragon Seekers: How an Extraordinary Circle of Fossilists Discovered the Dinosaurs and Paved the Way for Darwin*. Cambridge: Perseus, 2001.

McMurtrie, B. "Darwinism under Attack." *Chronicle of Higher Education* 48, no. 17 (December 21, 2001): A8–A10.

McNamara, M. *Targum Neofiti 1: Genesis, Translated, with Apparatus and Notes*. Collegeville, Minn.: Michael Glazier, 1992.

Meshel, Z. "Kuntillet Ajrud." In *The Anchor Bible Dictionary*, ed. D. N. Freedman, 4:103–9. New York: Doubleday, 1992.

Miller, K. R. *Finding Darwin's God: A Scientist's Search for Common Ground between God and Evolution*. New York: Cliff Street Books, 1999.

Minot, S. *Surviving the Flood*. New York: Atheneum, 1981.

Monastersky, R. "Seeking the Deity in the Details." *Chronicle of Higher Education* 48, no. 17 (December 21, 2001): A10–A11.

Montgomery, J. W. *The Quest for Noah's Ark*. 2d ed. Minneapolis, Minn.: Bethany Fellowship, 1974.

Navarra, F. *The Forbidden Mountain*. Trans. Michael Legat. London: Macdonald, 1956.

———. *Noah's Ark: I Touched It*. Plainfield, N.J.: Logos International, 1974.

Nelkin, D. *The Creation Controversy: Science or Scripture in the Schools*. San Jose, Calif.: toExcel Press, 2000.

Nhat Hanh, T. *The Stone Boy and Other Stories*. Berkeley, Calif.: Parallax, 1996.

Numbers, R. L. *The Creationists: The Evolution of Scientific Creationism*. Berkeley: University of California Press, 1992.

Oard, M. J. *An Ice Age Caused by the Genesis Flood*. El Cajon, Calif.: Institute for Creation Research, 1990.

Oden, R. *The Bible without Theology*. Urbana: University of Illinois Press, 1987.

Paine, T. *The Age of Reason*. New York: Freethought Press, n.d.

Paley, W. *Natural Theology: or, Evidences of the Existence and Attributes of the Deity, Collected from the Appearances of Nature*. 1802. Reprint, Houston: St. Thomas Press, 1972.

Parrot, A. *The Flood and Noah's Ark*. New York: Philosophical Library, 1955.

Parrot, F. *Journey to Ararat*. Trans. W. D. Cooley. London: Longman, Brown, Green, and Longmans, 1845.

Patrides, C. A., ed. *Sir Walter Ralegh, The History of the World*. Philadelphia: Temple University Press, 1971.

Perryman, W. *The 1993 Trial on the Curse of Ham: With Liberty and Justice for All*. Bakersfield, Calif.: Pneuma Publishing, 1994.

Peterson, T. V. *Ham and Japheth: The Mythic World of Whites in the Antebellum South*. Metuchen, N.J.: American Theological Library Association, 1978.

Pleins, J. D. *The Psalms: Songs of Tragedy, Hope and Justice*. Maryknoll, N.Y.: Orbis, 1993.

Polo, M. *The Travels*. Trans. R. Latham. New York: Penguin, 1958.

Price, G. McCready. *Illogical Geology: The Weakest Point in the Evolution Theory*. Los Angeles: Modern Heretic Company, 1906.

———. *Q.E.D. or the New Light on the Doctrine of Creation*. New York: Fleming H. Revell, 1917.

———. *The New Geology: A Textbook for Colleges, Normal Schools and Training Schools, and for the General Reader*. Mountain View, Calif.: Pacific Press Publishing Association, 1923.

Pritchard, J. B., ed. *Ancient Near Eastern Texts Relating to the Old Testament, Third Edition with Supplement*. Princeton, N.J.: Princeton University Press, 1969.

Raikes, R. L. "The Physical Evidence for Noah's Flood." *Iraq* 38 (1966): 52–63.

Ralegh, W. *The History of the World: A New Edition, Revised and Corrected, Volume 1*. Edinburgh: Archibald Constable, 1820.

Rank, O. "Die Symbolschichtung im Wecktraum und ihrer Wiederkehr im mythischen Denken," *Jahrbuch für psychoanalytische und psychopathologische Forschungen* 4 (1912): 51–115.

Rimmer, H. *Monkeyshines: Fakes, Fables, Facts concerning Evolution*. Duluth, Minn.: Research Science Bureau, 1926.

Roberts, J. H. *Darwinism and the Divine in America: Protestant Intellectuals and Organic Evolution, 1859–1900*. Notre Dame, Ind.: University of Notre Dame Press, 1988.

Robinson, J. M. *An Introduction to Early Greek Philosophy*. New York: Houghton Mifflin, 1968.

Robinson, S. "Negro Slavery at the South." *De Bow's Review* 7, no. 3 (September 1849): 206–25.

Romer, J. *Testament: The Bible and History*. New York: Henry Holt, 1988.

Rudwick, M. J. S. *The Meaning of Fossils: Episodes in the History of Palaeontology*. London: MacDonald, 1972.

Rupke, N. A. *The Great Chain of History: William Buckland and the English School of Geology (1814–1849)*. Oxford: Clarendon Press, 1983.

Ruse, M. *The Evolution Wars: A Guide to the Debates*. New Brunswick, N.J.: Rutgers University Press, 2000.

Rushdie, S. *Haroun and the Sea of Stories*. London: Granta, 1990.

Ryan, W., and W. Pitman. *Noah's Flood: The New Scientific Discoveries about the Event That Changed History*. New York: Simon and Schuster, 1998.

Saggs, H. W. F. *The Encounter with the Divine in Mesopotamia and Israel*. Loneon: Athlone, 1978.

Satinover, J. *Cracking the Bible Code*. New York: Morrow, 1997.

Schüssler Fiorenza, E. "The Will to Choose or to Reject: Continuing Our Critical Work." In *Feminist Interpretation of the Bible*, ed. L. M. Russell, 125–36. Philadelphia: Westminster, 1985.

Schwartz, H. *Reimagining the Bible: The Storytelling of the Rabbis*. New York: Oxford University Press, 1998.

Schwartz, R. *The Curse of Cain: The Violent Legacy of Monotheism*. Chicago: University of Chicago Press, 1997.

Sedgwick, A. "Address to the Geological Society." *Proceedings of the Geological Society of London* 1 (1831): 281–316.

Segal, R. A. *In Quest of the Hero*. Princeton, N.J.: Princeton University Press, 1990.
———. *Jung on Mythology*. Princeton, N.J.: Princeton University Press, 1998.

Smith, G. *Assyrian Discoveries*. New York: Scribner, Armstrong, and Co., 1875.

Smith, J. Pye. *Scripture and Geology, on the Relation between the Holy Scriptures and Some Parts of Geological Science*. New York: D. Appleton, 1840.

Stander, H. F. "The Church Fathers on (the Cursing of) Ham." *Acta Patristica et Byzantina* 5 (1994): 113–25.

Steno, N. *The Prodromus of Nicolaus Steno's Dissertation: Concerning a Solid Body Enclosed by Process of Nature within a Solid*. Intro. and trans. J. G. Winter. London: Macmillan, 1916. Reprint, New York: Hafner, 1968.

Stiling, R. L. "The Diminishing Deluge: Noah's Flood in Nineteenth-Century American Thought." Ph.D. diss., University of Wisconsin–Madison, 1991.

Stringfellow, T. *Scriptural and Statistical Views in Favor of Slavery*. Richmond, Va.: J. W. Randolph, 1856.

Thompson, T. L. *The Historicity of the Patriarchal Narratives: The Quest for the Historical Abraham*. New York: Walter de Gruyter, 1974.

Tigay, J. *The Evolution of the Gilgamesh Epic*. Philadelphia: University of Pennsylvania Press, 1982.

Trible, P. *Texts of Terror: Literary-Feminist Readings of the Biblical Narratives*. Philadelphia: Fortress, 1984.

Unger, R. W. *The Art of Medieval Technology: Images of Noah the Shipbuilder*. New Brunswick, N.J.: Rutgers University Press, 1991.

Van de Fliert, J. R. "Fundamentalism and the Fundamentals of Geology," *Journal of the American Scientific Affiliation* 21, no. 3 (1969): 69–81.

Van der Toorn, K. "The Babylonian New Year Festival: New Insights from the Cuneiform Texts and Their Bearing on Old Testament Study." In *Congress Volume: Leuven 1989*, ed. J. A. Emerton, pp. 331–44. Leiden: Brill, 1991.

Van Seters, J. *Abraham in History and Tradition*. New Haven, Conn.: Yale University Press, 1975.

Vandermeersch, P. "Where Will the Water Stick? Considerations of a Psychoanalyst about the Stories of the Flood." In *Interpretations of the Flood*, ed. F. G. Martinez and G. P. Luttikhuizen, 167–93. Leiden: Brill, 1998.

Verbrugghe, G. P., and J. M. Wickersham. *Berossos and Manetho, Introduced and Translated: Native Traditions in Ancient Mesopotamia and Egypt*. Ann Arbor: University of Michigan Press, 1996.

Veyne, P. *Did the Greeks Believe in Their Myths?* Chicago: University of Chicago Press, 1988.

Voltaire. *Philosophical Dictionary*. Trans. P. Gay. New York: Harcourt, Brace, and World, 1962.

Wacholder, B. Z. *Nicolaus of Damascus*. Berkeley: University of California Press, 1962.

Wenham, G. "The Coherence of the Flood Narrative." *Vetus Testamentum* 28 (1978): 336–48.

Whiston, W. *A New Theory of the Earth*. New York: Arno, 1978.

Whitcomb, J. C. *The World That Perished*. Grand Rapids, Mich.: Baker Book House, 1988.

Whitcomb, J. C., and H. Morris. *The Genesis Flood: The Biblical Record and Its Scientific Implications*. Philadelphia: Presbyterian and Reformed, 1961.

White, A. D. *A History of the Warfare of Science with Theology in Christendom: In Two Volumes*. New York: D. Appleton, 1925 [1896].

Wilber, K., ed. *Quantum Questions: Mystical Writings of the World's Great Physicists*. Boston: Shambhala, 1984.

Wilde, O. *Epigrams: Phrases and Philosophies for the Use of the Young*. Boston: Aldine, 1910.

Witham, L. A. *Where Darwin Meets the Bible: Creationists and Evolutionists in America*. New York: Oxford University Press, 2002.

Wolde, E. van. *Mr. and Mrs. Job*. London: SCM, 1997.

Woodmorappe, J. *Noah's Ark: A Feasibility Study*. Santee, Calif.: Institute for Creation Research, 1996.

Woodward, J. *An Essay toward a Natural History of the Earth and Terrestrial Bodies, especially Minerals: As also of the Sea, Rivers, and Springs. With an account of the Universal Deluge: And of the Effects that it had upon the Earth*. London: Ric. Wilkin, 1695. Reprint, New York: Arno, 1978.

Woolley, L. *Ur of the Chaldees: A Revised and Updated Edition of Sir Leonard Woolley's Excavations at Ur by P. R. S. Moorey.* Ithaca, N.Y.: Cornell University Press, 1982.

Wright, G. E. *God Who Acts: Biblical Theology as Recital.* London: SCM, 1952.

———. *The Old Testament Against Its Environment.* London: SCM, 1950.

Youngblood, R., ed. *The Genesis Debate: Persistent Questions about Creation and the Flood.* Nashville, Tenn.: Thomas Nelson, 1986.

Zukav, G. *The Dancing Wu Li Masters: An Overview of the New Physics.* New York: Morrow, 1979.

Index